Shaping the
Christian Life

Shaping the Christian Life

Worship and the Religious Affections

Kendra G. Hotz
Matthew T. Mathews

Westminster John Knox Press
LOUISVILLE • LONDON

Book design by Sharon Adams

First edition
Published by Westminster John Knox Press
Louisville, Kentucky

This book is printed on acid-free paper that meets the American National Standards Institute Z39.48 standard. ♾

PRINTED IN THE UNITED STATES OF AMERICA

06 07 08 09 10 11 12 13 14 15 — 10 9 8 7 6 5 4 3 2 1

Library of Congress Cataloging-in-Publication Data is on file at the Library of Congress, Washington, D.C.

ISBN-13: 978-0-664-22938-2
ISBN-10: 0-664-22938-7

Contents

Foreword

In *The Humanity of God*, Karl Barth claims that it is "imperative to recognize the essence of theology as lying in the liturgical action of adoration, thanksgiving and petition."[1] This sounds a theme that echoes throughout the early church: theology is doxological. This in turn sounds a primordial claim of Christian life and faith: worship of God is not some optional extra, but is the church's love in response to God's lavish incarnate gift of love in Christ. To worship God is to praise, thank, and bless God. Yet at worship the Christian community also laments the injustice, sin, and suffering of the world, and pleads for grace, mercy, and forgiveness. To worship the God of Abraham and Sarah, Moses and Miriam, Joshua and Deborah is to enter into the deep patterns of biblical memory and experience. To worship the God of all creation and history revealed in Jesus Christ is to bring all of life and death, love and struggle, sorrow and hope before the Holy Three-in-One. This places the human heart at full stretch before God. Put another way, the theological character of worship demands both that we shout, "Glory!" and cry out "Mercy!" If these things are so, then Christian worship demands that we attend to what Jonathan Edwards called the "religious affections."

The appearance of this book carries the work of liturgical theology in a new key. While there are increasing numbers of liturgical scholars and theologians writing about worship, none has articulated how a distinctive theological anthropology of the affections illuminates central practices of Christian worship. The authors' interpretive proposals and depictions of the worshiping assembly's practices are remarkably relevant to a number of issues facing Christian churches in North American culture today. They do not set out to "solve" questions of the so-called "worship wars," but I am convinced that their framework and approach will be of immense help to any who are currently struggling with such pastorally and liturgically demanding conflicts.

Our authors, both skilled theologians, place themselves solidly within the Reformed traditions of Christian faith, drawing especially on the resources found in the Presbyterian (PCUSA) *Book of Common Worship*. While citing patterns of prayer, proclamation, and ritual action found therein, Kendra Hotz and Matt Mathews are concerned to go well "beyond the text" to the matrix of living worship. As music is more than the score, so for them worship is much more than directives and printed texts. Their work is a kind of theological "sounding" of the soul of worship.

These pages explore in a fresh way how worship may shape and give expression, over time, to our humanity at full stretch before God. The study of what Christian congregations do in gathering about Word, the Lord's Table, and the font of baptism to worship the living God requires tracing ways in which human emotional dispositions are essential to participation in divine life. Of course there are wide differences with respect to how "emotional" the actual experience of worship may be. Some Christian traditions, including some in the lineage of the Reformed churches, have shown a deep ambivalence about emotions and feelings. But their conception of "religious affections" avoids the popular misunderstandings of human subjectivity that often cloud our vision of religious experience. There is clearly a marked sobriety about the ordering of common worship here. Yet because the book draws upon insights from Eastern Orthodoxy as well as Schleiermacher, Edwards, and more recent moral theologies, we are led to a generous ecumenical vision of worship as well.

I am persuaded that their work provides the groundwork and specific instances of how all authentic Christian faith must aim to cultivate a thankful heart, sorrow over sin and death, hope for a world of peace and justice, compassion for neighbor, and even love for enemies. These are theological matters, not merely "psychological" matters. This book thus sets an important agenda for future work in comparative liturgical studies as well. Our understanding of and, *above all*, our faithful participation in Christian worship can only be deepened by what is proposed in this volume.

Don E. Saliers
Wm. R. Cannon Distinguished Professor
of Theology and Worship
Candler School of Theology
Emory University

Preface

This book arises out of the conviction that how we worship both expresses and shapes who we are as people of faith. In it, we attempt to account theologically for those powerful experiences of the heart that are rooted in Christian worship and essential to Christian life. More specifically, we explore how worship makes us who we are "at heart" by cultivating the religious affections of awe, humility, gratitude, a sense of mutuality and interdependence, a sense of rightness, a sense of well-being, delight, obligation, self-sacrificial love, contrition, hope, and a sense of direction. We explore how these religious affections come together in our identities to orient us in the world so that we live to the glory of God and in relationships of beauty and harmony with all God's creatures.

We are convinced that taking account of these affective experiences of the heart necessarily involves bringing the resources of academic theology into conversation with the practices and experiences of Christian life and worship. When theology intersects the lived experience of the Christian faith, the relationship between the two is mutually enriching. Theology may help us to express and interpret the meaning of our Christian lives, and the shape of the Christian life will frame the nature of our theological projects. The intersection of theology with Christian life and worship can fund rich new visions of the meaning of the person and work of Christ, the nature of God, the eschatological renewal of all things, and the work of the Holy Spirit in preserving, sustaining, and strengthening the church. In this book, however, we focus on the way in which the intersection of theology and worship funds a new vision of human nature and on how we might interpret Christian worship in light of this new understanding. In the first half of the book, we develop a liturgical theological anthropology, an interpretation of human life that focuses attention on the nature and importance of the religious affections in human experience. In the second half of the book, we interpret the meaning and significance of the central acts of Christian worship in light of this affectional understanding of human nature.

We offer this interpretation of the relationship between the religious affections and worship practices with the hope that it might provoke thought and conversation among pastors, seminary students, and interested lay people about worship practices in local congregations. Our aim is to offer a broad, ecumenical vision of human life under God that can spark useful exchanges about the nature and purpose of the worship life of the church among Christians of many different communions. We offer this work as theology for the church and as theology that emerges out of the life of the church. In our case, it is theology that has emerged out of participation in mostly Presbyterian congregations, and our Presbyterian-Reformed theological perspective shapes the work in some obvious ways. Our intention is to speak out of one tradition, but to speak as those who have listened to and learned from other traditions. We offer this work as one perspective that may illumine certain features of our common heritage and that can be critiqued and corrected by others in places where that perspective may conceal important truths from us.

Because this book centers on the intersection of theological anthropology and worship, it should not be mistaken for a general introductory textbook in Christian worship. We do not attempt to offer a general survey or comprehensive treatment of Christian worship. Neither do we explain basic concepts in liturgical theology or offer a history of worship. Instead, we intend this book to be a supplementary work—a work that stands alongside many well-written and useful textbooks that are already used by seminarians and pastors.

While we aim to offer a fresh, new contribution to the field of theology and worship, our work has been shaped by a number of theologians. First, our work has been deeply informed by the Reformed moral theologies of H. Richard Niebuhr and James Gustafson, both of whom have highlighted the importance of character formation in the moral life. We draw especially on Niebuhr's deeply social and relational model of the self, his sustained attention to the role of affectivity in the moral life, and his treatment of the relationship between revelation and the religious imagination. Gustafson's high theocentrism and attention to the role of common religious discourse in shaping the affective patterns of Christian personhood also stand near the heart of this project.

Second, Jonathan Edwards and Friedrich Schleiermacher are undisputedly the central figures in the Reformed tradition who focus attention on the nature and place of affectivity in our theological understanding of human nature. Both Niebuhr and Gustafson were deeply influenced by these two theologians and indeed synthesized much of their work. We also draw heavily on their germinal insights and appropriate them constructively for the contemporary church and its worship. We are indebted to Edwards for his penetrating and sophisticated analysis of the religious affections, his innovative use of aesthetic categories in theological analysis and reflection on the Christian life, and his unwavering theocentrism in the face of a growing awareness of the ways in which religion might be used to validate a revaluation of God and the world around human interests and ends. We are indebted to Schleiermacher for drawing attention to the centrality of feeling and affectivity in the Christian life, for linking our experience of the affections to an underlying sense of dependence, and for highlighting the social formation of our affections in the context of the church.

Third, we have been influenced by the traditions of Eastern Orthodoxy, which have a long history of granting worship a central place in theology. We have been especially influenced by the Pseudo-Dionysius, a sixth-century figure foundational for Orthodox thinking about the nature of the church and its sacraments. The Pseudo-Dionysius attended especially to the ways that the sacraments and our invocations of God draw us toward a love of God that forms us for love of our neighbor. We are especially indebted to the Pseudo-Dionysius for drawing attention to the centrality of desire in shaping our identities, for highlighting the relationship between that desire and liturgical practices, and for his analysis of the central role that embodied practices play in our purification and illumination.

Finally, we are deeply indebted to Don Saliers, whose imaginative and synthetic work in liturgical theology has shaped our thinking in direct and significant ways. Saliers's attention to the mutually enriching relationship between theology and worship practices, his careful distinction between feeling and affection, the connections that he draws between particular religious affections and forms of prayer, and his careful explication of the logic of the religious affections provide insights central to the proposals advanced in this book. Don also read and commented on a draft of the prospectus for this book, and we thank him for the clarity of thought that he brought to that task and for the consistent encouragement that he has offered since our days as graduate students at Emory University.

This book was produced during a sabbatical leave from Calvin College in 2004–05. We are grateful to the college board of trustees for granting our sabbatical leave. We especially wish to thank the Louisville Institute for the generous grant that allowed us the leisure of a full-year sabbatical, which enabled us to complete the manuscript without interruption. We owe a special word of thanks to Jim Lewis, executive director of the Louisville Institute, for his wise and patient counsel and enthusiasm for the project. We are also grateful to the Wabash Center for Teaching and Learning in Theology and Religion for two summer research grants that were crucial in the early planning and writing stages of the book. Special thanks belong to Paul Myhre and Tom Pearson, associate directors of the Wabash Center, for the direction and guidance that they provided as mentors to two young scholars. We appreciate, too, the early support for our work provided by Westminster John Knox Press and Donald McKim, academic and reference editor.

We are deeply grateful to four pastors who generously gave of their time, energy, and intellect by serving as readers and conversation partners during the production of this book: the Reverend Michael C. Fedewa, rector of St. Andrew's Episcopal Church, Grand Rapids, Michigan; the Reverend Helen Havlik, pastor of North Park Presbyterian Church, Grand Rapids, Michigan; the Reverend Linda Knieriemen, pastor of First Presbyterian Church, Holland, Michigan; and the Reverend Seth Weeldreyer, pastor of First Presbyterian Church, Marshall, Michigan. With careful thought, generosity of spirit, and much good humor, each pastor brought distinctive insights and contributions that clarified our thinking and writing, rooted our theological reflection in the concrete pastoral and worship life of the church, and gave us cause for continuing hope for the mission and resilience of the church in the contemporary world. We are also grateful to Shirley Roels, John Witvliet, and Janel Curry for reading and commenting on early drafts of the book prospectus.

We are grateful to a number of friends and colleagues who have offered support and encouragement over the years and especially during the year of our sabbatical. Our profound thanks go to Arie and Kris Griffioen, whose friendship has sustained us and whose hospitality has delighted us. We are especially grateful for their generosity in allowing us to use their cabin in northern Michigan while we wrote chapter 6. We are also deeply grateful for David Crump, Chris deGroot, Ken Pomykala, and Richard Whitekettle who have always been wonderful conversation partners and supportive colleagues.

Finally, we wish to express our thanks to our families for their love and support and to the pastors and members of the congregation of Westminster Presbyterian Church, Grand Rapids, Michigan, for the liberating and expansive vision of the church that finds expression in the weekly worship which has cultivated and nourished our own religious affections and Christian identities.

Part One

Religious Affections

1

An Introduction to the Religious Affections

When you worship, what do you know by heart? Do you ever find yourself humming the doxology as you drive to work or recalling the Twenty-third Psalm when facing a difficult decision? There is more to knowing something "by heart" than just memorizing it. Some elements of worship work themselves so deeply into our hearts that they become a permanent part of who we are and how we interpret and engage our world. Think of the doxology: In it all of the "creatures here below" join their voices to the choir of the heavenly host in order to "praise God from whom all blessings flow."[1] Part of being Christian is to be a person who experiences the good things in life as gifts of God, as blessings. By singing the doxology in worship Sunday after Sunday we learn to interpret our world in such a way that we see it as good and offer praise to God for this goodness. We learn that God is the source of all goodness, the one from whom all blessings flow. Likewise, the doxology places us within a broad cosmic context in which all creatures praise God. Humanity finds its place within a vast created order that includes everything from angels to cosmic dust, and each of these creatures exists to glorify God.

We may not think about these things each time we sing the doxology; we may not unpack its meaning and remind ourselves of these truths, but it works its way into our souls anyway. The doxology becomes part of us, and as a result we become doxological beings. We are not simply people whose minds have grasped the truths the doxology teaches; we are people whose hearts have been changed by that truth. The things we know by heart are like that. They intensify the colors of our lives; they transform the whole shape of who we are as children of God. We become who we are in part through our acts of worship, as those acts of worship work themselves into our hearts.

REASON AND EMOTION:
A CULTURAL PROBLEM

But to say that worship is about the heart introduces a difficult problem for modern people: We do not know how to think about the relationship between reason and emotion. Our confusion over how to explain the nature and place of these matters of the heart often manifests itself in two competing impulses, both of which exercise a powerful sway over how we think about the emotional dimensions of our experience.[2] The first is an impulse to elevate reason over emotion, seeing in reason and its practical fruits the path to human progress and flourishing. The cultivation of human reason has carried our culture to its greatest scientific discoveries and technological advances. Emotion only gets in the way of scientific objectivity and technological progress. It clouds our reason. Reason, so we think, deals with cold, hard facts, whereas emotion deals with slippery values and private feelings. Scientific and technological reason, not emotion, has given us the vaccine for polio, the microprocessors that run our computers, and the well-crafted business plans and marketing studies that ensure our economic prosperity and upwardly mobile way of life. Reason quantifies, categorizes, arranges, and manipulates the unquestioned, given realities of our world, harnessing them for human flourishing. We come to believe that while emotion may have its place in the private sphere of values and relationships, it does not belong in the public realm of clear thinking and prudent action.

To this way of thinking, emotion is suspect for several reasons. First, it is too subjective. Emotion give us no traction on objective reality. It does not put us in touch with the really real, with the world of objective, reliable facts and realistic courses of action. Second, emotion is essentially private, personal, and not subject to verification by other people. You cannot quantify, measure, or record matters of the heart and then offer them up to public scrutiny and scientific testing. Matters of the heart are endlessly contestable, and for this reason, emotions cannot provide a shared foundation for a common social life. Finally, emotions are deceptive. Anger, love, and hatred, for example, cloud our judgment, bias our perceptions, draw us into illusion, and provoke actions that we will later regret. How many of us in the heat of argument have blurted out to our opponent, "You're being too emotional! Why can't you listen to reason?" How many of us, swept away by the emotional intensity of the moment, have made a decision or spoken words that we later regretted?

While scientific and technical rationality has often contributed to human flourishing and expresses an important dimension of human goodness and creativity, it is not, however, immune from our sinfulness. Our rationality bears the marks of our fallenness no less than all other dimensions of our lives. The rationality that produces the polio vaccine likewise produces the nuclear bomb whose aim is to annihilate indiscriminately innocent civilian populations.

Additionally, this view of rationality artificially separates it from our emotional lives. But we do not experience ourselves as knowers in this moment and feelers in that moment. Was it not a deep compassion for suffering people and a driving passion to alleviate pain that motivated scientists to create the polio vaccine? Because in experience our knowing and feeling are always united, it is impossible in practice to suppress emotion. And when we try to do so, we often find that emotion erupts into the supposedly pure realm of reason, sometimes in destructive ways. The drive to banish emotion and matters of the heart to the margins of human experience is both impossible and undesirable.

The impulse to elevate reason over emotion, however, is matched by a second, competing impulse, to elevate emotion over reason. While reason has in fact improved many aspects of our lives, our experience is not reducible to the merely rational. Deep, undeniable yearnings within the human heart seek expression and fulfillment in social life. Matters of the heart, so the thinking goes, are really what is most true and authentic about our lives. While we may of necessity be thrust into the public world of work and stencil-drawn social roles, this public world is ultimately alien to the deepest sense of who we are. Public life demands conformity, rational action, and the artificiality of carrying out roles that eclipse our authentic inner world of deeply felt convictions and emotions that are the genuine source of our identities. Who am I? I am the person who loves so-and-so, who delights in photography or needlework, who is overjoyed in the presence of my grandchildren, who is angered and bewildered in the face of poverty and homelessness. The key to who we are and who we want to be lies here, in the inner world of the heart with its unique pattern of emotions and deeply felt convictions.

There is something right about this impulse, but it can also tempt us toward a shallow emotivism. We are tempted to lose ourselves in the immediacy of our feelings, to focus our energies too exclusively on ourselves, and to lead impulsive, unreflective lives that open us to the manipulation of others. Theologian H. Richard Niebuhr noted that this protest of emotion over reason perhaps expresses itself most poignantly in our prevailing culture of amusement. We seek in the amusement offered by film, television, theater, art, sport, and even shopping an outlet for our emotions that will somehow express aspects of our authentic, genuine selves. In a series of lectures given just months before his death, Niebuhr describes this new role of amusement:

> We watch our baseball games and have our aggressive feelings kindled, our hopes of victory inflamed, and having killed the umpire in words and realized the great eschaton of the ninth inning with rejoicing, or accepted the grief of defeat, we go away and that is that. So we read

the whodunits and view the TV shows—spectators by and large—with spectators' vicarious and immediately discharged emotions. So also we tend to make a game even of human love, [humanity's] most perennial occasion for the emotional involvement of being with being but now so often reduced to an amusement that is supposed to have no consequence beyond the moment.[3]

If the domain of science, technology, and business is the domain where reason eclipses emotion, then the domain of amusement and entertainment is for many of us the domain where emotion eclipses reason. We seek in amusement opportunities to express, validate, and confirm the importance of matters of the heart. Entertainment, as Niebuhr points out, serves an important vicarious function because through it we come into contact with important but neglected affective dimensions of our personhood.

However, Niebuhr also points us to a profound danger inherent in this fusion of emotion and amusement. The danger lies in the particular way that emotion is related to amusement. In the context of amusement, the point of arousing the emotion is simply to make it felt. The emotion involved in amusement is immediate and intense, but also ephemeral and temporary. It arises with a wave of intensity, delights in the experience of that intensity, but quickly subsides when the event of the amusement ends, and thus remains disconnected from the deepest structures of our personality. The emotion sparked by amusement spends itself completely in the event of amusement; such emotion does not endure beyond the momentary experience to wear a groove in the soul capable of channeling the deepest affective currents of the human heart toward wholeness and fulfillment. While the emotion of amusement is fleeting, it is also intense and seductive and, for this reason, dangerous. The danger lies in the ever-present temptation to trivialize the most sacred experiences of life by transforming them into events of mere amusement. When Christian worship is accommodated to the culture of amusement, it ceases being the occasion to come reverently into the presence of God and becomes instead an entertainment event produced and packaged for the sake of evoking warm feelings, generating excitement, and expanding the membership rosters of the organization with the names of satisfied spectators.

REASON, EMOTION, AND WORSHIP

This tug-of-war between suppressing emotion and celebrating it leaves us in a difficult position, because neither approach answers well to our experience of ourselves. We are not thinkers at one moment and feelers at another. We are unified persons whose capacity to perceive the world rationally can never be separated from how we relate to it emotionally. We know this about ourselves, but are at a loss as to how to explain it. We know that "the things we know by heart" are more than information we have memorized; we know that they have soaked into our bones and have become like the frame over which the canvas of our lives is stretched. Our experiences of the heart belie the effort to impose a simple bifurcation on the personality, with reason on one side and emotion on the other. Our experiences of the heart reveal to us something about who we most basically are.

But once we have acknowledged the centrality of the heart to our personhood, our analysis of worship becomes all the more difficult. Worship has such a profound effect upon us that it forms us, changes us, renews us, and opens us to experience the world as Christians. Who we are "at heart" and how we worship are deeply interconnected. But why does worship have such a powerful effect on us? How exactly does the act of praising and thanking God transform who we are as the people of God? The answers given to these questions are increasingly contested, especially among Protestants in the United States. Arguments about just what constitutes proper Christian worship take place not only between denominations and congregations, but often within them. When these conversations take place in the absence of a theology that links our understanding of what it means to be human to our concrete worship practices, they can quickly degenerate into "worship wars" that are rooted in nothing more than expressions of preference.

Worshiping is as natural to being human as breathing. We have a deep and natural longing to direct our ultimate loyalty to that upon which we ultimately depend. We want to know to whom or what we belong, because knowing that tells us who and what we are. The question is never *whether* we will offer our ultimate loyalty to some powerful other in worship, but rather to *what* or *whom* we will offer such loyalty and worship. We are worshiping creatures; this is what it means to be human. Therefore, to give an account of worship necessarily involves giving an account of who we are and who we want to be. This is, at least in part, why worship is so hard to think about.

Because what we do in worship is connected to fundamental questions about what it means to be human in relation to God, we should expect that debates about the nature and function of worship will be passionate. Although it often remains implicit, what is contested in the worship wars is this more fundamental question of theological anthropology. What remains undeveloped is a theology of human personhood that explains why worship is natural to us, why worship is so powerful, and how worship contributes to the renewal and transformation of humanity. To forge the link between human personhood and the power of worship, we contend, requires a new understanding of what it means to be a human being, an understanding that integrates reason and emotion. Debates about worship practices, if they are to become fruitful occasions for congregational reflection, must always be linked explicitly to a theological interpretation of the human person. This book seeks to make explicit this link between worship practices and theological anthropology in order to facilitate productive dialogue about worship practices. In order to do this, we need to offer a proposal about how worship practices transform and renew worshipers.

Specifically, this book explores the link between worship practices and human personhood by focusing on the religious affections. Although the idea of a religious affection is a very old one, many modern Christians are unfamiliar with it, so we spend the remainder of this chapter describing the religious affections and explaining how they are both like and unlike emotions. In the remainder of the book we develop an affectional theology of human personhood that accounts for the power of communal worship to shape the deeply seated dispositions that orient us with reverence and awe toward God and God's world. We first develop a theology of human personhood that focuses on the religious affections in chapters 2–5; we then deploy this affectional understanding of human personhood in an analysis of specific worship practices beginning in chapter 6.

WHAT IS A RELIGIOUS AFFECTION?

Although there are many religious affections, we will be working with twelve primary ones: awe, humility, gratitude, a sense of direction, a sense of rightness, a sense of well-being, contrition, a sense of mutuality and interdependence, a sense of obligation, delight, self-sacrificial love, and hope. On first glance, this may seem to be simply a list of emotions, and indeed emotions and affections are closely related. Because religious affections and emotions are closely related, it is easy to confuse them, but they are not identical.[4] Emotions are feelings that come and go. Sometimes we feel them; sometimes we do not. But what endures is who we are as persons, who sometimes feel these emotions and sometimes do not. We may, for example, describe someone as being "a delightful person," even when that person is not currently experiencing the emotion of delight. Likewise, we may understand ourselves as grateful persons even when we are in the midst of a crisis that prevents us from feeling gratitude. When we think about that enduring feature of our identity that specifies who we are regardless of what we are currently feeling, we are thinking of an affection. Religious affections endure whether or not we are experiencing a particular emotion. Emotions are about what we *feel*, but religious affections are about who we *are*.

When we refer to a religious affection, then, we mean a deep, abiding feature of the human personality that grounds and orients us in all that we know, do, and feel. The religious affections form our fundamental disposition and attunement to the world around us. They are the enduring features of our identities that lie at the root of how we see our world, how we enter into and sustain relationships with others, and that constitute in us a kind of readiness to experience the world in certain kinds of ways.[5] The religious affections come together to form our basic temperament. Persons with a hopeful temperament are apt to find cause for hope in the midst of terrible darkness. Persons with temperaments of self-sacrificial love engage the world with a readiness to set aside their own interests for the sake of others. When these twelve affections come together in a well-ordered way, they form in us a distinctively Christian temperament.

Emotions that come and go are not utterly separate from the religious affections. The affectional current of our personhood is subtly moved in its course by the emotions that we experience. We need concrete emotional experiences of awe, contrition, and gratitude, for example, to cultivate in us their corresponding affections. Before we can become grateful people, in other words, we need to have been prompted to feel the emotion of gratitude on a number of occasions. That emotion may eventually settle down in us and become a permanent feature of our identities. When that happens, the emotion has passed over into an affection.

Religious affections, then, are connected in important ways to the emotions that we experience in the here and now, so that what we feel, and how we are made to feel, matters; but the main current of the religious affections runs far deeper than the eddies of emotion that swirl on the surface of daily experience. It is helpful to think of a religious affection as an enduring disposition that we become aware of as we experience a particular emotion. We can discover dimensions of underlying religious affections when we experience one of them as an emotion. In order to get at what a particular religious affection is, then, we need to tunnel down to it through its corresponding emotion.

PRELIMINARY DESCRIPTIONS
OF TWELVE RELIGIOUS AFFECTIONS

When do you feel *awe*? Many of us feel it in the presence of vast natural beauty such as the Grand Canyon. In such situations, our affective response is mixed. On the one hand, we are drawn in wonder toward that which is beautiful; on the other hand, we feel almost swallowed up by its vastness and push back against it. Awe, then, involves a disorienting awareness that disrupts our normal ways of interacting with everyday objects. We are aware of our smallness before and our dependence on something larger than ourselves for life itself.

Humility is closely related to awe. In the presence of vast beauty, we are prompted to reassess our own significance. Humility involves a proper estimate of one's own significance. We are humbled to find ourselves in relationships with other creatures that indicate to us that while we do not provide the central value and purpose for the creation, neither are we irrelevant to its value and purpose. Humility emerges from a sober estimate of our limited place, power, and influence in the cosmos, but it also involves an affirmation of our fundamental goodness even in the midst of our limitations.

Gratitude, like humility, flows out from awe. When we experience awe and are prompted to reassess our place in relation to the whole, we also come to see how deeply dependent we are on others if we are to have life and to have a meaningful life. Gratitude is the religious affection underlying our capacity to recognize that life comes to us as a gift and to be thankful for it.[6]

A *sense of mutuality and interdependence* emerges out of humility and gratitude when we realize that we are not self-sufficient, but instead rely on others, even as we provide for some of their needs. Our sense of interdependence expands as we come to recognize the interdependent structure of the entire cosmos. We are aware that creatures live in mutuality and harmony.

This awareness of the mutuality and harmony of the creation gives rise to a *sense of rightness*. Our sense of rightness is our sense that everything in the world, ourselves included, fits together to form a whole that is beautiful and good. The world is not simply an amalgamation of pieces; it is more akin to a living organism whose every member contributes to the goodness and proper functioning of the whole. We sense not simply that the world happens to be this way but that it *is supposed to be* this way—that it is *right* to be this way. We sense that what the world *is*, despite its flaws and shortcomings, comports in large measure with what it *ought* to be. Our sense of rightness is our sense that the world is, at bottom, good.

The sense of mutuality and interdependence also flows into another religious affection, the *sense of well-being*. The religious affection of well-being emerges when we sense that the order of this world is not hostile to our existence and that there is a place for us to flourish in it. It is the awareness that we belong here and can flourish here; we sense that this world is our home, that the forces of life and the powers at work in the cosmos are fundamentally supportive of our ability both to have life and to have a meaningful life.[7]

The sense of mutuality and interdependence that emerges from our combined affections of humility and gratitude also flows into the religious affection of *delight*. Delight is the joy and pleasure that attend the appreciation of other creatures. Our sense of enjoyment and pleasure are evoked by our awareness of the beauty, complexity, and goodness of other creatures in our world.

The awareness that we were made to live in mutuality generates in us a *sense of obligation.* Other creatures rightly make claims on us, and we are responsible for their well-being. Other creatures need us, and those needs create obligations when we are able to meet them.

Self-sacrificial love emerges from our awareness that the love we bear for others makes demands on us that intensify our sense of obligation to the point where we are ready not only to meet the need of another but to set aside our own good, or at least our own immediate good, for the sake of that other.

In spite of our awareness of our limitations, in spite of how our dependence calls for gratitude, and in spite of our awareness of our obligations, we sometimes fail to act in ways that honor our limited place within God's grand scheme; we sometimes fail to acknowledge the giftedness of life and to be grateful; we sometimes fail to meet our obligations. And these failures prompt *contrition.* Contrition involves sorrow for wrongdoing and a sense that we have diminished ourselves—made ourselves less—through some violation of another.

Contrition prompts *hope.* Hope emerges when we sense that the present situation of our lives is not entirely what it ought to be, and yet, in spite of the difficulties of the present, we yearn for and sense that there are seeds of possibility, newness, and openness for the future. Hope is the anticipation that such possibility, newness, and openness will translate into a fuller, richer form of life.

Finally, our capacity to see possibility and to be hopeful depends upon our *sense of direction.* A sense of direction undergirds our sense that our lives are meaningful, that they have a purpose. We sense that the course of our lives has brought us to a certain place and given us momentum and a trajectory for the future. We are ordered to some end, and when we find it difficult to discern what that purpose is, we feel that we have lost our way. The acute experience of unsettledness and disorientation that often accompany such experiences of being lost bear witness to our natural, persistent sense that our lives are ordered toward and made meaningful by a larger purpose that we are to pursue.

It should be clear, even from this preliminary description of these twelve religious affections, that they are not twelve discrete features of our identities. The religious affections are interrelated. Each one flows into and out of the others. Whenever we experience the emotion that corresponds to one of them, and identify its underlying affection, we are still only at the very tip of the iceberg. In fact, every emotional experience of a particular affection is ultimately related to the total affectional structure of our identities.

Our task in the chapters to come will be not simply to list and describe these twelve affections as we have done here, but to discover how they become *religious* affections when they are properly oriented toward God, to explain how worship works to orient them toward God as their proper object, and to demonstrate the pattern that binds them together in such a way that they bring unity and coherence to our identities. Worship renews and transforms us because in praising and glorifying God, it graciously shapes, sustains, and directs the religious affections that lie at the very heart of who we are.

2

Four Features of
the Religious Affections

The Lord be with you. / And also with you. / Lift up your hearts. / We lift them up unto the Lord. / Let us give thanks to the Lord our God. / It is right to give our thanks and praise.[1]

I greet Thee, who my sure Redeemer art, / My only trust and Savior of my heart, / Who pain didst undergo for my poor sake; / I pray Thee from our hearts all cares to take.[2]

Joyful, joyful, we adore Thee, / God of glory, Lord of love; / Hearts unfold like flowers before thee, / Opening to the sun above. / Melt the clouds of sin and sadness; / Drive the gloom of doubt away; / Giver of immortal gladness, / Fill us with the light of day.[3]

These are words that many of us know by heart, and "heart" is right at the center of them. Language of the heart in Christian worship is undeniably emotional language. But, as we have noted, the language of emotion is fraught with difficulties in our culture. We are deeply ambivalent about the nature and place of emotion in our lives. We sometimes try to suppress emotion in the name of reason, and at other times we celebrate emotion uncritically. We find ourselves at a loss to explain those deeply felt experiences of joy, awe, sorrow, contrition, or gratitude. That these experiences are essential to who we are is undeniable, but when we try to explain them, we often find ourselves without adequate concepts to do so.

We find ourselves with a difficult task then: to acknowledge and affirm the deeply emotional nature of Christian life and worship in a way that moves us beyond the impasse that would either suppress emotion in the name of reason or celebrate emotion uncritically. Moving beyond this impasse requires that we develop new concepts and that we attend to the important distinction between an emotion and an affection. It is the concept of affection rather than emotion, we believe, that will provide us with a richer vocabulary for exploring matters of the heart. While the remainder of this chapter is devoted to the task of exploring and explaining the meaning of an affection, we need to keep in mind the distinction between an emotion and an affection. By *affections* we do not mean the particular emotions that we feel in one moment or another. Instead, we mean the deep-seated dispositions, the settled and abiding postures of the heart, that qualify or color everything that we know or do. When we focus on the affections, we are referring not to the immediate experience of this or that emotion in this or that moment, but to the deep dispositional structures of our personalities, the foundations of who we are as creatures of God and how we are oriented toward God and the world that God has made. By *emotion*, in contrast, we mean the particular way that an affection comes to expression in a given moment of experience. In short, we *feel* our emotions, but we *are* our affections.

A DESCRIPTIVE ACCOUNT OF
THREE EXPERIENCES OF THE HEART

Worship is thick with the language of the heart, but we often struggle to account for the validity and significance of the experiences of the heart. If we are not unfeeling thinkers or unthinking feelers, then the language of the heart in worship must gesture toward a richer sense of personhood. One way of understanding this richer sense of personhood is to describe and explore particular experiences of the heart and to see what they indicate about the affectivity that shapes our personhood. In this section, we will offer descriptions of three experiences of the heart: awe, contrition, and gratitude. In the following section, we will draw on these descriptions to develop a theology of the religious affections that focuses on four of their chief characteristics.

Let's begin with *awe*. It is a rare person who can stand at the foot of a great sequoia and not feel small. The sheer size and longevity of that living being inspire in us a sense of awe. Standing amidst a forest of such great trees and gazing upward at just one of them, we fall silent. In such moments, the magnitude of what we are seeing presses in on us with an intensity that is almost overwhelming. This experience of awe is disorienting. We feel attracted and connected to something much larger than ourselves. Yet at the same time we feel ourselves recoiling from it almost in fear of its overwhelming presence. There is something in the life of that great tree that has nothing to do with the one who gazes upon it. It has its own beauty, majesty, and life that do not derive from or depend upon the one who gazes upon it. This means that in the forest of great sequoias we stand, in a sense, where we do not belong and amid that which does not belong to us. It is as though we stand unworthily on holy ground. In such moments we sense that we are not of such great consequence that the meaning, value, and purpose of the cosmos depend upon us. This realization generates a wonder that is disorienting and that suspends our normal ways of being in the world. This experience of awe has in it both the awesome and the awe-full.

A second experience of the heart is *contrition*. All of us at some time or another have found ourselves in conflict with someone whose love has sustained us and whom it is important that we love if we are to be the person that we want to be. There is something sacred about such relationships because the love of God comes to us through them in the love extended to us by the other person. Being open enough to love someone in this way makes us vulnerable to that person. We know and love one another well enough to know precisely what will hurt one another the most, and in moments of anger we sometimes exploit that knowledge and speak to our beloved in ways that are intentionally hurtful. We throw words like daggers aimed at the soft spot that only a loved one would know is there. In the aftermath of such conflict, we begin to feel the magnitude of the damage we have inflicted and grow sorrowful. Such sorrow is a chief ingredient in contrition. Contrition involves the sense that we have violated another and in so doing have diminished ourselves. It is the awareness that we have taken the sacred and used it for the purposes of the profane, and regardless of how hard we try, we will never be able to restore it completely. Contrition encompasses sorrow for the wound inflicted on the beloved; humiliation for the diminishment of the self resulting from that act; a sense of guilt, defilement, and unworthiness for having profaned something sacred; and mournfulness over the realization that some of the goodness and beauty we have corrupted may be lost forever.

Alongside awe and contrition stands *gratitude*. Think of the birth of a new child, a daughter, anxiously awaited and eagerly hoped for. We receive this new life with fear and trembling, with delight and humility. But above all we receive her with gratitude. She comes to us as gift, as something we have not earned and do not deserve. Theologian James Gustafson describes gratitude in this way:

> In certain moments of experience we recognize that we have been loved by others beyond our deserving, we have been forgiven when we dared not believe it was possible, we have been sustained by the patience of others when they have had sufficient reasons to reject us, we have benefited from nature and society more than we have contributed to them. We have received more than we have earned or deserved, and we are thankful.[4]

At its most basic, gratitude is thankfulness, but it is thankfulness colored by an awareness that we are not self-sufficient. We are dependent on others. From cradle to grave, we rely on others as we come into being, are sustained in existence, and seek meaning and purpose in life. Gratitude is the joyful acknowledgment of this dependence. It entails a deep sense of the giftedness of life.

FOUR THEOLOGICAL THEMES

With these three experiences of the heart before us, we can turn to a theological explication of the affections. What do such experiences of the heart indicate to us about the deepest structures of our identities? What theological insights are implicit in our experiences of awe before the great sequoia, or contrition for having wounded a loved one, or gratitude for the gifts of life? In this section, we develop four themes that help us to understand what an affection is, what a *religious* affection is, and how religious affections are theologically significant.

1. Religious Affections and the World of Our Senses

Experiences of the heart are object-oriented.[5] We do not simply feel awe, contrition, and gratitude in the abstract or generically. Our awe, contrition, and gratitude are always inspired by and directed toward a particular object or event in creation that is perceptible to us through our senses. Every creature has its own peculiar beauty, its own particular goodness. It is precisely the individuality and particularity of that object that is crucial for eliciting the affection. We feel awe *before the great sequoia*, contrition *over the harsh words spoken*, and gratitude *for a particular child*. It is the great tree, here and now—in this forest, at dusk—that evokes awe. It is the wounded friend—with whom you rode bikes last weekend—who elicits contrition. It is the new daughter—with her father's eyes and her mother's nose—who provides the occasion for gratitude.

What we feel in the here and now, in the presence of this tree or that child, may be simply an emotion, in the sense that it erupts within us spontaneously and quickly passes away. In such a case, we are not yet dealing with an affection. But perhaps the felt awe or contrition or gratitude, as we experience it in this moment, points to something more. Perhaps it points to something about who we are as persons who are dispositionally ready, constitutionally open, and pervasively attuned to experiencing the world as a place that properly calls for awe, contrition, and gratitude. We are not, in this case, simply people who feel awe or contrition or gratitude from time to time—though we do that, and it can be good. Instead, we are people constituted by awe, contrition, and gratitude. We are people whose hearts are pervasively attuned to the world as a place that calls for awe, contrition, and gratitude.

This means that emotions and affections are related in complex and recip-rocal ways. The inner chords of our being are attuned to the world in such a way that the ordinary and mundane become occasions that evoke and form the affections within us. On the one hand, ordinary and mundane experiences call out emotional expressions of what we already are at heart, that is, what we are affectively. On the other hand, we cannot become what we are in our affec-tions—persons who are attuned toward the world with awe—until we have first experienced the emotion of awe on numerous occasions. We might say that an emotion can pass into an affection when it becomes a settled and abid-ing disposition in us. Once that has happened, the emotion is the outward, expressed form of an inward, enduring feature of our identity. Emotions, then, are oriented toward objects that we perceive through our senses. Affections are the underlying readiness to experience the world in a particular way. But those affections enter the world of experience—that is, the world in which we *feel* them—only when elicited by a particular, sensible object and expressed through a particular emotion.

So far we have addressed the affections only as they are elicited by the cre-ated order, but for people of faith there is another dimension to them. For peo-ple of faith, the experiences of awe, contrition, and gratitude are directed not only toward a created object or event. Such experiences also gesture toward and are related to the God who creates, sustains, and gives purpose to those created objects and events. Our sense experience points us toward that which is beyond our capacities to see, hear, taste, touch, or smell. God, however, does not replace the created objects or events that serve as the object of our religious affections. Rather, a sense of God's presence, power, and grace accompanies and shines through such experiences. Ultimately, then, our gratitude is thank-fulness for God's bounty; our awe is awe of God's majestic beauty; and we stand contrite before the God who both loves and judges us. God is ultimately the object of our affections, and this is what makes them *religious* affections.

But to acknowledge God as the ultimate object of our affections is not to say that God is the only or immediate object of our affections. God's presence is always mediated to us through God's creation. And while we must never con-fuse creator and creature, we must acknowledge that God is present in the cre-ation and becomes present to us through other creatures. While it is true that "we live and move and have our being" in God (Acts 17:28), it is also true that we live and move and have our being through food, family, and meaningful work. Scripture provides ample witness to the fact that "no one shall see [God] and live" (Exod. 33:20), but it also provides ample witness to our indirect "see-ing" and "hearing" of God. A sacrament is "an outward and visible sign of an inward and spiritual grace."[6] We may say, then, that there is a sacramental quality to all of creation and that we bear witness to this reality in our celebration of the sacraments of baptism and the Lord's Supper as water, wine, and bread mediate to us the redeeming presence of God in Christ. Through these objects that are accessible to our senses—through water, bread, and wine—we come into the presence of the God who is beyond the world of our senses.

For the Christian, awe before the great sequoia is always also awe directed toward the majesty of the creator God in whose life the great sequoia participates, for it too lives, moves, and has its being in God. For the Christian, contrition is never simply sorrow and remorse for wounding the close friend with whom you rode bikes; it is always also sorrow and remorse for the estrangement from God that was included in that act. For the Christian, gratitude is never simply thankfulness to families that provide support through the pregnancy and for the nurses and physicians who work to ensure a safe delivery; it is always also thankfulness to the "God from whom all blessings flow." In short, affections become *religious affections* when the ordinary objects and events of creation mediate the presence, power, and grace of God to us.

But why is it that creatures can mediate the presence of God to one another? They can do so because the world that God creates is good and bears witness to God's majesty, sovereignty, wisdom, and power. In the first creation story, narrated in Genesis 1, Scripture concludes its description of the work of each of the six days of creation by noting with an almost liturgical repetition that "God saw that it was good." The entire drama of the story concludes with an even more resounding divine acknowledgment that "indeed, it was very good" (Gen. 1:31). In Genesis, God calls out the goodness of creation; in the Psalms, the creation responds by calling out the goodness of God: "The heavens are telling the glory of God; and the firmament proclaims [God's] handiwork. Day to day pours forth speech, and night to night declares knowledge" (Ps. 19:1–2). In the antiphonal play of praise and delight between a good creation and its good creator, we catch a glimpse of the doxological character of life in God. In both its particularity and in the relationships that bind together all of those particulars into a coherent and beautiful whole, the creation is good in itself and participates in the goodness of its creator. Each creature is a token of the divine that participates in and points to the God who is sovereignly and preeminently beautiful.

Christian religious affections are evoked and formed in this primordial liturgy in which God and creation sing praises to their shared goodness and beauty. John Calvin was acutely aware of the way the beauty and goodness of creation bestowed upon it by God are intimately related to the affectional dimensions of our identities. Calvin spoke of the entire creation as a "dazzling theater," a set of "insignia whereby [God] shows his glory to us," and as a "mirror in which we can contemplate God, who is otherwise invisible." The revelatory power of created beauty is ubiquitous and floods the senses for Calvin, and at every moment reveals the invisible through the visible. When people of faith encounter such created beauty, Calvin adds, they are "overwhelmed by the boundless force of its brightness," and their "mental powers are suspended in wonderment." The ordered beauty of nature "stirs us deeply," and we "break forth in admiration of the Artificer." Calvin goes on to note that the revelatory power of creation gives to the faithful a "devout disposition" and an affectional form of knowledge of God that is "more of the heart and more of the dispositions than of the understanding." For Calvin, the goodness and beauty of creation work upon the affectional chords of our identities. Encountering God in and through the creation stirs the affections and offers us a knowledge of God that does not merely "flit about in the top of the brain."[7]

When we affirm that the creation is good, that it is the "dazzling theater" in which God is revealed to us, we do not mean that the creation is good in spite of its physical existence, as though it can point us to a God who is pure spirit only if we can get past its physical nature. We mean that the creation is good precisely *in* its materiality. Creatures do not act as tokens of the divine in spite of being bodily beings. Rather, their bodily natures are precisely what allow them to act as vehicles of revelation. What is it that we marvel at in the great sequoia, after all, but its immense physical presence? At the birth of a child, don't we stand in grateful wonder, counting her fingers and toes, watching her eyelashes grow in, and looking for signs of a well-functioning central nervous system? Even in our sorrow over harsh words spoken to a friend, we are sorrowful for the sake of one who is inseparably ensouled flesh and enfleshed soul. Precisely because we can sense the beauty of the world, it "stirs us deeply" and points us toward God.

Christians are often tempted by a spiritualizing tendency that would eschew the physical for the sake of gaining salvation. We sometimes speak as though at death our souls joyfully flee the wretched bodies that have trapped them. This impulse is especially pronounced in Protestant worship, with our reduction of the sacraments to mere signs and our deep discomfort with bodily acts of reverence such as making the sign of the cross and kneeling. We worry about stimulating the senses too much with incense or icons. Simplicity of form in worship can be a virtue, but not if it is funded by a spiritualizing tendency that runs contrary to the central witness of the Christian faith that in Christ, God became human, really human, flesh and blood. Such a spiritualizing tendency also runs contrary to the Christian hope for the final restoration of all things. We hope, not for a disembodied heavenly existence, but for a kingdom with resurrected bodies, where lions and lambs lie down together, where the hungry are satisfied and the sick made whole. We hope, in short, for a kingdom where "the conditions of heaven" come to an earth made new.[8]

Individual creatures and the beautiful web of being that binds them all together, then, point us toward the divine life in a way that evokes and shapes our affectional lives. But we must remember that other creatures do not exist merely for the sake of forming our affections; they exist to glorify God. The Westminster Catechism begins by asking us, "What is the chief end of [humanity]?" It answers that question by affirming that we were made to "glorify God and to enjoy [God] forever."[9] This affirmation conveys an important truth about human life. We do not exist for our own sakes. We exist to glorify God. The catechism might have continued by asking, "What is the end of every creature?" The answer would remain the same. The whole creation and every creature in it—including human beings, dogs, trees, rocks, and cosmic dust— exist to glorify and enjoy God. This means that although creatures act as tokens of the divine, pointing us toward God and evoking and shaping our affections, we may not reduce them to this function. Creatures exist to glorify God, and a wondrous secondary consequence of that purpose is that they also shape our affectional lives. Proper Christian affections, moreover, incorporate this theocentric insight. Our affections, in other words, are shaped and ordered by a deep awareness that God and God's purposes in creation exceed human interests and that our own interests, therefore, ought to be conformed to God's delightful celebration of the goodness of the whole of creation.

2. Religious Affections and Community

In the previous section, we argued that the good creation mediates the presence of God to us through our senses in an affection-forming manner. In this section, we want to investigate a second important way in which our religious affections are formed: through the shared life of the communities of faith in which we are embedded. To understand how our affections are formed in community, though, we must first address a common misconception about the relationship between individuals and their communities.

Modern people, perhaps especially Americans, are prone to think of themselves first and foremost as individuals. We imagine ourselves to be "self-made" and the sole authors of our own lives. We bristle at the suggestion that we are shaped by the practices, beliefs, traditions, and shared assumptions of the communities from which we come. We imagine that to be a genuine adult—an autonomous individual—is to rise above such determinants of our identity through the free choices and rational decisions that we make as individuals. We think of ourselves as masters of our own destiny, as rational individuals who rise above mere social convention and conformity to craft an autonomous identity for ourselves. We resist blind conformity to tradition, the suffocating effect of the social expectations and assumptions that constrain us, and we resent the suggestion that our lives and choices are limited by the circumstances into which we are born.

Much of this mindset is rooted in the philosophy of the eighteenth-century Enlightenment. In Immanuel Kant we find one of the clearest articulations of this vision of life.[10] Kant described human beings as self-generated beings who ought to be autonomous, a law unto ourselves. We generate our identities through the rational act of prescribing a law for ourselves. He wanted us to grow out of the stage of human development when we were heteronomous, under the law of another. Just as children pass from the governance of their parents into adulthood where they govern themselves, so Europeans, according to Kant, were moving from a time when they were the subjects of kings and queens into a time when they would be citizens of a democracy. They were moving from a time in which tradition and institutional religion determined what they ought to believe and how they ought to behave, to a time when individuals would decide such matters for themselves based on rational grounds.

When this idea of autonomous individualism becomes coupled with a romantic valorization of emotion, it can lead us to believe that religious affections first well up from the inner recesses of the heart of the isolated individual and then overflow in a sincere and authentic expression of piety. Church provides the context for an aggregation of individuals to gather so that they may express their individual inner religious emotions in worship. To borrow and adapt a term from George Lindbeck, we may call this an experiential-expressivist model of Christian life and worship.[11] In this model, the inner emotional life of the individual comes first and is only afterwards expressed in communal life and practice. The church is effectively an aggregation rather than a congregation; that is, the church comes into existence through and continues to exist as a voluntary gathering of like-minded, like-feeling individuals. The glue that holds the church's identity together is the continued exercise of the free choice of the individuals who gather in worship to express their inner emotional experiences.

The problem with the theory of autonomous individualism, whether in its rationalistic Enlightenment form or its emotivistic experiential-expressivist form, is that it does not answer well to human experience. We don't experience ourselves as simply appearing in the world as self-made individuals, isolated from one another. Instead, we grow into who we are, how we think, and how we experience the world emotionally through our relationships with others. Friedrich Schleiermacher argued that he had been formed in the womb of piety before he was ever able to think for himself.[12] Many of us likewise find ourselves gratefully indebted to the traditions and institutions that have shaped us. We identify ourselves by our relationships. We are daughters to parents, members of congregations, friends of coworkers, and citizens of nations.

Social relationships and inherited traditions can go wrong in many ways, and become damaging and destructive to our development as children of God. But these are, after all, distortions and should not deflect attention from the fact that social relationships and inherited traditions of belief and practice provide the rich soil in which our identities take root, are nourished, flourish, and bear fruit. Such social relationships are not merely inescapable; they are good. After all, in the second creation story narrated in Genesis, God declares that it is not good for us to be alone.

Instead of thinking of ourselves first as individuals, who secondarily come into relationships, we ought to acknowledge that we are relational beings, whose identities as individuals emerge only from within a community.[13] We are, that is, social selves at the outset. And this is good. If we return to our descriptions of awe, contrition, and gratitude, we see clearly the generative and shaping power of communities. When we feel contrition over breaking faith with a friend, we acknowledge not only that we have hurt our loved one, but also that we have diminished ourselves. But only if we are socially formed and relationally defined is it possible to diminish the self by breaking a relationship. Gratitude at the birth of a new daughter highlights most poignantly the relational web in which our lives and affections are embedded. We receive her as daughter, granddaughter, new patient, new citizen, child of the covenant, and, above all, we receive her as a gift—as that which we have not earned and do not deserve. Gratitude grows out of a deep sense of our dependence on others. We depend on others for life, for joy and meaning, and for all that we cannot provide ourselves. Our capacity to respond to the world in awe is also cultivated socially and relationally. Awe extends our sense of community beyond the confines of the human community. It embeds us in a cosmic order that sustains us and to which we have responsibilities. But our capacity to locate ourselves within that order and to respond to it in awe must be learned in a community that acknowledges that all creatures are connected to the sacred purposes of God.

We are formed as social and relational selves within particular communities, but there is no one, single community that forms us. Neither is there broad consensus among the various communities in which we are embedded about what values ought to shape us, what affections ought to be cultivated, and what object or objects those affections ought to be oriented toward. Indeed, there is stiff competition among a variety of social forces for dominance in the business of forming persons. Some of these social forces would generate and shape our affective lives in destructive or superficial ways. Nationalism, consumerism, and the culture of amusement are but three examples.

We are all citizens of a nation, and that citizenship rightly entails a degree of love of one's country, loyalty to its cause, and service to its common good.

Being formed in the political order for citizenship and the cultivation of civic virtue does not conflict with the Christian faith, and action in the political life of the nation often provides a venue for the translation of the commitments of the Christian faith into action. But such citizenship should not be confused with nationalism. Nationalism does not form us to be citizens; it forms us to be uncritical patriots. Nationalism asks us to replace our ultimate loyalty to the kingdom of God with loyalty to the nation. It does not form us to be citizens who can question and critique particular forms of national life when they conflict with the values of the Christian faith. Bleeding together Christian identity and national identity, nationalism is idolatry. Nationalism transforms the affection of humility into pride. Humility reminds us of our own limitations and allows us to find our proper place in relationship to others who are likewise limited. It allows us to relate to those who do not share our citizenship as fellow children of God. Nationalism makes us incapable of contrition for the sins of the nation. It perverts hope by replacing the coming kingdom of God as its object with imperialism. It replaces our capacity for self-sacrificial love with militaristic aggression and paternalism toward others.

If nationalism shapes us to be uncritical patriots rather than citizens, consumerism shapes us to be bargain hunters and conspicuous consumers rather than economic beings who seek just exchanges and meaningful work. Part of being human, being a relationally and socially formed self, is to participate in the economic order. How we earn a living is an important part of our identity. Sometimes we even identify ourselves by vocation: we are construction workers, waitresses, nurses, managers, teachers, farmers, and homemakers. The work that we do and the economic exchanges that we enter into shape us deeply. But when just participation in the world of work and exchange is distorted into consumerism, we become identified by what we can purchase, consume, dispose of, and put on display so that others will be impressed with us. Consumerism undermines our capacity for awe by reducing all other things to raw materials or products to be bought, sold, and harvested for narrow human ends. It impairs our capacity for gratitude because when everything has a price, nothing is sheer gift. It distorts our mutuality and interdependence by reducing all relationships to market exchanges. It undermines our sense of obligation by blinding us to the claims made on us by those who are marginalized from the community of consumers.

Like consumerism and nationalism, the culture of amusement has a powerful "person-forming" capacity.[14] There is an appropriate role for leisure activity in forming us as persons. Play, sports, and the arts participate in the goodness of creation. Participation in these activities should cultivate certain affections, such as sportsmanship, a species of mutuality. They open us to delight and sometimes to humility. But as we discussed earlier, leisure can degenerate into a culture of mere amusement that converts audience members who are the attentive listeners into fans and voyeurs. Since the function of emotion in the culture of amusement is simply to be *felt*, the emotions never settle down and become affections; they never become part of who we are. Once discharged, they simply evaporate. Though often intense, the emotions are superficial, immediate, and evanescent. The culture of amusement may accidentally distort particular affections by sentimentalizing them, but more importantly it trivializes the emotions by refusing to connect them to anything beyond the amusing event. They never attach themselves to the deepest affectional structures of our personhood.

Because we are social selves, and not autonomous individuals, our identities are generated and shaped within a variety of communities. Nationalism, consumerism, and the culture of amusement provide three competing social forces that would shape our personhood. They are, in a sense, countercommunities to the church. The church is also a community that can shape our affections, and it ought to be a chief context in which we as social and relational selves become who we are. But how does the church do that? How do communities generate and shape the affections that are at the core of our identities?

"The church," wrote Schleiermacher, "is . . . called the common mother of us all." Schleiermacher's words echo those of Cyprian of Carthage in the third century and John Calvin in the sixteenth.[15] Throughout the centuries Christians have affirmed that even as our mothers bring us into life when they give birth to us, the church brings us into the life of faith in Christ. This coming into the world and coming into the world of faith are bedrock to who we are. Covenant is a central theme in the Christian doctrine of the church. When God calls Abraham out of Ur of the Chaldees, God makes a covenant not simply with Abraham as an individual, but with all of his descendants and with all of the nations to whom they shall be a light. The divine initiative for salvation is extended first in the formation of a community of faith, and through that community the initiative reaches the individual. To affirm that the church is a covenant community is to recognize the social nature of faith. Even as our mothers precede us and bring us into life, so the church as a covenant community, as "the mother of us all," precedes the individuals whom the church brings into the life of faith.

If we are to understand how the church generates and shapes the affections in individual lives, we will have to attend to the central activities of the church when it is engaged in its central work, the worship of God. As the community of faith gathers around Word, Table, and Font, it enters into a set of practices that are powerfully person-forming. In gathering around the Word, we are invited not simply to hear Scripture, but to participate in and perform it. Our own life stories are joined to the great narrative of faith. Its story becomes our story; its hope becomes our hope; its awe at the grandeur of God becomes

our awe; its sense of human brokenness and contrition becomes ours; its gratitude and delight become ours. Our lives are interpreted by and incorporated
into its grand narrative. In gathering around the Table and Font, we are invited
not simply to observe but to be bathed and fed.[16] The material substances of
water, wine, and bread act on us bodily to renew us spiritually, bringing us to
new life and sustaining us in that new life. Through these sacred rites we begin
already here and now to live into and participate in the new creation. As we
are washed in baptism, the old self begins to pass away. As we are fed at the
Lord's Table, the new self begins to lean into the promised future. We sit at a
Table that anticipates the heavenly banquet, and we are washed at the font that
immerses us already in the death and resurrection of Christ who makes all
things new. Our broken, disordered, and distorted affections begin to become
whole and coherent, reorganized and reoriented. In worship we encounter
afresh the divine initiative of grace coming to us to renew and transform our
religious affections, that is, to make us new creatures in Christ.

3. Religious Affection, Desire, and Dependence

There is a logic to the religious affections. To say this, however, runs contrary
to our common way of thinking about emotions and affections. We rarely
associate them with logic. Instead, we contrast matters of the heart and logic,
pitting them against one another. In so doing, though, we are blinded to a central truth about our religious affections, namely, that our individual religious
affections such as awe, contrition, and gratitude come together in our personalities in a patterned way. Individual religious affections are like stars that come
together in a patterned way in the night sky to produce a constellation. Or, to
change metaphors, each religious affection is like a musical note. When musical notes come together in a well-ordered way, they produce a song. Likewise,
our religious affections come together in an ordered way to produce our identities. Our ordinary language reflects this reality. Think, for example, of how
we characterize someone as having a "pleasant disposition" or an "even temperament." Such phrases indicate that we see in the affections of such people
a unifying order or pattern that manifests itself in visible, predictable ways in
their behavior. When we speak of the logic of the affections, then, we are referring to the order or pattern that binds the affections together in a meaningful
way and provides our identities with stability, order, coherence, and purpose.

In chapter 4 we will describe this ordering of the affections in greater depth,
giving special attention to twelve religious affections. But here we want to
explore the source of this affectional order. What is the glue that binds our affections together in a patterned way and thus organizes our identities? There are
probably innumerable factors and forces that affect how we become who we are.
Our dispositions are shaped by our genetic heritage, social circumstances, faith

commitments, and life experiences, among other things. While we cannot focus on all these factors in the ordering of our affections, we want to highlight two crucial components that have deep roots in the Christian tradition and are especially open to theological analysis. Augustine captured both components well when he confessed to God that "our hearts are restless till they find their rest in Thee."[17] The human heart is animated by an endless yearning to be related properly to the God upon whom we are utterly dependent for our being and life. Augustine points us to the fact that the deepest structures of our identities are shaped by what we want and what we depend upon; who we are, in short, has to do with *desire* and *dependence*.

What do you want? On what and whom do you rely? We answer these questions in a wide variety of ways. We want ice cream cones, security and happiness for our families, world peace, and peace of mind. We rely on food producers, transporters, and retailers; on municipal authorities that provide police forces, education, and public art; on governments that strive to avoid conflict and bring about justice; and on our work, family, and faith to provide these things. What we desire and what we depend on are intimately connected and serve as root indicators of what kind of persons we are. When spouses long for and lean on one another, they weave a common life that deeply shapes who they are as individuals. When the church receives a new member through the sacrament of baptism, a complex network of desire and dependence is revealed and enacted. In the covenant of baptism, God demonstrates a desire that all persons should come to faith and be sustained in faithfulness. Members of the congregation come to share this desire and to depend upon God and one another as they guide, nurture, and encourage the new member.

The ancient and enduring language of Jewish and Christian worship found in the Psalter reflects the centrality of desire and dependence in our affectional lives: "As a deer longs for flowing streams, so my soul longs for you, O God" (Ps. 42:1); "O God, you are my God, I seek you, my soul thirsts for you. . . . My soul clings to you; your right hand upholds me" (Ps. 63:1, 8). More often, however, desire and dependence are expressed through particular affections in the context of worship. In the prayer of Great Thanksgiving that precedes Communion in the Alexandrian Liturgy of St. Basil, we pray: "Fountain of all life, source of all goodness, you made all things and fill them with your blessing; you created them to rejoice in the splendor of your radiance."[18] The prayer accentuates the affection of delight, and this delight flows directly out of a recognition that we depend upon God for life and goodness. Moreover, to "rejoice in the splendor of [God's] radiance" is at the same time to experience the satisfaction of our deepest desires in relation to God.

Another example of how dependence and desire shine through particular religious affections can be found in that moment between the corporate confession of sin and the assurance of pardon. In this moment, we stand in humility and hope between the contrition expressed in the prayer of confession and the gratitude evoked by the forgiveness offered in the assurance of pardon. In this moment, many congregations sing one of two pleas for God's mercy.[19] In the Kyrie Eleison, we pray, "Lord have mercy. Christ, have mercy. Lord, have mercy." In the Trisagion, we pray, "Holy God, holy and mighty, holy immortal One, have mercy upon us." Both prayers accentuate the affections of humility and hope, but ingredient in this humility and hope are our deep desire to be related rightly to God and a heartfelt trust that the God upon whom we depend for mercy will not withhold it. This desire and dependence are bedrock to our identities as Christians, and it is important to remember that our desire and dependence are a desire for and dependence on the God revealed to us in Jesus Christ. This means that the desire and dependence at the core of our affections, and therefore at the core of our identities, are shaped by the character of the loving, self-giving, sovereign God. In the context of a liturgy where we know that our plea for mercy will always be followed by an assurance of pardon, the hope for a reconstituted relationship with God is not mere wishful thinking because our desire finds its object in a God who wants the same. Our humility is never cowering fearfulness because our dependence is on a God who never fails to forgive. The plea for mercy is always followed by an assurance of pardon. We are never surprised and never disappointed. The God whom we worship, the One whom we desire and on whom we depend, is the God who comes to us in love and forgiveness in Jesus Christ.

We have noted that desire and dependence are often expressed in worship through a particular religious affection like delight, humility, or hope. In fact, every religious affection will display this same pattern. We will find desire and dependence in every religious affection, because the affections are specifications of dependence and desire. It is precisely this dependence and desire that provide the order, pattern, or unifying logic to our religious affections. We might say that desire and dependence are basic organizing forces of the personality. By themselves, these unifying energies communicate nothing about who we are, but when they take particular form in the affections, they form the settled and abiding dispositions that mark who we are.

If we return to our descriptions of awe, contrition, and gratitude, we can see how desire and dependence run through every religious affection. Desire is, after all, about attraction. We are drawn toward the beauty of the great sequoia. That attraction is part of the awe. But the great tree also reminds us of our small place in the vastness of the cosmos, reminding us that we are dependent on the cosmos in ways that it is not dependent on us, and this sense of our dependence is also part of the awe. Likewise, desire and dependence run through our gratitude. We are innately attracted to whatever we perceive to be good and beautiful. The experience of the new child as sheer gift is a recognition of the goodness and beauty of that child. It is precisely this goodness and beauty for which we are grateful. But our gratitude also places us in a broader context of dependence. We are grateful for having received that which we do not deserve. We are dependent on a vast network of others for the gifts that allow us to have life and to have meaningful lives. Contrition also carries with it both desire and dependence. We yearn for restoration with both God and friend. And perhaps no experience reminds us of our dependence more than that of needing a friend's forgiveness. Because we are relational beings, wounding our friends diminishes our very selves. If we are again to be fully who we are, then we depend on our friend's and God's mercy.

All of these affections are linked. The desire and dependence that run through each of them also bind them together like pearls on a string. Our awe at the great sequoia reminds us of the vastness of the cosmos; it reminds us that we have received from the creation and its Creator far more than we have contributed, and this recognition prompts gratitude. But awe also prompts contrition, because when we realize the vastness of the creation in which we are embedded and of the God before whom we stand, we also recognize how wide is the chasm between God's holiness and our brokenness. When we see the bonds that tie together everything in the creation and orient it toward the glory of God, we see also how our actions have violated that goodness. Awe, then, prompts contrition. But contrition always prompts gratitude, for of all the gifts that we have undeservingly received, forgiveness is one of the greatest. There is, then, a pattern or logic that binds together all of the affections, and this pattern or logic is grounded in the desire and dependence that run through them all.

The interconnectedness of all of the affections means that every outward, emotional expression of an affection carries with it overtones of the other affections. The plea for mercy in worship is an act of humility, but it carries with it hope. The awe we experience at the foot of the great sequoia carries with it gratitude, contrition, and delight. The complex interrelations of the affections mean not only that individual, expressed affections contain overtones of the other affections, but also that as each affection is formed, every other affection is also shaped, modified, and integrated in fresh ways with the broader nexus of affections. We are constituted not simply by the individual affections, as settled and abiding dispositions, but also by the whole web of affectivity, by the order and pattern of the affections as they are related to one another.

Our hymnody often speaks of the "heart," and when it does, it is referring precisely to this patterned web of affectivity. When we invite God, the "Fount of every blessing," to come and "tune my heart to sing Thy grace," we are asking that God realign all of our affections so that they are focused on divine glory.[20] The hymn speaks of our delight, hope, gratitude, and humility. It asks that God would "take and seal" our hearts, the full spectrum of our affections. Calvin's famous hymn "I Greet Thee, Who My Sure Redeemer Art," also speaks to a range of religious affections and petitions God to reorient these affections, to "come . . . and our whole being sway."[21]

Our hearts, our whole beings, are "prone to wander." They may be drawn toward reverent love of God, or seduced by nationalism, consumerism, and amusement. What we do in worship, when we touch on one or another of the affections, has an impact on the whole web of affectivity, on our hearts. Which direction will our worship move us? Will it invite us into an abiding relationship with our maker and redeemer? Or will it merely entertain us, giving us occasion to develop and express superficial emotions? What we do in worship has the capacity to be deeply person-forming, and this truth should prompt in us hope for the work of the church. But it should also give us pause. If we are about the work of shaping persons for reverent life before God, then we must be very intentional, humble, and cautious about how we do that. Beginning in chapter 6 we will investigate particular components of the worship service to find ways in which we can become more intentional, humble, cautious—and, yes, hopeful—about our work in worship.

4. Religious Affections, Knowing, and Doing

If God comes to us in worship to sway our "whole being," then we should not be surprised to find that the gracious transformation of our affections radiates out over and influences all our knowing and doing in the world. If the religious affections are identity-constituting realities, it is natural for them to shape the way we perceive and understand the world around us, as well as how we translate that knowledge into action and behavior. The affections cannot be relegated to the private, inner sphere of the individual heart; they shine over, color, and shape all that we know and do. Jonathan Edwards, perhaps the most astute observer and theological analyst of the religious affections, saw this clearly. In his monumental *Treatise on the Religious Affections*, Edwards draws attention to the interaction of the affections with our normal knowing and doing in the world:

> Such is [human] nature, that [it] is very inactive, any otherwise than [it] is influenced by some affection, either love or hatred, desire, hope, fear, or some other. These affections we see to be the springs that set [us] agoing, in all affairs of life, and engage [human beings] in all their pursuits. . . . We see the world of [humankind] to be exceedingly busy and active; and the affections of [humankind] are the springs of the motion: take away all love and hatred, all hope and fear, all zeal and affectionate desire, and the world would be, in a great measure, motionless and dead.[22]

The web of affections in the human heart colors and shapes the way we perceive, understand, and lean into our world, and serves as the spring that generates and shapes our motion, activity, and behavior in that world.

Let's begin by exploring how our religious affections are related to our knowing. In every act of knowing, there is a subject, the knower, and an object, the known. The question is, how are these two related? Perhaps we know an other as a purely objective "thing." We investigate it objectively and are essentially unaffected by the other. Jewish philosopher Martin Buber called this an "I-It" relationship.[23] Edwards called it "mere notional understanding." But if we are affectional knowers who are essentially relational and social, then this cannot be our truest form of knowledge. Buber proposed another way of knowing, a way that requires us to enter into a relationship with the other in which we are open to change. He called this an "I-Thou" relationship. Edwards called it "experimental knowledge," and said that in this way of knowing "the soul does not merely perceive and view things, but is [in] some way inclined with respect to the things it views or considers."[24]

Edwards' explanation of these two kinds of knowing is derived from a very common experience. Think of two people, both of whom are trying to understand honey. The first person tastes the honey and delights in its sweetness. The second person simply observes the honey in its jar; this person does not smell or taste the honey or feel its texture on her tongue. While each may have some knowledge of the honey, only the first person, the one who tasted the honey, has known it affectionally. Part of knowing honey entails being pleased (or, perhaps, displeased) by its taste. We know the honey by participating in it. Ultimately, even the more distant form of knowing is still affectional. The scientist who examines the honey for its chemical makeup and potential medicinal properties is drawn by curiosity to participate in the honey in a different way.

This simple example highlights the kind of affectional knowing that is participatory in nature. In participatory knowing, we enter into "affectional communion" with the one we come to know and are "infused or pervaded" by that other.[25] What this means is that, for example, when we stand in the presence of the great sequoia, its presence surrounds us and dominates our awareness in a way that invites us, however briefly, to become a part of its life; and it becomes a part of ours. In this kind of knowing, the rigid boundary that separates the knower from the known becomes permeable, is partly dissolved. The tree and the whole cosmos in which we and it are situated are never utterly other than and unrelated to us. To know a thing is to come into a relationship with it.

This affectional attunement to the other as thou prevents us from reducing the other to a mere means to our ends, a product to be purchased, consumed, and discarded. Affectional knowing always stands in judgment over our tendency to tear ourselves out of the fabric of interdependence and then, as so-

called autonomous individuals, to relate to the rest of reality in purely strategic ways, assuming that all other things exist to serve us. Knowledge that pre-
tends to pure objectivity exists only as a distortion of the true form of knowing
that reflects our affectional, relational lives. In affectional knowing we are
attuned to our own embeddedness in the interdependent web of creation, and
this means that while other creatures may contribute to our well-being, they
may also make claims upon us, nurturing in us the affection of obligation. In
affectional knowing we are sensitized to the mutuality that brings all the parts
of creation into dynamic relationships with one another. This same dynamic
relationality contributes to the beauty of the whole so that both individual
creatures and the whole web of creation glorify God. In participatory knowing we are pervaded with a sense of the interdependence and interconnectedness of all things and perceive that "indeed, [the creation] is very good."

There is a special relationship between such participatory knowing and the
perception of beauty. In experiences of beauty, we feel drawn toward the beautiful other in a way that heightens our sense of connection to it. We should
not, then, be surprised by nor fearful of the age-old presence in the liturgy of
concentrated moments of beauty. Think of the "Ode to Joy." For many people that hymn does not merely describe joy; it calls us into it. As the notes soar
through us and above us, they fill the sacred space, and our hearts are drawn
upward with them "in the triumph song of life." We feel our hearts opening
before God as flowers "open to the sun above." And it is not humanity alone
that praises God; we join a whole creational symphony of praise: "All Thy
works with joy surround Thee, / Earth and heaven reflect thy rays, / Stars and
angels sing around Thee, / Center of unbroken praise. / Field and forest, vale
and mountain, / Flowery meadow, flashing sea, / Chanting bird and flowing
fountain / Call us to rejoice in thee."[26] Here the forest is not surveyed for its
lumber, nor the mountain for its mineral deposits, nor the chanting bird for
its tender breast meat. Instead we immerse ourselves in a song of praise with
all of our fellow creatures and are called to "join the happy chorus which the
morning stars began." Such moments of concentrated beauty draw us out of
the narrow confines of our so-called autonomy and invite us into a form of
affectional, participatory knowledge that involves fellowship with those with
whom we worship, with all our fellow creatures, and with the God whose very
life as Father, Son, and Holy Spirit, is relational.

Over the course of a lifetime, moments of beauty in the liturgy cultivate in us
an enduring openness and pervasive readiness to recognize and respond to
beauty in the world. The affections, in other words, are not only integrally
related to our knowing (our capacity to recognize beauty); they are also integrally related to our doing (our capacity to respond to that beauty). Beauty in
worship begins to wear a groove into our souls through which the Holy Spirit

flows into us, reforming our affections, and enabling us to "relate to all things in a manner appropriate to their relations to God."[27] Worship, with its power to shape and direct the religious affections, is thus organically related to the moral life. Worship is not an occasion for escape from the world, but is instead the occasion to renew our hearts in preparation for participating in God's renewal of the world. Worship tunes our hearts by reorienting our religious affections, and those affections are the hinge that joins the frame of knowledge to the door of action.[28] Christian ethics are always liturgical and affectional ethics.

The moments of beauty in worship that accumulate over the course of a lifetime open us to the beauty of the world, but they also attune us to that which is ugly, incongruous, and improperly related in our world. Worship makes us notice the injustices of sexism, racism, homelessness, and poverty that deny other human beings their rightful place in the social network. Worship makes us notice the degradation of the natural environment that would convert all "flowery meadows" to parking lots and subdivisions. When such ugliness becomes the object of our affective attention, for example, delight properly manifests itself as anguish, our sense of well-being properly expresses itself as anger, our sense of obligation and self-sacrificial love are heightened, and contrition at our complicity in such injustice is paired with a sense of hope and possibility that arises from an awareness that God forgives us still and empowers us to struggle toward the new creation.

When we reflect on experiences such as standing at the foot of the great sequoia, wounding a friend, or beholding a new child, we find that they are rich experiences of the heart. They are experiences in which we may neither dismiss emotion in the name of reason nor celebrate it uncritically. We find instead that these experiences of the heart point us to deep structures of our identities that lie beneath the outward emotional expressions. They point us to the religious affections. A careful investigation of such experiences of the heart reveals four important theological truths about the religious affections and their relationship to worship. First, the religious affections are grounded in the goodness of creation and its capacity through our senses to mediate to us the presence of God. Second, the religious affections are socially generated and formed by the communities in which we are embedded. As the covenant partner of God, the church ought to be a chief community for organizing the religious affections of Christian people. Third, the religious affections are interrelated and organized by the desire and sense of dependence that run through them all. And finally, the religious affections, when cultivated in worship, open us to participatory knowing that organically translates into fitting moral action.

3

Fallen Religious Affections

We have seen that religious affections are related in complex ways to desire and dependence. Desire and dependence run through each of the individual affections but also bind all of them together like pearls on a string. It is this binding function of dependence and desire that imparts to our affectional lives a logic, order, and pattern. But precisely how desire and dependence exercise this binding and ordering power depends upon the object toward which they are directed. The Christian faith affirms that the ultimate object of our desiring and depending is the sovereign, loving, and gracious God who makes, orders, and sustains all things beautifully and well. We were made to focus our desire and dependence on God, and thus to order our affections around the sovereign, loving, and gracious God. Our chief end is to glorify and enjoy God forever.

But, of course, we do not experience ourselves simply as God made us. We do not experience ourselves as beings who are primarily oriented toward the glory of God. Instead, we experience ourselves as those who have been broken by sin and—in spite of that sin—claimed and restored by God in Christ. In this chapter we want to explore the contours of our religious affections under the aspect of sin. How does our sinfulness disrupt our religious affections by distorting our desires and sense of dependence? In the next chapter we will explore the contours of our religious affections under the aspect of redemption.

ORIGINAL SIN

There is a balm in Gilead to make the wounded whole. There is a balm in Gilead to heal the sinsick soul.[1]

Dona nobis pacem.[2]

Sin has a particular feel to it, a specific shape in our lives. It feels like brokenness, like being at war with ourselves and everyone else. We often sing of this brokenness in worship. "There is a balm in Gilead," we remind ourselves, "to make the wounded whole." This traditional African American spiritual points to our sense that sin is a fragmentation of that which used to be whole. Sinfulness feels like brokenness. It leads us to "feel discouraged, and think [our] work's in vain." The ancient Latin "Dona nobis pacem" points us to the same reality. "Grant us peace," we plea. Sung in canon, the plea to end the warfare that rages within us and between us is repeated over and over. These two hymns, emerging from dramatically different cultural and historical contexts, express the same reality about our sinfulness. What they say about sin is simply this: what ought to be peaceful and whole is now mired in conflict and fragmentation.

We often think that sin simply refers to the bad things we do—the "thou shalt nots" that we have done and the "thou shalts" that we have not done. At one level, sin does refer to these acts of commission and omission that violate the will of God. It is right, then, that in prayers of confession we ask God to forgive us for what we have done and for what we have left undone. But we ask for more than this. We ask God not only to forgive what we have *done* but also to "amend what we *are*."[3] If we attend only to our *doing* in sin and ignore our *being* in sin, then we are like a poor physician who treats symptoms while neglecting the underlying disease that produces those ill effects. Before we can think well about lying, cheating, stealing, and failing to honor our parents, we need to gain clarity about the disease that generates these symptoms.

Christians call the disease *original sin* and describe it in myriad ways. Augustine identified pride as the root cause of sinfulness. Evagrius explained that "the passions" disrupted our capacity to bear the image of God. Jonathan Edwards described original sin as "a powerful astringent" that leaves the soul a dried-out and shriveled remnant of the full and open source of life that God intended it to be. For Tertullian all sin grows out of idolatry. Søren Kierkegaard identified sin as despair. And Reinhold Niebuhr argued that all sin grows out of a natural human anxiety and insecurity about the limitations built into creaturely life.[4] All of these accounts of original sin hold in common the idea that an inner flaw issues in outward manifestations of sinfulness.

But how is this tear in the inner tissue of our being related to the religious affections? To answer that question we can turn again to the insights offered by the "Dona nobis pacem" and "There is a balm in Gilead." God made us to be whole and at peace, but we experience ourselves as broken and divided, disharmonious and fragmented, and in conflict. A sixth-century theologian called the Pseudo-Dionysius offered a helpful analysis of this fragmentation and how it is connected to the desire and dependence that generate, order, and give pattern to our religious affections. We employ the image of a mirror to explain his idea. We are like a mirror that reflects whatever it is directed toward. The Pseudo-Dionysius explained that we are "shaped by what [we] yearn for."[5] The qualities of the object of our longing write themselves into our souls. In some measure, we become what we want.

This image allows us to recognize the important role of desire in shaping our religious affections. Like all of creation, human beings are made to desire God, on whom we depend for life, meaning, and direction. If we are oriented primarily toward the glory of God, then we, like a mirror, bear the image of God. We may certainly love, appreciate, and even desire and depend on other creatures, but we do so because we recognize that they belong to God. Because our desire is directed primarily toward God, our religious affections have a kind of coherence and wholeness. All of our other desires are organized around our central desire for God. All of our other relative dependencies point to our ultimate dependence on God.

Properly ordered desire for and sense of dependence on God organize the affections, thereby giving us a stable center of personality that can hold in harmony all of our other relationships. Well-ordered affections allow us to maintain the boundaries that preserve the integrity of our identities, even as we enter into relationships with others. Depending on God allows us to rely on others without being subordinated to them. Desiring God allows us to long for others without losing ourselves in them. Longing for and relying on God, in fact, always move us into appropriate relationships with other creatures. We are, as the Pseudo-Dionysius explained, brought together in "an alliance in which nothing is confused and all things are held inseparably together."[6] Living in community means maintaining our integrity while being open to others. It means cultivating relationships that value others because they belong to God. Relationships with creatures that grow out of a central desire for and dependence on God are relationships in which we learn to accept guidance from others without resentment, to exercise power in liberating ways, and to delight in relationships of companionship where we simply keep company, neither leading nor being led.[7] Both our desire and our sense of dependence are ordered relationally.

If we are like mirrors that reflect whatever our desire and sense of dependence are focused on, what happens when the mirror is directed toward something other than the glory of God? Since the stability of our personhood and our capacity to enter into healthy relationships with other creatures depend upon our cleaving to God, when our desiring and sense of dependence are directed elsewhere, it as though the mirror has been dropped and has shattered into a thousand slivers. The fragments still reflect whatever they are directed toward, but there is no longer a central, unifying image to bring coherence and harmony to the religious affections. Because God is the only object capable of sating our desires, misdirected desire leaves us unfulfilled. Because God is the only one in whom our sense of dependence will settle permanently, in whom are hearts can find rest, disoriented dependence leaves us filled with anxiety. Because longing for and depending on God bring coherence to our personhood, misdirected desire and a disoriented sense of dependence leave us broken and in conflict. Increasingly governed, then, by insatiable desires, fallen humanity submits in its longing to every passing whim. Overcome by the anxiety that accompanies our disoriented sense of dependence, we wander desperately in search of security. We write fragmentation into our souls. If we were made to be reflections of God—the image of God because we desired and depended upon God above all else—now that reflection is cracked, broken, and distorted because our desires are all out of order and our sense of dependence is disoriented. Thus, the unifying principle of our affectional lives has been lost.

We experience the power of this fallenness in our affectional lives in two ways. First, we experience an inner fragmentation, a brokenness of the affectional structures of our personhood. Second, we experience an outer fragmentation, a brokenness of relationships with God and other creatures.

INNER FRAGMENTATION

Inner fragmentation manifests itself by distorting particular religious affections. Think of humility, the religious affection that grows out of a proper assessment of our value and place in God's purposes. We might assess our value and place improperly, coming to believe that we are nothing before God and that our lives are insignificant in comparison with the vastness and majesty of the cosmos. This disordered form of humility imprisons us in despair and self-negation. We might assess our value and place in God's purposes in another improper way, coming to believe that the rest of the creation can be meaningful and valuable only when measured by our desires and goals. In this case, the affection of humility inverts itself and becomes a self-deifying form of pride.

The religious affection of hope grows out of our recognition of the "already" and "not yet" qualities of God's final restoration of all things. Sin disorders hope in two distinct ways. On the one hand, when hope lacks an awareness of the ways in which God's kingdom is *already* in our midst, it gives way to an otherworldliness that excuses us from the need for action directed toward social justice in the here and now. On the other hand, when hope fails to trust that *final* restoration comes ultimately at God's initiative, it gives way to a naive trust in human progress that simply confuses cultural change with divine intentions.

Likewise, sin disorders affections such as gratitude, contrition, and direction into obsequiousness, self-loathing, and rigid imperiousness.

We are not cookie-cutter sinners. The fall affects us in different ways. For some of us, a distorted sense of direction comes to dominate our personalities. We are certain of where God intends for the world to go and that we have the map that will get us there. We impose our will on others for their own good and alienate those who do not share our vision. For others of us, a distorted form of delight comes to reign in our personalities. Pleasure in the goodness of creation gives way to unbridled hedonism. We revel in the pleasures of the world to such a degree that we lose ourselves in it. We lose ourselves in the endless products made available to us by our consumerist culture, defining ourselves by the latest fads and fashions, the square footage of our homes, and what we drive to work. For still others of us, the religious affection of self-sacrificial love is distorted into a form of self-negation. We lose ourselves in caring for and giving to others to such a degree that we thoroughly deplete our own reserves, neglect our own well-being, and refuse to receive from others. The popular children's story *The Giving Tree* perhaps demonstrates more about the destructive power of self-negation than it does about the healing power of self-sacrificial love. In the story, the tree is devoted to a young boy in whose company "she" delights. At first she gives him her branches to swing in and her apples to eat, but as the boy grows, she sacrifices her branches, then her limbs, and finally her trunk. In the end, all that is left of her is a stump, and even this she offers so that the boy, now turned old man, has a place to sit and rest.[8] Caring for children, spouses, aging parents, and the marginalized victims of society leaves us no time or energy to care for ourselves or to receive care from others.

Inner fragmentation does more than distort the individual religious affections. It also distorts the pattern that binds them together. When one distorted affection or another comes to dominate the personality, the distortion reverberates across the full range of our affections, disrupting the pattern that binds them together in healthy ways. The coherence and pattern of our affectional lives gives way to fragmentation and brokenness. Notice, for example, how a disordered sense of direction eclipses our sense of mutuality, how disordered delight blunts our sense of self-sacrificial love and awe, and how disordered self-sacrificial love exaggerates our sense of obligation.

While there are many variations in the way that distorted affections show themselves in our individual lives, we can nonetheless see in this variety the tangle of our misdirected desire and disoriented sense of dependence. A singular yearning for and trust in the sovereign God has yielded to a divided yearning for and false dependence on created realities. When we lose the unitive force of the religious affections that bind our personalities together, by

multiplying our desires and misidentifying the basis of our dependence, we
find ourselves looking for ways to restore that unity, or sometimes despairing
of the possibility of doing so. On a quest for the wholeness that we sense is
natural to our being, we find ourselves constructing a false sense of wholeness,
when ultimately nothing less than God can satisfy us and give us peace. If God
is not the ultimate object of our desiring, then we must seek satisfaction for
those yearnings in the creation. If God is not the one on whom we ultimately
depend, then we must seek security in the creation.

The person dominated by a disordered sense of direction feels personally
responsible for imposing order on the rest of the world. The person with the
disordered sense of delight has simply become immersed in the multiplicity of
created things. The person with a disordered sense of self-sacrificial love seeks
to restore security by becoming the one on whom all others can depend. In
each case, we find ourselves with an acute sense that we are broken and at war
with ourselves, and we seek to cope with that fragmentation in a variety of
ways: by imposing order, by insatiably seeking fulfillment in the pleasures of
creation, by becoming self-sufficient. There is an inner fragmentation that
manifests itself in an almost infinite variety of affectional permutations. This
inner fragmentation of our affectional lives ultimately derives from our misdirected desires and from our disoriented sense of dependence.

A life governed by false objects of desire and dependence is a life lost in the
tragedy of idolatry. When our desires are misdirected and our sense of dependence is disoriented, we invest the fragile, finite creation with infinite significance. We expect the creation to do for us what only its Creator can. We expect
it to satisfy our deepest longings and to provide us with ultimate security,
meaning, and purpose. The mind caught in the swirling chaos of fallen affections becomes, as Calvin put it, "a workshop of idols."[9]

Idolatry is complex. We tend to think of it simply as the worship of a material thing, and we think it is sin that we have outgrown. After all, we no longer
carve wood or chisel stone and call our handiwork gods. But while we may well
have outgrown these crudest forms of idolatry, we are master practitioners of
far subtler and more pernicious forms of it. For while idolatry may well
encompass the worship of material things, at bottom the problem is not the
materiality of such objects, but rather the improper value that we assign them.
Idolatry involves the value or status that we assign to an object, to the place we
give it in our lives. Idolatry involves investing *any* finite reality with the ultimate status of the infinite. When we think of idolatry in this way, we can recognize it, for instance, in hope that confuses cultural change with the
intentions of God, in a sense of direction that becomes rigid imperiousness,
and in a sense of delight that becomes hedonism. Sometimes our idolatry takes
the form of investing some other creature with the status of ultimacy; at other

times it takes the form of investing ourselves with such status; but usually our idolatry involves us in both at once. Paradoxically, we often find ourselves investing with the status of ultimacy the very creatures that in an earlier moment we had reduced to mere objects to enlarge ourselves.[10] We move erratically between deifying ourselves and deifying other creatures, and this dynamic movement of idolatry ensures that the inner fragmentation of our affectional lives translates itself into an outer fragmentation of our relationship with other creatures.

OUTER FRAGMENTATION

The distortion of our religious affections, which derives from the fragmentation of the desire and sense of dependence that runs through them and organizes them, manifests itself outwardly in our relationships with God and other creatures. Distorted affections give rise to distorted, destructive ways of relating to others. But the relationship between religious affections and outward behavior is complex and multidimensional. Not only do distorted inner affections generate and distort our outward behaviors and relationships, but also, over time, living in the context of these distorted relationships and behaviors further distorts our religious affections. The distortions in our relationships and behavior are not simply the result of the distortion of our religious affections; they also serve to aggravate, amplify, and worsen the distortion of those very affections from which they arose. The traffic between distorted affections and outward relationships and behaviors runs in two directions. Inner and outer fragmentation flow in and out of one another, and each generates, exaggerates, and reinforces the other.

Outer Fragmentation as Self-Deification

Our outer fragmentation sometimes manifests itself as self-deification. We make ourselves the measure of all things. We dethrone God and enthrone ourselves in God's place, claiming for ourselves the powers and prerogatives that belong to God alone. We seek to rearrange the creation to serve and glorify ourselves; we redefine the purposes of the world to match our self-centered vision for it. In this state of self-delusion, we come to believe that the chief end of creation is to glorify humanity and to be consumed by it forever. We deify ourselves because, in the midst of our fragmentation, we still sense that we were made for order, pattern, goodness, and beauty, and we seek that order wherever we can find it. We seek wholeness amid all the wounded parts of our lives. When we are unable to find this wholeness, we begin to construct

it, declaring ourselves to be the orderers. Humanity, we say, is the measure of
all things.

If humanity is the measure of all things, then the meaning, value, and purpose of all things will be measured by the degree to which they serve our ends,
satisfy our desires, and provide us with a sense of ultimate security. We become
blind to the intrinsic value and worth that God has assigned to other creatures.
We fail to recognize their integrity and inherent beauty. We no longer address
other creatures as "thou," but speak of them as "it"; they can be used, consumed,
and disposed of in whatever way serves human good or pleasure. All creatures
become for us mere instruments or means that serve the great end of our self-
aggrandizement. In "the flowery meadow" we see only wasted space that can
be better used as a parking lot, and in the "flashing sea" only an inconvenient
barrier to the vast pockets of oil and natural gas that will continue to fuel our
consumer lifestyle. In a culture that has lost a deep sense of sexual fidelity and
intimacy, we expand the number of our sexual partners even as we reduce those
partners to mere objects for our genital gratification. Our "lovers" are no longer
our beloved but are instead disposable goods that can be traded in for newer,
more exciting models. We rely on migrant farm workers to provide us with
inexpensive and readily available produce. We need them to pick our tomatoes,
blueberries, grapes, and lettuce cheaply, and we want them to do it without
making any demands about fair labor practices, adequate housing and sanita-
tion, a decent living wage, or access to healthcare. We need them to be invisible and anonymous, not children of God who have a moral claim on our lives.
We want to know and use them as mere objects, rather than know them in a
participatory way. We want no genuine affectional communion with them, no
mutuality and interdependence; we want to maintain the rigid boundaries that
separate us. We feel no obligation toward them, no gratitude for their work,
and no contrition for our complicity in their exploitation.

Whether such self-deification manifests itself in environmental exploitation, sexual infidelity and promiscuity, or economic injustice, the relationship
between distorted affections and distorted outer behaviors and relationships is
complex. Environmental exploitation, sexual infidelity, and economic injustice
may arise from and be perpetuated by the distortions of our religious affections; but once caught in their cycle, such distorted patterns of relating and
behaving work back upon the religious affections to aggravate, amplify, and
exaggerate their distortion. Such outward behaviors and fragmented relationships both arise from and generate inner fragmentation. While our distorted
affections may lead us out into the world to exploit the earth or the sexuality
and labor of others, over time such exploitation also redounds to us, further
fragmenting our affective lives. Our capacity for some religious affections,
such as gratitude, humility, and contrition, may become blunted, while other,

distorted affections may come to dominate the personality. A distorted sense of mutuality, for example, may lead one out in confusion and desperation to seek intimacy in sexually faithless relationships, and such sexual encounters may become a habitual part of one's lifestyle. As they do so, they become fundamentally exploitative of the other so that what began in confusion and desperation eventually so utterly distorts our sense of mutuality that we become blind to the possibility of genuine mutuality and callous toward the affective lives of our sexual partners. When we learn to disregard our moral obligations toward sexual partners, it is only a matter of time before we become callous with respect to our broader obligations to others. Hence, our distorted sense of mutuality will eventually infect our senses of obligation and interdependence. But exploitative sexual behavior not only further fragments the affections of the one who exploits; it also disrupts the affective life of the one being exploited, as that person's sense of well-being and delight will be eroded.

When we dethrone God and reorder the creation so that it serves and glorifies us, we also relegate God to the status of a creature whose purpose is also to serve and glorify us. We retain the vestiges of genuine faith only to enlist them for our self-serving ends. God is envisioned as creator only in the sense that God generates a world tailored exclusively for human dominance. It is as though God created a hierarchy of creatures specifically so that human beings could occupy the top position and hold sway over all that is beneath them. We imagine God's function as sustainer to be that of showering us with blessings, intervening to shield us from the consequences of our foibles, and working providentially to keep us from becoming one of "the least of these." We conceive of God's work of redemption as spiriting us away to heaven, where we live happily ever after. Being God becomes about serving humanity.

We were made to be theocentrically oriented, that is, to glorify and enjoy God forever. But our sinful self-deification reverses this orientation, making us egocentric and anthropocentric, displacing God from the center to the margins, where God can cater to our every desire. A thin veneer of piety conceals our egocentric instrumentalization of God and gives us license to demonize those not so "blessed" with abundance and divine favor as ourselves. In its most pernicious form, such self-righteousness passes from the individual human heart into our social identity. Those who do not share our race, ethnicity, national identity, social status, party affiliation, faith tradition, or sexual orientation, for example, simply cannot be recognized as full recipients of the love of God. It is but a small step from there to concrete acts of oppression, discrimination, marginalization, and even violence. With time, such attitudes and behaviors take on a life of their own within social institutions. They become part of the powers and principalities of the present age. Even when we are able to root racism and sexism out of individual human hearts, we find that these are perpetuated in our economic, educational, and religious institutions. Outer fragmentation in the form of self-deification, in short, expresses itself in both personal and institutional sin.

Outer Fragmentation as Self-Negation

Self-deification is not the only form of outer fragmentation. We can also exhibit such fragmentation as self-negation. We have already discussed some of the main features of self-negation when we considered how inner fragmentation manifests itself in the distortion of self-sacrificial love. However, there are other forms of self-negation as well, and these manifest themselves more broadly in our relation to other creatures. We may relate to our world by simply losing ourselves in it, refusing to exert ourselves as moral agents, as image-bearers of God with a God-given affectional sense of direction, purpose, and possibility for our lives. Instead of overextending the self as god and seeking to rearrange the world to serve our narrow ends, as we do in self-deification, in self-negation we simply fail to develop the self into the being that God calls us to be, preferring instead to be absorbed and defined by the things of the world. In self-negation, we lose ourselves among a myriad of things, and such things become for us the false gods that rule our lives.

Self-negation has not always been recognized as a form of sin. Historically, theologians were much more likely to focus almost exclusively on pride and self-deification. But in recent years, feminist theologians have drawn attention to sin as self-negation, especially as it shows itself in the lives of women.[11] Any woman walking through a shopping mall, for example, is presented with a number of models of womanhood, and she is expected to want to be all of them. The ideals presented to her do not merely say, "Purchase and use these things." They also say, "Become these things." They communicate that she ought to subordinate her "self" to the ideal type. She should *be* the mannequin in the store window with the perfectly sculpted body. She should *be* the mother with the name-brand-attired children. She should *be* the domestic goddess with the right home furnishings and the well-equipped kitchen. Making these purchases is not primarily about acquiring things needed for daily living; it is about being absorbed into a scripted set of social roles. It is about giving up the self and becoming the mannequin-mother with the perfect home.

The shopping mall is not the only place where women are presented with scripted roles that are supposed to take the place of their real selves. It happens at church too. "The good Christian woman" is the happily married mother who, if she works outside the home, is careful never to let her professional life cast a shadow over her calling as nurturer and caretaker of husband or children. She is above all else nurturer, caregiver, supporter, and helpmate who is to expend herself in the service of others. Her faithfulness is best expressed by extending her domestic gifts to the "church family"—baking and serving cookies after church, volunteering in the nursery, and attending women's Bible studies that often focus on how to negotiate the endless details of care-giving that divide her identity without remainder. She is supposed to be the happy caretaker, and we give her no place to rage against injustice, to question the distribution of social power, to raise profound questions about her faith or world, or to express hurt and confusion about her life. And we certainly have no place for her to be unmarried or without children. The unquestioned goods of motherhood, nurturance, and self-sacrifice have become the gods around which her affectional life is organized. She has simply lost her "self" in the "wonder, love, and praise" of the "cult of domesticity."[12]

The feminist theological insight into self-negation in women's lives helps us to recognize it even beyond women's experience. Take, for example, national-ism, in which the self is lost in a fervent patriotism that demands ultimate loy-alty to the values, symbols, and activities of the nation. The uncritical patriot does not—indeed cannot—offer criticism or suggest a moral corrective to the policies, values, and activities of the nation. To exert oneself as a moral agent—as a citizen with a sense of moral obligation—in such acts is to become a trai-tor to the god of our fathers. God and country are so thoroughly intertwined that a sacred aura is cast over the nation, bathing it in the warmth and light of piety. To question the nation is to question God, and to speak a word of criti-cism or protest against a national policy is to utter blasphemy. Such national-ism and patriotism are often intoxicating. We can be swept away by the tide of patriotism, losing our moral bearings, our sense of moral obligation, and finally our "selves." We sacrifice our individuality and moral agency on the altar of the national god.

The example of nationalism points us to a curious and paradoxical feature of idolatry: self-negation and self-deification are intimately intertwined. On the one hand, we cede our moral agency and negate our individual identity in unquestioning worship of the nation and its god. On the other hand, in deify-ing the nation we are indirectly deifying ourselves. In short, we take back with one hand what we gave away with the other. The nation becomes the Mount Olympus on which we dwell as gods, looking down upon the mere mortals of other nations who have no standing to question or resist our will and no means by which to ascend to the dwelling place of the gods.

Throughout this chapter, we have explored the nature of our fallenness, the shape of original sin in our lives, and have noted that it results in a fragmen-tation of our personhood and a fragmentation of our relationships. Inner frag-mentation disorders our affections, grows out of misdirected desires and a disoriented sense of dependence, and leads us into idolatry. And this inner fragmentation manifests itself in and is exacerbated by an outer fragmentation that prevents us from entering into harmonious relationships with others. That is, the war within ourselves leads us into war with others. The broken-ness of our affectional lives leads us into broken relationships with others, and those broken relationships further fragment our inner lives. A vicious circle of inner and outer fragmentation throws us into a downward spiral of conflict and disharmony.

4

Redeemed Religious Affections

> This is the joyful feast of the people of God. They will come from east
> and west, and from north and south, and sit at table in the kingdom
> of God.[1]

The good news of the gospel is that the spiral of conflict and disharmony of
our fallenness is not the end of the story. After all, there *is* a balm in Gilead to
make the wounded whole. There is healing and peace for the wars that rage
within us and between us. There is a vision of a banquet where people from
every culture and race gather in joy to feast together, and this hope for and
vision of restoration grow out of our participation in Jesus Christ. God, the
source of all peace, goodness, and beauty, becomes broken for us so that we
who are broken both inwardly and outwardly may be healed and restored.
Christ, who is beauty incarnate, redirects our desires and reorients our sense
of dependence. Christ becomes the new object of our affections, and when he
does, God redirects the desire and reorients the sense of dependence that run
through and give pattern to our religious affections. The gracious renewal of
our desires and sense of dependence lays the foundation for a gracious renewal
of both our individual religious affections and the pattern that binds them
together in our personalities.

THE BEAUTY OF THE INCARNATION

But how exactly does Christ become the new object of our affections? Perhaps a clue can be found in our everyday experiences of beauty in the world.
Beauty attracts us and binds us to itself. It impresses itself upon us. Have you
ever witnessed an ocean raging as a storm blows in? It is powerful, dangerous,

frightening even. But it is also beautiful, so beautiful that you almost cannot tear your eyes away from it. Its beauty draws us in and impresses itself upon us. It attracts us; it disturbs us; it changes us. We are not the same for having witnessed its beauty. We have known it in a participatory way and that knowing has changed us. Jesus is like that for us. Jesus Christ—God with us, God among us, God as one of us—attracts us, disturbs us, changes us.

Protestants do not often speak the language of beauty. We are sometimes suspicious of physical beauty and rarely think in aesthetic terms more generally. There is good reason for this reluctance; accounting for what is beautiful and what is not and why some things are more beautiful than others is notoriously difficult. But there is much to be gained if we can recover a sense of beauty. For example, we all recognize intuitively that there is a difference between the sound of pots and pans clanging as they strike the kitchen floor and the sound of Beethoven's *Ode to Joy*.[2] In both cases we have struck many of the same notes. Why is one simply intolerable noise and the other inescapably beautiful? Why does the one drive us away, while the other draws us in? Part of the answer lies in the pattern, order, and harmony inherent in the relationships between the notes in Beethoven's work, but missing when the pots and pans strike the kitchen floor. Beethoven has arranged the individual notes in a complex pattern. Beauty is a way of being related. It involves relationships of order, harmony, and pattern. It involves not merely an aggregation of parts, but an arrangement of parts into a coherent whole. In the whole, individual parts that seem to be incompatible and contradictory are reconciled and brought into harmony.

In Jesus Christ we find that unique individual in whom are united peacefully and harmoniously the otherwise incompatible elements of time and eternity, creator and creature, the infinite and the finite. Jonathan Edwards, perhaps more than any other theologian of the Protestant tradition, drew attention to the centrality of beauty in God and its relationship to our religious affections. "God is God," wrote Edwards, "and is distinguished from all other beings and exalted above them, chiefly by [God's] divine beauty." God's beauty, for Edwards, consists in the order, harmony, and pattern that characterizes God's being and actions. In the incarnation, Christ becomes the preeminent display of divine beauty, and Christ's beauty consists in "the admirable conjunctions" of seemingly contradictory, conflicting qualities and attributes.[3] In the incarnation of Jesus Christ, the quality of "infinite highness" is joined to "infinite condescension," "majesty" is joined perfectly with "meekness," "justice" is reconciled with "mercy," "glory" is harmonized with "humility," "equality with God" is united with "reverence" for God, "sovereignty" and "dominion" are conjoined with "resignation" and "obedience."[4] The beautiful way that these characteristics are embodied in Jesus of Nazareth works to "draw our affection" toward him, thereby luring us into the new life of faith.[5]

Edwards helps us to see two important things. First, he points us to the fact that while God is made known to us in the beauty of creation, God's fullest self-revelation comes only in the beauty of the incarnation—in the person and work of Jesus Christ. Second, Edwards also points us to the power that such divine beauty has in redirecting and reshaping the religious affections. In coming to see the beauty of Christ, our religious affections are reoriented around this beauty in such a way that our personhood is reshaped and reformed by divine grace. By divine grace, we enter into a participatory knowing of Christ's beauty, and such affectional communion with God in Christ becomes person-forming. It redirects our distorted desire and sense of dependence, laying the foundation for a new ordering of our religious affections freed from the tragedy of our idolatry. We are attracted to Christ by his beauty, and that beauty is redemptive.

Let's look at an example of how Christ's attracting beauty can reshape a particular religious affection and repattern its relationship to other affections. When desire moves toward whatever is perceived to be beautiful, the religious affections through which that desire runs will be deeply shaped by the object of our longing. When we are attracted by the beauty of Christ, when we come to desire and depend on God in Christ, it has profound consequences for both our individual affections and the relationships among them. Think, for instance, of our distorted sense of direction, which often leads us to dominate and control others. If this sense of direction is united to a deep longing for and dependence on the beauty of Christ—whose life embodied and holds before us a new model of power rooted in servanthood and humility—it will be reformed into a sense of our cooperative searching for a common direction and will be coupled with a desire to empower others. When this happens, our sense of direction will be colored by our sense of mutuality and interdependence in such a way that it no longer shows itself as a dominating form of "power over" others but rather as a form of empowering others to achieve a shared, cooperative purpose.[6]

We are drawn toward Christ, attracted by his beauty, but we are also disturbed by it because it calls us out of our comfortable way of life. Christ's beauty demands that we give up our self-deification and self-negation, that we turn away from our destructive patterns of relating to others, and that we subordinate ourselves to the glory of God. The life of Christ is no less disturbing in our time than it was in his own. Christ upsets all of our expectations about who a redeemer ought to be, with whom a redeemer ought to converse and eat, and how a redeemer ought to relate to the religious and political establishment. He takes women seriously as conversation partners and disciples. He violates racial and ethnic boundaries in his interactions with the woman at the well and the Syro-Phoenician woman and in his use of a Samaritan as an example of virtue. He eats and drinks with sinners and outcasts. He accepts physical affection from a woman of ill repute, who bathes his feet with her tears and anoints his head with oil. He touches the diseased. His teachings and parables subvert our common-sense way of organizing the world. The first are last; the last are first; the poor inherit a kingdom the rich cannot enter. In short, he violates all of the social conventions that let us build walls between the holy "us" and the soiled "them." He breaks down the hierarchy that sometimes lets us exercise domination over others and at other times gives us permission to cede our moral agency to them.

The disruptive power of Christ's beauty has the power to reorient the desire and sense of dependence that run through and give pattern to our religious affections, thus transforming them. We can see this clearly if we return to the example of the economic exploitation of migrant workers. We noted that our senses of obligation, gratitude, and contrition are both distorted and blunted by our complicity in their marginalization. When we come to long for and depend upon Christ, who called attention to the blessedness of the poor, who preached a kingdom in which the last shall be first, and who cautioned a rich young ruler against the blinding, seductive power of wealth and privilege, then we are invited into a life of beauty where harmony and hospitality stand in judgment over conflict and exploitation. Attentiveness to the beauty of Christ disrupts our earlier blindness and sensitizes us to the marginalization of laborers inherent in our economic system. Having glimpsed Christ's beauty, we become attuned to the ugliness of injustice. Our sense of obligation is now extended beyond our immediate circle of family and friends. We are opened to a richer, more expansive sense of gratitude. We become contrite for our complicity in institutional sin. Our sense of mutuality and interdependence is heightened. These graciously restored religious affections transform what we perceive as moral problems, how we perceive them, and how we respond to them. The affection-forming power of Christ's disruptive beauty ultimately translates into an ethical imperative for the Christian life.

We sometimes circumvent this disturbing feature of the beauty of the incarnation by focusing almost exclusively on the death of Christ. When we think about how God in Christ acts to reconcile the world, we tend to focus on Christ's death on the cross. That, we think, is where the saving act happened. It is almost as though Christ had been born merely to die. His life and teaching are important, of course, but we think that if you want to know what saves us, what Christ does to atone for us, to reconcile us to God, then go to the cross and witness the martyr bleeding for you. All of this is true and important, but there is something missing from it. The cross is powerful because it bears witness to a more fundamental reality. It is the incarnation that infuses the world with God's grace. The cross completes the incarnation and is redemptive only because it is the culmination of it. The cross, in fact, happens only because of Christ's subversive life, which the powers that be cannot allow to continue. Despite this injustice, Christ does not refuse to bear the consequences of his disruptive life. On the cross, Christ enters fully even into our suffering and death, even into our alienation from God. The fact that the Son of God became human sets aright all of the relationships that sin has put awry. It is the totality of a life lived, lost, and resurrected that redeems us. And that means that we must come to terms with the disturbing life of Christ.

We are attracted and disturbed by the beauty of Christ, but we are also changed by it. The beauty of Christ transforms our affectional lives by offering us an image of God and humanity so irresistibly attractive that the desire and sense of dependence that run through and unite all of our religious affections are redirected and reoriented. When we turn our attention to Christ, we find that we cannot tear our eyes away. We are attracted, and if that attraction by divine grace becomes the central, unifying desire that governs our religious affections, it provides the basis for the restoration of harmony and coherence to our identities and relationships. Because we are once again oriented toward the glory of God, and because we bear the image of that which we desire and depend upon, we are restored as the image of God.

Just as we do not choose what will attract us, so we do not choose the redemptive power available in the incarnation. We simply find ourselves attracted, simply feel ourselves claimed by God. We may recognize in an instant that God has claimed us and experience that instant as a conversion, or we may slowly awaken to God's claim on us so that, as Horace Bushnell put it, we may "grow up a Christian and never know [ourselves] as being otherwise."[7] In either case, the power of God's claim in our lives makes its effects felt over long periods of time. The life of faith is one of growth.

How we worship is an important part of how we grow in the life of faith. The Westminster Catechism explains that in worship "Christ communicates to us the benefits of redemption."[8] Worship needs to be attentive to all of the ways that the incarnation attracts, disturbs, and changes us. There need to be moments in worship that offer us the opportunity to experience each of these. Sermons, for example, ought to focus on the life and teachings of Jesus, as well as on his death and resurrection, and need to highlight the disturbing features of the incarnation as much as they do the comfort it offers. In the celebration of the Lord's Supper, rather than prompting a fear of "eat[ing] and drink[ing] judgment against ourselves" (1 Cor. 11:29), the liturgy should emphasize that it is indeed a *joyful* feast of the people of God that *invites* all people of faith to participate in anticipation of the heavenly banquet. Children should be invited to come, "taste and see that the LORD is good" (Ps. 34:8). The sacrament is a celebration that invites, attracts, and draws us into mystical union with and participatory knowledge of the living Christ who meets us in the bread and

wine. In the words of assurance spoken after the prayer of confession, worshipers should experience the way that the incarnation changes us before God
and in relationship to one another. We are assured that our sins are forgiven,
that we are strengthened for goodness, and that by the power of the Holy
Spirit we are kept in life eternal. We are assured that the old life has gone and
the new life has begun.

THE WORK OF THE HOLY SPIRIT IN THE CHURCH

When, by the grace of the Holy Spirit, we are able to experience the attracting,
disturbing, and changing power of the incarnation through worship, then worship becomes the occasion for both purification and illumination. Although
these categories may be unfamiliar to many Protestants, they have deep roots
in Eastern Orthodox theology, and they offer us helpful vocabulary for expressing two ways in which the power of the incarnation meets us in worship and
reorders our lives. The concepts of purification and illumination help us to connect the doctrine of the incarnation to the doctrine of the church. The Holy
Spirit enlivens the body of Christ and actualizes the sanctifying power of the
incarnation in the lives of individuals and communities, and this sanctifying
work of the Holy Spirit has both purifying and illuminating dimensions.

In purification, through the grace and power of the Holy Spirit, we learn
to turn away from our false valuation of ourselves and the creation. In illumination, through that same grace and power, we relearn the true value of ourselves and creation, and our relationships to God and other creatures are
restored. Purification focuses on the dying away of the old self, the self governed by idolatry, the self fragmented both inwardly and outwardly. In worship practices that engage us in purification, we emphasize what John Leith
has called "the polemic against idolatry" that is inherent in the Christian life.[9]
Illumination focuses on our rising again in Christ, becoming new creatures in
Christ whose affections are reoriented properly toward God and the world. In
worship practices that engage us in illumination, we emphasize the capacity of
the good creation to mediate God's grace and presence to us. In purification
we reject the world as idol; in illumination we learn to see it as icon, as a window onto the glory of God. Dying and rising with Christ, purification and illumination, always occur together in the Christian life. It is not as though we
begin with purification, and once having completed that task, take up the work
of illumination. Always, we are being purified. Always, we are being illuminated. We are always destroying idols, and discovering icons.

By the work and sovereign will of the Holy Spirit, public worship extends
the redemptive work of the incarnate Christ by drawing us into this process of

purification and illumination. It does so by presenting us with the beautiful image of Christ, by calling us out of fragmentation into harmony, by redirecting our desires, by reorienting our sense of dependence, and by repatterning our religious affections. In short, the Holy Spirit sanctifies us.

There is probably no place in worship where we see this dynamic of dying and rising more clearly than in the sacrament of baptism. In baptism we are symbolically buried with Christ, and the old self is put to death. Then we rise again with Christ, and a new self is resurrected. The whole structure of the baptismal liturgy reflects this dynamic of mortification and renewal. The baptismal vows, for example, begin with renunciations. We renounce the power of evil in the world, our sinful ways, and all the demonic powers that would pull us apart. In the liturgies of the early church, catechumens prepared to receive baptism would be stripped of their old clothing as they were also putting off their old lives. They would face west, the direction of the ending day, and make their vows of renunciation. The baptismal vows then continue with affirmations. We say what we believe, often using the words of the Apostles' Creed. In the early church, the catechumens would face east, the direction of the coming new day, to make their affirmations, and they would receive baptism and be robed in fresh garments, symbolic of their new life in Christ. The renunciations come first. After all, how else can we learn to see the true value of things unless we first reject our false valuation of them? But, it is not as though we make our renunciations—or have them made for us in infant baptism—and then are finished with the work of purification. Instead, baptism offers a paradigm of the Christian life in which we are constantly dying and rising, always being purified, always being illuminated.

THE GRACIOUS REORDERING OF
THE RELIGIOUS AFFECTIONS

The process of purification and illumination renews not only our individual affections, but also the order, pattern, and logic that bind them together in our personalities. In the example used above, we noted that when a distorted sense of direction is purified and illuminated, it is restored by being reordered with reference to other religious affections such as humility. The order of the Christian religious affections, the pattern in them that gives our identities shape, derives from the way that a common desire for and dependence on the God who is revealed in Jesus Christ runs through them all. Earlier we argued that desire and dependence run through the religious affections, binding them together like pearls on a string; while that image is useful, it is also limited. Perhaps it would be more accurate to use the image of a cobweb. Desire and dependence unite the religious affections the way every point on a cobweb is connected to every other point. If you pluck on one strand of the web, every part feels the vibrations. Likewise, the unitive power of desire and dependence binds together and orders the religious affections so that every one of them is affected by every other. When we evoke a sense of delight, therefore, we are indirectly evoking and shaping gratitude, a sense of rightness, and every other affection too.

But this common Christian ordering of the religious affections does not mean that all Christians will or should have the same personality. The nexus of affections will intersect our lived experience in very different ways. The affections will be cultivated through emotional experiences differently in the course of different lives. Those affections will work back on the emotions in response to the different events in the unique life story of each individual. To say that there is an order or logic to the religious affections, then, is also to affirm that there is great and good diversity among Christians, even as those Christians share the common identity rooted in "one Lord, one faith, and one baptism" (Eph. 4:5).

Exploring how worship orders the religious affections requires respecting both the multiplicity of Christian identities and the common identity given us as the body of Christ. There is great diversity among us as individuals, and this diversity is good. The sense of direction will be stronger in some, while others bring the strength of a deeply rooted sense of mutuality. So long as these affections are related to and balanced by other affections within individuals, it is good that the Christian community can encompass and celebrate such variety. Just as we are not cookie-cutter sinners, there is no reason to expect that we should be cookie-cutter saints. God made each of us to be unique and redeems each of us in ways that honor and preserve our differences.

But we also know that there are better and worse ways of living out our identities as children of God. We have already seen how an exaggerated sense of direction can lead us to become rigid and hegemonic, while a distorted sense of self-sacrificial love can lead us toward self-negation. There must be ways, then, to discern when the religious affections are well ordered and when they align themselves in patterns that are distorted and destructive. On the one hand, we do not want to suggest that there is a singular right ordering for the religious affections that issues in an "ideal" Christian personhood. On the other hand, we want to affirm that there is a discernible common pattern of the religious affections that binds Christians together as recipients of the grace of the one God. What we propose here is a structure for thinking about the religious affections that indicates how the affections are or ought to be related to one another but that also allows for flexibility and diversity within that structure. We believe that this approach will allow us to celebrate diversity within the Christian community and identify what is desirable in and distinctive about the shape of Christian personhood.

Awe: The Gateway Religious Affection

When our desire is graciously redirected toward God as its proper object and when our sense of dependence is graciously reoriented so that we seek ultimate security in God alone, then they begin to flow into the religious affections in new ways. Desire and dependence are always expressed in and specified through particular religious affections, and first among these is awe. Awe, which is ordered as reverence, serves as the gateway religious affection. All of the other religious affections flow out of our first response to God as the one before whom we stand in awe. Unless the other affections are rooted in a sense of the majesty of God, unless they emerge from a sense of the profound otherness of God, they will not ultimately be *religious* affections. Awe is that affection that radically relativizes us. The experience of awe is disorienting, and this disorientation prompts us to acknowledge that we are not gods. Awe jolts us out of our self-deification. But because attraction is part of awe, it also jolts us out of our self-negation.

Christian worship, across its wide swath of traditions, always begins with adoration. We begin with a call to worship, a hymn, or a prayer of the day that calls us out of ourselves. These acts of adoration call us to the awe-ful experience of standing before the God who made us, who sustains us, who gives us meaning and purpose, but who is also a profound mystery to us. This adoration both attracts us and disorients us. It calls us to worship and frames worship as our creaturely response to God's disorienting love. The opening acts of adoration in worship acknowledge awe as the gateway religious affection.

Because every religious affection is connected to every other, it can be difficult to find a place to begin when exploring the proper ordering of the religious affections. To simplify this task, we consider three clusters of religious affections that organize themselves around awe, the gateway religious affection. The first cluster consists of humility, a sense of rightness, a sense of well-being, and a sense of mutuality and interdependence. The second cluster consists of gratitude, delight, a sense of obligation, and self-sacrificial love. The final cluster consists of contrition, hope, and direction.

Humility, Rightness, Well-Being, and a Sense of Mutuality and Interdependence

In the purification that frees us from self-deification, we recover a proper sense of where we fit in the context of God's broader creative purposes. We discover that we are not, in fact, the center of all things and that our desperate attempts to be so are self-destructive and illusory. We are freed from the burden of being God, and we have a renewed sense of what Karl Barth called the "Godness of God."[10] But *humility* does not mean humiliation; it does not mean that we count for nothing. Being purified of our self-deification does not reduce us to insignificance. Instead, purification opens us to illumination, and as we are illuminated, we joyfully and humbly embrace a new perspective in which we find our genuine meaning and purpose in conformity with God's great ends for the creation. We discover that being a creature is good and that our worth need not derive from an exaggerated sense of ourselves or from the subordination of others.

In laying aside the burden of being a god, we rediscover two other religious affections, the sense of rightness and the sense of well-being. A *sense of rightness* is our sense that despite its flaws and shortcomings, the world is as it ought to be. It is our sense that despite the incursion of sin and evil into the world, it is right and fitting that the world is ordered and arranged as it is. This sense of rightness is as simple as our affirmation of the goodness of the material world; our deep sense that creatures are not meant to live autonomously, but in relationships of interdependence with one another; and our awareness that we were meant to live as social creatures. The sense of rightness includes an awareness that all things have a place in the creation, that the world displays an order that is good.

Our *sense of well-being* involves the awareness that while this rightly ordered world does not revolve around us, it is not hostile to us. While God's purposes for creation and the powers and forces of creation itself are larger than us, we nonetheless experience a confidence that God has taken account of our well-being and that we have a proper place amid the power and purposes of the creation. Together, our senses of rightness and well-being tell us that it is fitting and appropriate that the world is the way it is and that while we are not the source and center of all things in this rightly ordered world, God has nonetheless created a place for us in it where we may flourish.

Purified and illuminated humility and the senses of rightness and well-being naturally flow into yet another religious affection, a *sense of mutuality and interdependence*. We sense that our well-being in this world depends upon a thick web of reciprocal relationships that connect our lives to the lives of other creatures. We sense that I-It relationships, which objectify and exploit others, compromise our flourishing, and that I-Thou relationships, in which we interact with other creatures in ways that respect their integrity and goodness, enhance our flourishing. Purifying and illuminating grace reorients our religious affections and reorders them in relation to one another, and by so doing begins to replace our inner and outer fragmentation with a new wholeness that enables us to relate properly to God, ourselves, and other creatures.

Gratitude, Delight, Obligation, and Self-Sacrificial Love

A second cluster of religious affections begins with *gratitude*. When awe becomes a religious affection, it profoundly alters our identities. We become persons who meet the world with an openness to its awe-inspiring nature and who recognize the hand of God within and behind the creation's capacity to inspire awe. When that happens, when we become persons constituted by awe, we naturally also begin to experience the creation as gift. We did not bring the world or ourselves into being, and we cannot hold them in existence, let alone give them meaning and direction. We simply find ourselves in this world, find ourselves sustained by it, find ourselves with a sense of meaning and purpose, and for all of this we are grateful. Through awe we become grateful, and when that gratitude becomes a religious affection, we become persons who meet the world with a readiness to respond in gratitude. We find in nearly every occasion some cause for gratitude to other creatures that sustain and delight us. And we find in all things, or nearly all things, cause for gratitude to God who makes, sustains, and directs all things.

Gratitude is deeply connected to a *sense of delight*. We experience the goodness of the creation as delight. Delight entails the capacity to enjoy others in a way that does not diminish or objectify them, but instead honors their intrinsic goodness and integrity. We are delighted, tickled pink, by the beauty of the world. Who can resist laughing with delight while watching a young lion discover and then chase its own tail? It is good, of course, that lion cubs develop and express chasing instincts that allow them to survive. But that instinct is more than just a good survival instinct. It is funny; it is playful; it is delightful. We might similarly dismiss the delight of sexual intimacy as merely an evolutionary mechanism that encourages species to procreate; and it is that. But sexual intimacy is also a beautiful, playful, delightful gift from God. The world's goodness goes far beyond its already gratitude-inspiring capacity to sustain us in existence. That level of goodness is covered over with a thick layer of the Creator's sheer whimsy, and we rightly respond to it with delight.

But this description of delight becomes absurdly unrealistic if we do not acknowledge that our existence also prompts anguish. The chasing instinct that ensures the lion's survival also assures the agonizing death of others. The sexual intimacy that delights us also leads us into relationships with others where our openness and vulnerability may be abused. In a world that is broken by sin and distorted by natural evil that we simply cannot explain, our sense of delight rightly expresses itself as anguish in some circumstances. The religious affection of delight, in other words, may enter the world of our experience either as a positive feeling of delight or in the painful form of anguish. Christian worship needs to provide opportunities for us to express and explore that anguish as much as it needs to prompt us to express our delight in its positive form.

The religious affection of gratitude also flows naturally into a *sense of obligation*, especially when gratitude is joined to a sense of mutuality and interdependence. We are grateful for others who support and sustain us, and that gratitude comes with the awareness that our dependence on others connects us to them in relationships of reciprocity. We are not unilaterally dependent on others, for others also depend on us. We are caught up in a delightful web of interdependence. That interdependence creates obligations both to those on whom we depend and to those who depend on us. Just as others contribute to our well-being, and we are grateful to them, so we contribute to the well-being of others. Think of the gratitude that accompanies the birth of a child; that wonderful, undeserved gift also generates obligations in parents, siblings, and other loved ones. But Christianity, with its theocentric orientation, expands the realm of our obligations far beyond the human community. The Christian faith calls us to consider our obligations to the broader creation, including its plants and animals. Our dependence on fertile soil to support the crops that sustain our lives, for example, implies obligations to the ecosystem. Our dependence on animals as a source of food creates obligations that we provide them with humane living conditions or even that we seek alternate food sources.

For Christians, obligation also includes *self-sacrificial love*. Self-sacrificial love is the religious affection that creates in us a readiness to set aside our own interests for the sake of others. When it becomes a feature of our identities, we become persons who are open to responding to others with such a depth of love that we are prepared to suffer willingly on behalf of others. The life and death of Jesus attest to the power of self-sacrificial love. Jesus sets aside his own interests, even to the point of setting aside his natural concern to preserve his own life, for the sake of bringing good news to all who are captive to sin. Jesus orders his life around meeting others with hope and healing, even when doing so comes at great personal cost, even when it means being rejected in his home town, even when it means giving up his own life.

Contrition, Hope, and Direction

A final cluster of religious affections arises when the combined force of humility and gratitude in our lives prompts *contrition*. Awe *should* prompt humility; awe *should* produce gratitude. Standing before the face of God in awe both attracts and disorients us. It points us to our place in the broader context of God's creative purposes. But often, rather than responding with humility and gratitude, we feel anxiety about our limitations and assert ourselves in prideful, self-deifying ways. Or else, we come to believe that we are insignificant and respond with self-negation that refuses to delight in ourselves and our place in the world. When we become aware that we have failed to respond with the humility and gratitude that ought to accompany awe, we feel contrition. When contrition moves beyond momentary, remorseful emotional responses and becomes a religious affection in us, it shapes our identities so that we become people who are dispositionally ready to recognize our own shortcomings and to repent. A contrite person is not one who constantly cowers before a vengeful God, but one who, having experienced God's endless forgiving love, learns to put off defensiveness and to be open to the correction of others.

Contrition and hope arise simultaneously out of an awareness of our failure to be humble and grateful. Just as humility and gratitude prompt us to be contrite about our failures, they also cultivate a deep *hope* that the world may yet come into a full and rich life of delightful interdependence. We can recognize our brokenness and lament over the inexplicable presence of natural evil in the world, and still see the seeds of possibility for renewal. We can be realistic about the damage sin has inflicted without falling into despair. When hope becomes a religious affection, it forms us as persons who meet the world with the expectation that, in the midst of pain and anguish, the world is good and that this goodness can be developed and expanded in ways yet to be fully discovered.

Finally, contrition and hope are inseparable from a *sense of direction*. Acknowledging our brokenness while meeting the world with hope depends upon our sense that the creation and every creature in it exists for some purpose, that we were made and ordered to some end. Hope seeks that end; contrition prompts us to repent of imposing our own purposes or following wrong paths. Our common language reveals how important the sense of direction is for us. We might say that a motivated young person "is really going places" or that people who are confused about what to do with their lives have "lost their way." The sense of direction, when united with humility, self-sacrificial love, and a sense of mutuality, moves us to seek meaning and purpose while not imposing our will on others. A Christian identity deeply formed by a sense of direction will seek to empower others and to contribute to their well-being.

There is, then, an order to the redeemed religious affections. The desire for and dependence on the God whom we encounter in Jesus Christ binds together and orders the religious affections in a way that ensures that they provide stability to our identities, but this stability is not rigid. Well-ordered religious affections will manifest themselves in diverse ways, and this is good. But this diversity will always be rooted in the unifying power of "one Lord, one faith, and one baptism" (Eph. 4:5).

When we reflect on our affectional lives, we find that, on the one hand, we are not as we ought to be. We find that we are fallen in ways that affect not only what we do but who we are. On the other hand, we experience ourselves as having been accepted by God despite our sinfulness. We find that God's grace reaches as far as our fallenness does, into what we do and who we are. A careful investigation of God's redeeming grace reveals three important themes relevant to our exploration of the religious affections. First, the structures of desire and dependence that undergird and order our religious affections are graciously lured back toward God, their proper object, through the beauty of the incarnation—a beauty that encompasses both the life and the death of Jesus Christ, who attracts, disturbs, and changes us. Second, the redemptive power of the incarnation intersects, transforms, and reorders our affectional lives through the purifying and illuminating work of the Holy Spirit in the worship and life of the church. And finally, the purifying and illuminating work of the Holy Spirit sanctifies and transforms not only individual religious affections but also the whole shape of our personhood, as these renewed affections come together into a well-ordered whole.

PART TWO

Religious Affections
and Worship

5

Religious Affections and
the Work of the Church

So far we have been pursuing a theory of the religious affections. We have looked at how they shape us as persons, how they are formed through our social contexts, how they express something about what we most fundamentally desire and depend upon, how they are distorted through sin, and how they are redeemed through the beauty of the incarnation. In this chapter we forge a link between the first portion of the book, which treats the theory of the religious affections, and the second portion of the book, which connects the religious affections to particular acts of worship. Before moving to particular acts of worship though, we need to address the general question of how worship practices are related to the formation and expression of the redeemed religious affections. In this chapter we will discuss more generally how the person-forming power of the incarnation is extended to the Christian community through its public worship.

FIVE MODELS OF WORSHIP

In this book we are presenting a model of worship that is affectional and theocentric. To clarify our proposal about the relationship between worship and the religious affections, it is helpful to distinguish it from five other ways of thinking about the nature and function of worship. Like all typologies, the one we offer here is intended to function only heuristically to illuminate certain features of Christian worship practices; no congregation will conform exactly to any one of these five types.

In the first model, worship functions as *evangelism*. In congregations that emphasize the evangelistic component of worship, services are thought of primarily as a means to attract the unchurched. The elements of the liturgy are changed or accommodated to make them accessible and meaningful for worshipers who have little prior church experience. Congregations who offer "seeker services," for example, are intentional about organizing the worship experience so that no one is alienated and so that each element of worship is adapted from and patterned on elements of contemporary culture to which everyone can relate. Worshipers who have no familiarity with singing the Gloria Patri, reciting the Apostles' Creed and Lord's Prayer from memory, listening to a carefully prepared sermon, or publicly confessing the sinfulness of the human condition might find these traditional liturgical elements both strange and alienating. But these worshipers are familiar with pop music, television sitcoms, and multimedia business and marketing presentations. To reach this audience, the worship experience must appropriate these familiar components of contemporary culture and adapt them for outreach and evangelism. The sermon might be replaced with a skit that acts out a Bible story, and congregational hymn singing might be replaced with a performance by a praise band. Traditional elements of Christian worship that cannot be translated into the idiom of pop culture are often omitted from the worship service.

The model of worship as evangelism commends to us the importance of the worshiping community remaining an open and hospitable place for all people. But an exclusive or primary emphasis on evangelism threatens to eclipse other important dimensions of worship. An uncritical adaptation to the popular culture of amusement, for example, threatens to disconnect the worship life of the congregation from the historic Christian faith and its ancient patterns of worship. It may also succumb to a form of cultural Christianity that loses its capacity to speak prophetically to contemporary culture. Finally, the emphasis on winning converts to the faith may eclipse the role of worship in cultivating, nurturing, and sustaining the faith of those worshipers over the course of a lifetime.

In the second model, worship provides the occasion for *the expression of individual, inner spirituality*. Worship services understood in this way grant us permission to be emotional in public in a way that is different from our ordinary public interactions. In our places of business, in shopping centers, at school, and in other civic contexts, displays of emotion are often unwelcome. Expressions of our deepest spiritual senses and displays of emotion are understood as private matters, out of place in the public world. But in worship, we find a public context in which we are supposed to be deeply moved, in which we are invited to express our spirituality, and in which we are welcome to display our deepest emotions. In such "experiential-expressivist" worship services, there is often a prominent place reserved for sharing one's testimony, for hearing special music that expresses deep personal meaning, and for sharing passages from Scripture that speak meaningfully to worshipers. Worship, in other words, is primarily about expressing our individual, inner experiences.

This model of worship rightly reminds us that if worship is not connected to our inner lives, it can become empty and formalistic. But an exclusive or primary emphasis on expressivism can become overly individualistic, failing to recognize that the church is not simply an aggregation of individuals. The church is to be active in shaping and forming our inner lives, not simply in receiving the outpourings from them. The church is not called into being by and organized around the subjective experiences of individuals. Rather, it is called into being by the will of God and organized around the truths of the gospel and the glory of God. There is objective content to the faith that ought to reform and even call into question our inner lives.

In the third model, worship is understood as *training in doctrine*. In this model, worship is thought of primarily as instructional and didactic; its chief function is to convey to worshipers a proper understanding of the truths of Scripture. Congregations that tend toward this model often offer worship services that include a carefully crafted sermon that is more lecture like than poetic and that exposits a particular text of Scripture to extract doctrinal content from it. Metaphorical language, if it is used in the sermon at all, will not be left to play freely on the religious imagination, but will instead be explained in terms of the doctrinal propositions implicit in the metaphors. Likewise the sacraments will be preceded by often lengthy doctrinal explanations that ensure that participants fully understand and assent to the truths being enacted in the rituals. Hymns are selected and valued primarily for their lyrics, and even then only insofar as such lyrics repeat and enhance the doctrines thematized in sermon and sacrament.

This model of worship rightly reminds us that good worship does instill and reinforce belief as a central part of the Christian life. But an exclusive or primary emphasis on doctrine can become coldly cognitive and polemical, and overemphasizing the doctrinal distinctives of a particular community can fail to honor the unity of the church. Additionally, focusing too exclusively on the cognitive dimensions of the faith can disconnect knowing from heartfelt piety and fail to attend to the way that the metaphors, symbols, rituals, and acts of worship shape Christian identity in multiple and complex ways.

In the fourth model, worship is understood as *empowerment for social action*. In this model, we gather in worship to heighten our awareness of injustice and oppression in the world and to motivate and equip ourselves with the spiritual resources necessary for combating them. Worshipers are keenly aware of the continuing brokenness of the world outside the church and seek in the worship life of the church to confess and discover resources to ameliorate that condition. Prayers of confession will emphasize the privileged position of worshipers and offer occasions to repent for our complicity in the marginalization of oppressed peoples. Liturgical resources such as hymns, prayers, and litanies are often selected for the purpose of making voices heard that have been silenced. They may draw on the folk musical traditions of African Americans, Hispanics, and Native Americans, for example. Litanies and prayers may highlight the experiences of women and draw on the neglected biblical tradition of feminine imagery for God. Sermons, too, will inform worshipers and raise consciousness about social injustice and oppression in the world, and they may even offer guidance about how to organize for action to resist and overcome such social sin.

The model of worship as empowerment for social action appropriately links worship and the moral life and models itself on the most ancient pattern of worship, with its liturgical rhythm of gathering and sending. But an exclusive or primary emphasis on social action and empowerment can contribute to the subordination of faith to ethics, and the identity and life of the congregation can become so tightly wed to particular social issues that it neglects other important dimensions of the faith such as doctrine, evangelism, and spiritual formation.

In the last model, worship is understood as *the repetition of tradition*. In this model, the worship life of the church initiates us into and sustains us in the rich traditions of Christian worship, the rites and rituals that have endured through centuries, and the liturgical patterns that have persisted since apostolic times. The church is understood to be a place of stability, tradition, and changelessness in a contemporary world swirling in the ever-changing currents of newness, spontaneity, and unpredictability. Worshipers gather each week to pray the same prayers, to hear the same assurance of pardon, to recite the same creed, and to approach the same Table, because these forms and rites bear deep meaning and power and ground them in a heritage that gives them a place and identity in a world where change is often arbitrary.

The model of worship as repetition of tradition rightly respects the communion of the saints, attends to the power of ritual in grounding Christian identity, and appropriately resists the excessive individualism of contemporary culture by acknowledging that our identities are formed in community. But an exclusive or primary emphasis on ritual can lead to an empty formalism when it fails to respect the continuing need of the tradition to speak in fresh and salient ways to the contemporary world. It may also overlook the multiplicity of worship traditions within Christianity.

Worship is complex and functions at multiple levels. Offering true praise and thanksgiving to God entails being open to outsiders, expressing our inner lives, learning and assenting to doctrine, equipping ourselves for social action, and placing ourselves within a rich tradition. Each of these models offers something useful and important for our understanding of worship that we do not want to dismiss or reject. Instead, we want to offer a model of Christian worship that preserves these dimensions of truth, even as it locates them within a more comprehensive understanding of the nature and function of worship in the Christian life. If we are to understand how worship renews and transforms worshipers in this more comprehensive way, we must attend to two often neglected themes in Christian theology. First, we must attend to the nature and importance of the religious affections and the role that worship plays in cultivating them. Second, we must recover a sense of the sovereignty and majesty of God and a corresponding humility about the place of humanity in God's broader purposes. In a word, we need to develop an affectional and theocentric model of worship that focuses on how worship reorients the deepest affectional structures of our identities and thereby attunes us properly to God and the world as the expression of divine sovereignty and glory.[1]

A BRIEF THEOLOGY OF THE CHURCH

To understand why a recovery of the religious affections and a theocentric orientation is important, we need to understand worship as the work of the church, and this requires a theology of worship embedded in a broader theology of the church. Although we cannot offer a comprehensive theology of the church here, we will offer four guiding theological principles.

The first principle that guides our thinking is that the church is *a covenant community* called into existence and sustained by the sovereign grace of God, not merely a voluntary society that arises out of or is defined wholly by the willful consent of its individual members. Understanding the church covenantally has several implications. First, a covenantal model of the church recognizes that God loves us and makes a claim on our lives before we are ever able to return that love or respond in faith. God initiates and extends this love to individuals through the community of faith with whom God has first made a covenant. God's covenant with the community of faith includes not only the promise that God will continue to extend redemptive grace to individuals through the ministry of the church; it also provides the means whereby this occurs. We are not first and foremost individuals who "join a church"; instead, we are from the outset embedded in a covenantal community of faith, called into existence and sustained by God, that opens possibilities for and sets limits on who we may become as individuals.

Second, this understanding of the church as a covenant community entails a theocentric orientation for the Christian life. Because the church in which Christian life is embedded arises wholly out of God's gracious initiative, continues to be sustained by this same grace, and exists to serve God's ends, the church along with every other facet of creation exists for the glory of God, and worship must reflect this. Any form of worship that places human goods and goals, however noble they may be, above or before the glory of God fails to recognize sufficiently the sovereignty of God. While God's glory certainly includes human flourishing, it locates that flourishing in a broader creational context in which God is working out purposes beyond the scope of human interests, and worship must reflect this broader scope of divine purposes.

When the Westminster Shorter Catechism affirms this theocentric orientation of the Christian life by saying the chief end of humanity is to glorify God forever, it adds that in so doing we are to *enjoy* God forever as well. The catechism's link between glorifying God and enjoying God points to a third implication of a covenantal model of the church, namely, that the Christian life is deeply affectional in nature. To pursue God's ends and to be oriented toward the celebration of divine beauty in the entire creation necessarily encompass the totality of who we are. We are called not only to know God and to act for God, but also to desire and depend on God with every fiber of our being. Our knowledge and action are to be permeated by a total dispositional response to God grounded in our religious affections.

The second theological commitment that frames our interpretation of worship is an understanding of the church as *a community of memory and hope*. This understanding means respecting both the communion of the saints and the continuing vitality of the Christian tradition. The church is the covenant community that God has called into a relationship since time immemorial, but it is also the community that lives today and that will pass on the faith to future generations. Our task, as Calvin put it, "is not just to transmit the tradition faithfully, but also to put it in the form we think will prove best."[2] Each generation both receives and shapes the tradition.

The church is a community of memory. In worship we come together to remember. We remember God's great works in the history of Israel; we remember the life, death, and resurrection of Christ; we remember how the Holy Spirit breathed life into the body of Christ, the church, at Pentecost, and how the triune God continues to sustain and nurture the church even today. In the weekly remembering of worship, the ancient and distant story of the Scriptures and saints becomes *our* story. In the liturgy, the smaller story of our lives is taken up into the larger story of God as it has unfolded since creation.[3] In worship our lives are joined through memory to the lives of the people of God in all times and places.

But we are also a community of hope. In worship we gather together to lean into a future that we eagerly anticipate, a future that has been promised, a future that has already begun but has not yet been fulfilled. We participate proleptically in that future when we gather at the Table both to remember the work of Christ and to hope for the heavenly banquet in which people will come from east and west, from north and south, and sit at table in the kingdom of God. The church is a community of memory and hope, and as we participate in its worship life of remembering and hoping, we are no mere spectators. We do not come to *watch* worship; we come to *participate* in it and to be transformed by it. When we worship together, we come into an active relationship with the saints who have gone before us and bind ourselves to a future of life in God. Our active remembering and hoping takes place within the covenant community that shapes our affections and orients us theocentrically.

The third guiding theological principle is that the church is *a confessional community*. This means, first, that the church is a community of beliefs and that its beliefs are inherited from Scripture and tradition. The work of the church is to confess Jesus Christ and to bear witness to the grace and majesty of God unfolding in the world. Our confession of Jesus Christ, however, is bound up with our existence as a community of memory. In witnessing to the work of God in the world, we do not speak simply with our own voices; rather, we join our voices with the great cloud of witnesses who have gone before us. When we read Scripture, recite the Apostles' and Nicene Creeds, and ask and answer the questions of our catechisms, we speak a language and message that we have inherited from the Christian tradition, but we speak these with the peculiar accents and idioms of our own age.

Second, to say that the church is a confessional community means that its belief shapes and is shaped by its worship life. The existence of the church as a confessional community finds fullest expression in its worship life; in fact, our term *liturgy* derives from the Greek word *leitourgia*, literally the "work of the people." Roman Catholic theologians have been especially mindful of the link between belief and worship. Catholic theology captures the essence of this truth that belief and worship are inseparable with the Latin phrase *lex orandi, lex credendi*, which means "the law of prayer establishes the law of belief"; more simply put, it means that we believe what we pray. Confession of faith and worship go hand in hand, and they are reciprocally related. Faith commitments inform the way that we pray and the content of our prayers, but the life of prayer also generates and shapes our capacity to have faith and confess it. We are shaped by the worship of the covenant community before we are yet capable of holding and confessing the faith as individuals.

Third, to say that the church is a confessional community means that its belief and worship shape and are shaped by its morality. *Lex orandi, lex credendi* has implications for ethics because confessing Jesus Christ and bearing witness to the glory of God arise organically from the worship life of the church and flow into its work in the world. The Armenian Orthodox theologian Vigen Guroian highlights this link between liturgy, belief, and ethics when he explores how *lex orandi, lex credendi* is related to *lex bene operandi*, which means that the law of prayer, which is the law of belief, is also the law of good works.[4] The moral life is intimately connected to the worshiping life of the community that confesses Jesus Christ. Being formed through the worship of a covenantal community of memory and hope that confesses Jesus Christ shapes the kinds of moral agents we become and affects how we frame and respond to moral problems.[5] The confessional nature of the church and Christian life is never simply about speaking what we believe, though, of course, it includes this; to speak of the church as a confessional community is to recognize that the confessional life of the church is fully actuated in its worship life and radiates across the beliefs we profess, the moral life we pursue, and the deepest patterns of our affectional and dispositional lives.

A fourth guiding theological commitment is to *the unity and diversity of the church*. When we affirm in the Nicene Creed that "we believe in one holy catholic and apostolic church," we acknowledge that in the midst of its diversity the church remains one across space and time. We are united by one Lord, one faith, and one baptism; but this unity does not mean uniformity. There is beauty in diversity. In every time and place where the Christian gospel has come into contact with the wealth of human cultures, it has affirmed the goodness of those cultures and appropriated and transformed their traditions, incorporating them into the one body of Christ.

The incarnation serves as a model for thinking about the unity and diversity of the church. In the incarnation God becomes human for the salvation of humanity, but God does this work on behalf of humanity through a particular person, Jesus of Nazareth, in a particular time and place. God came as a first-century Palestinian Jew, speaking in the local dialect, teaching in the accustomed manner of a rabbi. He was a man of his place and time, but he did not simply receive and affirm the culture and tradition of his place and time. Instead, he preached and established a kingdom of God that pressed against the boundaries of that culture and challenged many of its assumptions. Likewise, the church continues this incarnational pattern when it takes root in the soil of diverse human cultures across history. Worship is, perhaps, the place where we see most clearly the incarnational unity and diversity of the church. In all times and places, Christians have gathered on the first day of the week to celebrate the resurrection of Christ, and we still do. We come together to read from and proclaim a common Scripture, celebrate common sacraments, confess shared creeds, sing, pray, and confess our sins; but we do these things in strikingly diverse ways. Yet amidst the diverse forms of our worship, we affirm the common truth that our worship is a means of grace whereby God transforms and reshapes the deepest patterns of our lives.

Diversity is good, but this does not mean that every variant is equally good. There are better and worse ways to come into the presence of God. Unfortunately, many Christians have become rigid and intolerant of liturgical diversity in the midst of the "worship wars." Proponents of contemporary worship deride traditional, formal worship as merely "going through the motions." Proponents of more traditional worship dismiss all contemporary worship as mere entertainment. In the midst of this diversity, how are we to discern which worship practices are good and worthwhile and which are flawed and destructive without rejecting the goodness of the diversity of the church? We believe that developing a theology of human personhood that is attentive to the religious affections and linking the cultivation of those religious affections to worship practices will help us discern which among such practices are appropriately suited for Christian worship that glorifies God while renewing and transforming humanity.

SOCIAL SELVES, SPEECH ACTS, BODILY ACTS

The link between a theory of the religious affections and the concrete worship life of the church rests in the understanding of the church that we have just set forth. To speak of the church as a covenant community that precedes and generates individual faith highlights the fact that we are social selves and that God works the mystery of redemption precisely through this most basic feature of our nature. To speak of the church as a diverse community united in a shared memory and hope and confessing Jesus Christ in word and deed highlights the fact that we are linguistic and embodied beings and that God works the mystery of redemption precisely through these most basic features of our nature. To be Christian is to be socially formed through the speech acts and bodily acts that constitute the work—the *leitourgia*—of the church as the body of Christ. In this threefold claim that we are (1) socially formed, (2) linguistically constituted, and (3) embodied beings we discover the link between the theory of the religious affections and the concrete worship life of the church.

The first claim, that we are socially formed selves, means quite simply that we become who we are as persons in large part through the formative influence of the communities that shape us. The language, stories, and repeated actions of a culture or an institution shape us into certain patterns of life. To be formed in this way is part of our created constitution. God made us, that is, as social creatures who grow into our identities through our companionship with others. So when God comes to redeem us, this redemption comes in a form that both reflects and honors our social nature. In establishing the institutional church as the location of the continuing work of the Holy Spirit, God continues to create and re-create us through the pattern of our nature established in creation. This is not simply a sociological observation of the fact that the church shapes us; rather, the Christian faith makes the normative claim that the church is the institution established and sustained by God for the sake of extending the work of Christ. The church does that by shaping persons for lives of reverence and awe before God. The church, through the words and embodied acts of worship, shapes us to be worshipful people, people who stand in humility and awe, in hope and delight, in contrition and gratitude before the face of God.

The second claim, that we are shaped as social selves through the linguistic practices of our communities, is somewhat at odds with our common way of thinking about language. We often imagine that we use words merely to express ideas that emerge within the prelinguistic reservoir of our minds. We think that we first have an idea and then search for words to express it so that others may share this idea with us. We think that words are simply signs that stand in for reality. When we say "chair," for instance, that sound or mark on the page simply points to an external thing-we-sit-on reality.

This depiction of language, however, is too simple. While we do have ideas that can be expressed with words that act as stand-ins for reality, our capacity to generate ideas in the first place depends on having been formed by certain kinds of linguistic practices. Our capacity to use language to express ideas depends upon a more basic truth. Language does not merely stand in for reality in a static way; rather, language *generates* our perception of reality. Language is a living, dynamic, creative force that organizes the world for us conceptually so that, through our inherited languages, we are made able to experience the world in particular ways. As we mature and acquire ever more sophisticated linguistic abilities, we come to experience the world in ever more complex and particular ways. Ideas do not precede words. Words precede ideas and make them possible. Words organize our world into ideas and things.

Perhaps some examples will help to clarify this point. When we are children we learn our manners; we learn to say "please," and "thank you," and "excuse me." When we learn these things, we are still in a very egocentric stage of life. Children do not have a natural sense that food and fun come to them as gifts. They feel a sense of entitlement to the things that allow them to live, flourish, and enjoy themselves. But we insist that they say "thank you," even when they do not feel grateful. We insist that they say "please," even for those things to which they feel entitled. We insist that they say "excuse me," when inserting themselves into a situation where they feel they have every right to be. But a strange thing happens. If we say "please," and "thank you," and "excuse me" often enough, we come to feel grateful; we come to acknowledge the giftedness of life. We internalize the manners first made available to us through the external mechanism of language. The social network of polite exchange enacted by and perpetuated through our linguistic practices becomes so much a part of who we are that we feel a sense of shock and dismay when we experience rude behavior.

As another example, consider a child who grows up in a home where family members regularly use racial stereotypes and epithets. That child learns to divide the world artificially and arbitrarily along the lines of skin pigmentation and physiological characteristics. That child literally begins to "see" races, rather than to see a spectrum of humanity with no clean lines of division. Through language, the world has been constructed for that child in a racist way, and these racist linguistic practices, when internalized, generate a grid through which reality is interpreted and engaged. The language practice will determine how the child interacts with others. Whom she can love, hate, trust, or fear, and whom she can date or befriend, will be strongly influenced by the language practices she uses to characterize those others. If we are to change racist perceptions of the world, we would do well first to change our language practices. When it becomes simply unacceptable to speak in certain ways, it soon becomes unacceptable to think in those ways, and eventually racism becomes simply *unthinkable*.

These simple examples point to something very basic about being human. We are not simply beings who use language. We are beings whose capacity to see the world in certain ways depends upon having that world first "named" for us linguistically by others. We cannot think what we cannot say. Language does not first well up from within individuals; rather, individuals are always already immersed in a world of vibrant and dynamic linguistic practices. Through immersion in that world, individuals come to construe reality in particular ways, to be attuned to it, and to act in it in particular ways. This understanding of language profoundly affects our understanding of worship. It means that the language of worship generates a world of meaning grounded in the revelation of the gospel and draws us into this new world where our religious affections are trained properly, thereby moving us from the fragmentation of humanity's fall to the new wholeness and integrity made available through the incarnation.[6]

So far we have simply pointed out that we are shaped by language, but there is another important way in which language is related to worship and to the religious affections: language does not merely represent things; it *does* things. Our words, like the words of God, are creative and active. In Genesis 1, God speaks and in speaking creates a world. We do that too. We make things happen with our words. There is probably no moment in human experience in which we are more aware of our likeness to God through our capacity to speak creatively than when we witness the joining of two people in the bonds of holy wedlock. At a wedding we witness two people as they speak and, speaking, create a new reality. At a wedding two single people speak vows to one another in the presence of witnesses, and in doing so, they make themselves married. They speak a new reality into existence. If they make these vows, then they are married. If they do not speak them, then they are not married. But there are also other ways in which we do things with words. We hurt people with them; we offer comfort and reassurance; we issue commands; we beg for forgiveness; we establish relationships and destroy friendships. Our words are acts.

Worship has much to do with words. We do a lot of speaking and hearing in our services of worship. Those words form us for humility and gratitude, for hope and contrition, for delight and awe. But those words are also acts. Through them we praise God, thank God, implore God. Through them we greet one another in Christ, commit ourselves to one another in baptismal vows, and charge and bless one another to live peaceful lives. In worship our words do things. This is why we are not invited to *read* prayers together, but to *pray* them. The reading is only in service of the act of praying. The point is not to read prayers of adoration, but to *adore* God. We do not read prayers of confession; we *confess*. We do not simply recite the creed, we confess our faith. Even Scripture is not simply read; it is performed. Scripture generates a world and invites us into it. Scripture opens interpretive possibilities that help our world bear meaning differently. Worship is *leitourgia*. It is the work of the people. Worship is work. In the language of worship, we are accomplishing, at least in part, the work of the church.

We are social creatures, and we are shaped by linguistic acts. But there is a third link between the religious affections and worship practices: our constitution as physical beings. God's creative speech generates a world replete with every kind of creature. God's creative speech, moreover, generates a diverse, material world that is good. If we bear the image of God in part through our capacity to speak creatively, it is also true that we are *creatures* who bear the image of God. We are embedded within that vast, diverse, and material creation, and this is good.

We are shaped by material acts as deeply as we are shaped by speech acts. What we do with our bodies and how we interact with the physical world influences our spiritual lives. The world we experience through our senses profoundly affects the shape and direction of our spirituality. Even the most austere Protestant worship service—shorn of incense, banners, vestments, stained-glass windows, and other such aids to worship—is filled with sensory stimuli: the sound of music, the taste of wine and bread, the heft of the Bible or hymnal in our hands, that old-church smell that greets us when we step through the doors of certain churches, the feel of our fellow worshipers' hands when we pass the peace, the physical acts of standing to sing hymns or bowing one's head to receive a blessing or join in prayer. All of these work on the state of our souls. This is not magic; it is the simple reality of being embodied creatures. Magic is the practice of manipulating physical elements in an effort to influence God. What Christian worship does is precisely the opposite of magic. In Christian worship, we trust that God works through the physical world to bring us under God's influence.

Of course we must be careful with our use of the physical world, but not because there is something intrinsically dangerous or tainted about it. We must be careful with it for precisely the same reason that we are cautious with our use of words in worship, because worship is a concentrated time and space in which we become intentional about coming into communion with God through the incarnate Christ, and that is a powerful thing to do. In worship we model ourselves on the ministry of Jesus Christ, who came with both words and acts. He came teaching and healing. Jesus Christ did not simply impart words of wisdom to his disciples. He also laid his hands on the sick and infirm: he touched the woman with the issue of blood and mixed his saliva with mud to heal a blind man. Jesus also received the touch of others: a kiss from Judas, anointing from women. Our worship, like the ministry of Christ, centers on word and matter.

WORSHIP AND THE RESTORATION
OF THE RELIGIOUS AFFECTIONS

Because we are social, linguistic, and embodied creatures, and because in the worship life of the church the Holy Spirit provides a communal context centered on words and matter, Christian worship has the capacity to shape us for the Christian life. The speech acts and material acts of the church at worship are person-forming for us at the deepest affectional levels of our being. Specifically, worship participates in the restoration of the affections in six ways. Worship *evokes* particular religious affections. Even as worship evokes particular affections, it also *shapes* them individually and *orders* them by establishing relationships between the affections that assure that they comprise a coherent constellation rather than merely an aggregation. Worship gives us the opportunity to *express* these well-ordered affections.[7] Worship *sustains* our religious affections. Finally, worship *directs* our religious affections toward God in such a way that we are brought into fitting relationships with other creatures.

Worship *evokes* emotional responses that are tethered to particular religious affections. Different parts of the liturgy will evoke different sorts of emotional responses. Prayers of confession, for example, may be especially well-suited to evoking a feeling of contrition. Hymns of adoration may be especially likely to evoke feelings of awe. The complex relationship between emotions and affections means that simply evoking these emotions can, over time, cultivate the deeper corresponding affections in us. In this sense, evoking the emotion provides the context for the longer-range purpose of evoking the affection. Only those who have experienced awe as an emotion can let that emotion settle down in them to become a feature of their personalities. Even for those in whom gratitude, hope, and the like have become affectional structures of their personalities, evoking the corresponding emotion is important. When contrition as an affection, for example, comes to the surface of our consciousness in the form of felt remorse, we are able to attend to its shape and nuance in our lives. It is perfectly appropriate, then, for worship leaders to be intentional about planning services designed to evoke the full range of religious affections. In fact, it is crucial that worship planners ensure that services are not dominated by certain affections to the exclusion of others.

Worship does not simply evoke particular affections, it also *shapes* those affections in a Christian way. Worship sculpts the more generic affections into their particular Christian form by grounding them in the sacred stories of Scripture and the doctrinal affirmations of the church. It is the content of our beliefs (*lex credendi*) that through worship (*lex orandi*) gives shape and specificity to our religious affections. Hope, for example, can be thought of as a generic longing for a better future, but Christian worship sculpts this generic longing into Christian hope by grounding such newness and possibility in the miracle of the incarnation as the source of all newness and possibility in a fallen world. For the Christian, hope is not merely generic longing for a new future; it is specific longing for that kingdom of God that is initiated and sustained only by Jesus Christ as God with us. Moreover, Christian worship shapes generic hope into Christian hope by filling it with specific content. The newness and possibility that Christians hope for is not a newness and possibility to be found in some distant, disembodied, otherworldly existence. Instead, Christian hope sees the seeds of newness and possibility as existing already in the present and maturing into the future that embraces the entire material world. Christian hope longs not for a flight of our souls from our bodies to a purely spiritual realm that replaces the present creation; rather, we long for the "new creation" that embraces and restores the goodness of the present material order. Finally, Christian worship shapes hope into Christian hope by affirming that the ultimate triumph over evil will come at God's initiative, and this truth serves both to embolden us to work toward the new creation and to caution us against excessive confidence in our capacity to complete that new creation on our own. Just as hope is shaped through worship, so too are all of the religious affections. The sacred stories of Scripture and the doctrinal affirmations of the faith carried in the words, rituals, and activities of worship shape generic affections into specifically Christian affections.

Worship evokes and shapes particular religious affections, but it also *orders* them by establishing relationships among the various affections. We explored this ordering of the religious affections at some length in the last chapter, noting how every religious affection is intrinsically connected to every other through the desire and dependence that run through them all. To be Christian, in other words, is not merely to have a particular set of affections, but to have one's whole personality oriented in a particular way. The sense of direction, for example, is always connected to a sense of mutuality and to humility in ways that prevent us from becoming hegemonic. Self-sacrificial love is always connected to a sense of well-being and to hope in ways that prevent it from becoming self-negation. Christian personhood consists not only in having a particular set of religious affections, then, but in having those affections well ordered.

Christian worship also provides us with the opportunity to *express* these well-ordered religious affections. Although the experiential-expressivist model of worship poses serious problems, it does offer the important insight that we need not be ashamed of our emotional lives, and we need not hide expressions of emotion from one another. Jesus often expressed his emotions publically. The Gospel of John repeatedly tells us that Jesus was "deeply moved" when he learned of the death of Lazarus (John 11:38 RSV). Jesus lamented over Jerusalem and wept over what awaited him in his final days. It is perfectly appropriate that worship offer us similar opportunities to allow our affections outward expression in the form of emotions. Christian worship, moreover, will provide these opportunities to express our emotions in a way that honors the abiding connection between our emotions and our rationality.

Appropriate expressions of emotion in worship are different from their expression in the context of amusement. In the latter context, emotion is aroused only to be immediately discharged, and it remains disconnected from the abiding structures of our identities. In worship, by contrast, the expression of emotion is not an end in itself; rather, the expression of emotion serves to express and cultivate a deep and abiding affectional disposition that ultimately functions to reorient our understanding of God's world and our conduct in it. In worship, such expressions of emotion, furthermore, will not be understood as simply welling up spontaneously from the inner recesses of the isolated individual. Instead, such expressions will honor our deeply social nature and be understood to grow out of and maintain their integral link to the community that shapes the individual.

Worship also *sustains* our religious affections, training them on the divine over the long course of our lifetimes. Worship will sustain our affections even during those long spells of spiritual dryness in which the emotions that correspond to our affections seem long absent. Worship sustains us even when we feel that we are simply "going through the motions." Because worship forms the deep affectional current of our personalities, and not merely the emotional eddies that swirl on the surface, it sustains us even when we feel isolated from each other and alienated from God as the source of life, meaning, and purpose. Participating in the elements of the liturgy nourishes our religious affections in those brief or even protracted periods when we lack the emotional experience of them, and in time such nourished affections will once again bear fruit in our emotional lives.

We express awe, delight, and gratitude, for example, even when we do not feel them for the same reason that we say "thank you," even when we are not grateful, because the affection is called for even when the emotion, for one reason or another, escapes us. Sometimes these expressions will evoke the emotion sooner rather than later. Sometimes, we will call ourselves into worship with a "shout of joy" and actually feel that joy. We will sing a hymn of adoration, and it will evoke the feeling of awe. At other times worship will not evoke such emotional expressions, but this fact in no way undermines the sincerity or genuineness of the worship we offer. There is no hypocrisy in proclaiming our awe in those seasons of life when we simply do not feel it or in offering thanks in those moments in which we lack gratitude or using a psalm to exclaim the delight of which we are only dimly aware. We express our gratitude because we are people who experience the creation as a gift that properly calls for gratitude, and we experience it that way even in the absence of felt thankfulness. Likewise, even in the depths of anguish we acknowledge that the creation calls for delight.

Impatience with the slow work of sustaining the religious affections, even when we do not experience them in emotionally intense ways, is bound to leave disappointed those worship planners who aim to make us feel a certain way at certain times. Worship focused on evoking intense emotions, rather than on sustaining the abiding affections that ground such emotions, if it does not disappoint us, is likely to become manipulative. Worshipers, in turn, are likely to feel alienated for not having the right feelings at the right time. What if the praise song did not bring tears to the eyes of the woman in the third row? What if the man near the back harbors some deep doubts about his faith when he recites the creed? We are not machines with buttons we can punch to order up one emotional response or another, and if we expect to be able to do so, then what do we as a church have to say to the woman in the third row and the man at the back of the sanctuary? But if we offer Christians permission to worship God even when they do not feel like doing it, we can give worship the time and space that it needs to work its way into our hearts, to sustain our religious affections. If we admit to ourselves that being people of faith often involves doubt, fear, and hurt, we can speak more meaningfully to people precisely when they are in the midst of doubt, fear, and pain. Ultimately this patience with the affection-sustaining nature of worship will allow us to be more honest with ourselves in the presence of God, and that will make our worship truer.

Finally, worship *directs* our religious affections. Earlier we noted that the affections are object-oriented, that an affective experience is always connected to some specific object or event in the order of our experience. We feel awe in the presence of the great sequoia, contrition over harsh words, and gratitude at the birth of a child. We do not experience these affections generically, but only as they are occasioned by a particular object or event at a particular moment of time. For example, hymns of adoration that attune us to the beauty of creation also direct our sense of well-being toward God, who is the source of that beauty. A sermon on the parable of the Good Samaritan that invites us to ask, "Who is my neighbor?" will expand our sense of obligation by directing our attention to those whom we may have neglected. Prayers of confession will direct our contrition toward the brokenness of our being as well as the sinfulness of our actions. As a means of grace, worship redirects our affections toward their proper object, God. But as we have seen, our experience of God is always mediated through other creatures, and, therefore, redirecting our affections back to God necessarily involves reordering our relationships with other creatures. Ameliorating our inner fragmentation leads to healing the wounds of our outer fragmentation. This means that worship serves an important ethical function because as it reorients us properly toward God, it necessarily also reorients us properly toward one another and toward other creatures.

Throughout this chapter we have sought to connect the theory of the religious affections that we developed in the first four chapters to an account of how worship practices participate in the restoration of those affections. We have developed an affectional and theocentric model of worship. In contrast to five other models of worship, we have highlighted the ways in which worship practices reorient the deepest affectional structures of our identities and attune us properly to God and to the world as the expression of God's glory. This model of worship rests on an understanding of the church as a covenant community of memory and hope that confesses Jesus Christ through both its unity and its diversity. Emerging from this model of the church is a view of the human as social, linguistic, and embodied, and a view of worship that acknowledges six ways in which it restores our affections.

6

The Structure of Worship: Gathering, Abiding, Sending

Christian worship is ordered around a very simple pattern of gathering, abiding, and sending. We gather together in established times and places; we abide together in peace around Word and Table; and we are sent out again in peace with the promise that this pattern will sustain us until we gather again to repeat it. This threefold structure of worship has a very long history in the Christian church, and it has been tested for its person-forming power through time and across cultures. We gather, abide, and are sent, just as Christians in all times and places have, to glorify and enjoy God and open ourselves to the renewing power of the Holy Spirit as it comes to us through the words and works of worship.

We come together, abide together, and are sent as social, linguistic, and embodied creatures, and our worship services both reflect and honor this. Our worshipful gathering, abiding, and sending always include both linguistic and material embodied acts. In gathering, we move bodily into designated worship spaces at designated times, and as we gather we call ourselves into worship and speak a greeting to one another in the name of the Lord. As we abide together, we hear the Word proclaimed and come to the Table to be fed in body and spirit by the bread and wine of the Eucharist. We are sent out blessed with words of comfort and hope and charged with living in a manner that embodies and enacts peace and justice in our world by feeding the hungry, sheltering the homeless, and caring for the sick. Through the many speech acts and material acts of worship, organized around the age-old movement of gathering, abiding, and sending, God works to purify and illumine the affectional core of our identities, thus moving us from the fragmentation of our fallenness to the new wholeness of redemption.

The grace of God that illumines and purifies our affectional lives meets us in particular times and places. The people of God come together from their

scattered places of dwelling and working to a designated place at a designated
time for the purpose of worship. Of course, God is present to us in all places
and times, but when we come to worship, we come to a time and place where
we are intentional about seeking the presence of God in a more concentrated
way. But we are not content simply to seek God in worship; we *expect* to find
God. We expect God to meet us here and now, at Rock Spring Presbyterian
Church, on Piedmont Road, at 8:30 on Sunday morning, in a particular and
powerful way. We mark time and space as religiously significant. We designate
particular buildings as the places where we expect God to meet us. We designate a weekly and annual cycle of worship, marking times when we expect God
to meet us.[1]

    This audacious expectation that we will meet God in a particular time and
place is rooted in the biblical vision in which God enters human history, our
history, and makes new things happen. The God of the Bible is not just the
God who makes the sun rise and the seasons change, though God does these
things too. God is revealed in history, through a community of faith, acting to
establish, admonish, and redeem a covenant people. This God is the God of
Abraham, Isaac, and Jacob, of Deborah, Ruth, and Naomi, the one who wres-
tles with Jacob at Bethel, who makes a covenant with Moses and the children
of Israel at Sinai, who enlists the assistance of Rahab to secure the promised
land, who becomes human in Jesus of Nazareth, and who breathes life into the
church at Pentecost. Our God comes to us in this time and at that place, not
simply as an impersonal force of nature. In our gathering, abiding, and sending, we, like the people of the Bible, meet God in a particular place, at a certain time, amid a community of faith, and with the expectation that God will
speak to us, correct us, restore us, and comfort us.

    Worship is intensely physical. The pattern of gathering, abiding, and send-
ing calls us to move bodily into particular worship spaces at designated times,
and the physical dimensions of our gathering, abiding, and sending are crucial. Watching worship on television or listening to a recording of a service
may provide important access to worship for those unable to be physically present, but it can never fully substitute for bodily presence. We need to see one
another face-to-face. We need to greet one another with handshakes and embraces. We see in each other's eyes the signs of our joy and grief. We note in
each other's bodies the signs of vigor and decline. We need to be bodily present to each other if we are to be the body of Christ. Coming together in this
way also makes us mindful of those who are not able to be physically present
and may thus intensify our sense of mutuality and interdependence. Such a
heightened sense of mutuality and interdependence may prompt us to make
our space more hospitable for those with disabilities so they can enter with

ease, and to work to ensure that we are physically present through times of visitation to those too ill or frail to join us in the sanctuary.

The particular acts of worship that purify and illuminate us are set within the order of worship that expresses the general pattern of gathering, abiding, and sending. This means that we must pay special attention to the order of worship, that is, to the formal structure in which the various acts of worship are set. Attending to the order of worship, however, raises the question of how we ought to arrange the particular acts of worship within the broader pattern of gathering, abiding, and sending. In his *Introduction to Christian Worship*, James White notes that "quite clearly there is no one 'right' order of worship."[2] While we may agree—though sometimes we clearly do not—on what components are important to include in a worship service, there is great variety among congregations and denominations regarding when in the service those things ought to happen. Should prayers of confession be offered before the services of Word and sacrament or between them? Should the people pass the peace after the prayers of confession or after reciting the creed? How often should the Lord's Supper be administered? Should children remain for the entire worship service or leave for their own service? If they leave, when is the proper time for that to happen? If the choir sings an anthem, when should that happen? All of these questions can be answered in multiple good ways. So long as things are done in good order, the church, even from its earliest days, has allowed a certain latitude in the particulars of ordering worship within the basic structure of gathering, abiding, and sending.

For purposes of simplicity, throughout this chapter we will assume the following basic order of worship: The service begins with rituals of adoration and continues with a call to confession, collective prayer of confession, plea for mercy, assurance of pardon, and the passing of the peace. The middle part of the service is devoted to proclamation (including prayers of illumination, the hearing of Scripture and its proclamation in sermon, the recitation of a creed, and the prayers of the people) and the sacrament of the Lord's Supper. The service concludes with rituals of response and sending.

We maintain that there is a certain logic to this ordering that mirrors the ordering of the religious affections. We gather in reverence and awe, are moved by that awe to humility and contrition; we abide together in mutuality and delight; we go forth in gratitude and with renewed senses of obligation, direction, and hope. But just as there is great and good diversity of Christian personalities in the midst of a common, discernable pattern of the religious affections that lends a distinctive shape to Christian personhood, so also there are many good and faithful ways to order Christian worship within a basic pattern that is distinctively Christian.

An Outline of the Service for the Lord's Day
from the *Book of Common Worship*, Presbyterian Church (USA), 46.[*]

GATHERING
> ***Call to Worship***
> Prayer of the Day or Opening Prayer
> Hymn of Praise, Psalm, or Spiritual
> Confession and Pardon
> ***The Passing of the Peace***

ABIDING

THE WORD
> Canticle, Psalm, Hymn, or Spiritual
> Prayer for Illumination
> First Reading
> Psalm
> Second Reading
> Anthem, Hymn, Psalm, Canticle, or Spiritual
> Gospel Reading
> Sermon
> Invitation
> Affirmation of Faith
> Prayers of the People

THE EUCHARIST
> Offering
> Invitation to the Lord's Table
> Great Thanksgiving
> Lord's Prayer
> Breaking of the Bread
> Communion of the People

SENDING
> Hymn, Spiritual, Canticle, or Psalm
> ***Charge and Blessing***

[*]We have modified this outline in two ways. First, we have added the heading "Abiding" to encompass both the service of the Word and the Eucharist. Second, we have placed the elements of worship analyzed in this chapter in bold and italic typeface.

In the remainder of this chapter we will isolate three moments of worship, three material acts set within a formal structure, and explore how they evoke, shape, order, express, sustain, and direct our religious affections. We begin with rituals of gathering, discussing their place in the liturgy and how they cultivate our religious affections of humility, awe, gratitude, and delight. Next we turn to a ritual of abiding, the passing of the peace, exploring how it serves as the hinge in worship that moves us from a posture of purification to one of illumination, preparing us for the service of Word and Table. Here we examine especially how the passing of the peace cultivates the religious affection of mutuality and interdependence. Finally, we turn to a ritual of sending, the charge and benediction, and note how our prayer and belief (*lex orandi* and *lex credendi*) flow naturally into the Christian moral life (*lex bene operandi*), fostering in us the religious affections of obligation, hope, and direction. Well-ordered worship moves us through a full range of religious affections and prevents us from structuring worship in such a way that one or another of the religious affections comes to dominate our identities inappropriately.

GATHERING: HUMILITY, AWE, DELIGHT, AND GRATITUDE

The time of gathering encompasses several activities, some that happen before worship actually begins and others that are part of worship proper. Those activities that precede worship are acts of preparation, and they include physically entering the space of worship and listening to the prelude or waiting in silence for the service of worship to begin. The gathering activities that are part of worship itself include greeting one another in the name of the Lord, the call to worship, a hymn of praise and adoration, and a time of confession. In this section, we begin by examining the acts of preparation for worship, linking them to the religious affection of humility, and conclude by examining the call to worship, linking it to the religious affections of awe, delight, and gratitude. We will reserve treatment of the time of confession for chapter 7.

Preparation for Worship: Movement, Silence, Music

The first act of gathering that prepares us for worship is the act of moving into the church building and then into the sanctuary through the narthex. The importance of this physical, embodied act of gathering and the role of the narthex in preparing us for worship are often overlooked. The narthex is the space of transition that invites us to quiet ourselves and suspend all the nagging concerns that follow us throughout our daily living. The narthex is the transitional space where we focus on the process of purification, a process in which God strips away the clutter of our idolatries. We are purified as we set aside our false dependence on and distorted desires for the multiplicity of created things that divide and fragment our identities. The movement from a clutter of idols to a singularity of devotion should be mirrored in how congregations arrange and furnish the narthex. It should be a place that encourages the people of God to come together, but it should also direct their gathering toward reverence. The narthex should not be cluttered or dominated by displays about church programs. Instead, it should be a place that encourages the faithful to remember that what we do in this place is different. Though God is present everywhere, this is the place that we designate for the special purpose of bringing the people of God together for the worship of God, and so we treat it with a special respect.

Once inside the sanctuary, we continue our preparation for worship by listening to the musical prelude or sitting in silence. Attending to the musical prelude or silence that precedes worship prepares us for worship by directing our thoughts beyond ourselves and focusing us on the glory of God. The musical prelude or silence continues the process of purification by focusing our religious affections theocentrically because these acts of preparation remind us that we were made to glorify and enjoy God and that all creatures share this end with us. The meaning and value of our fellow creatures is not determined by our needs and wants, but rather by their belonging to God. All creatures, ourselves included, are ordered to God and God's purposes.

Protestants have long recognized the power of the spoken word, but we have often neglected the power of silence. Both Scripture and the Christian tradition remind us that we often meet God in silence, and in these silent encounters between God and people of faith a profound theocentric reorientation of our religious affections and identities occurs. The power of silence to reorder us theocentrically rests partly in its ability to remind us that the God whom we worship in words ultimately lies beyond our capacity to think and to speak. Theologians of the early church such as Gregory of Nyssa and the Pseudo-Dionysius argued that God is met in silence, and they drew inspiration from the biblical story of Moses ascending Mount Sinai.[3] Other biblical stories also bear witness to the transforming power of silence. Think, for example, of how Elijah encounters God at Mount Horeb (1 Kgs. 19:1–18). Elijah experiences an earthquake, a strong wind, and a consuming fire, but God is not in any of these. At long last, Elijah hears "the sound of sheer silence" (v. 12), and knowing that this silence signals the transforming presence of God, he covers his face with his mantle and steps out to the entrance of the cave to meet his God. Ultimately, God does speak to Elijah, but only after preparing him through silence. First, Elijah must remember that God is not a creature, not even a creature like the powerful forces of nature. Elijah must experience the profound otherness of God—an otherness that cannot be contained and manipulated for human ends through human speech. The silence confounds Elijah's natural impulse to let speech stand in for God and to order God to his own purposes. In the silence God effects a theocentric reversal of perspective for Elijah. Elijah does not find God; God finds Elijah.

The silence before worship functions in a similar way for us. It effects a theocentric reversal of perspective. In our fallenness and fragmentation, we often come to worship seeking a god to do our bidding; but in the silence preceding worship, God finds us and, in finding us, relocates us within God's broader purposes for creation. In silence, we remember that we do not provide the ultimate meaning and purpose of creation, and we rediscover ground for hope in the knowledge that genuine human flourishing arises from locating ourselves within the limits set for us by God, whose purposes we serve.

Speech is sometimes a form of control, a kind of cognitive mastery of one's environment. There is power in naming, and perhaps this is why God refuses to give us a singular name by which we might call on God. Because giving up speech involves giving up this power, we are often uncomfortable with silence and seek to fill it, if not with sound, then at least with familiar thought. We want to use silent time "efficiently," making mental notes of what we need to do after worship or thinking through some problem we want to bring to God in prayer. But the silence before worship is not designed for us to focus on ourselves, our needs, our wants, or our list of things to do. It is designed to reorient our religious affections theocentrically. Silence can become the occasion for quieting the constant stream of self-talk that fills our heads. Silence can become the occasion for decentering ourselves so that we are open to feeling the presence of God in our lives.

The musical prelude can function in a similar way. Filling our senses with music can make it easier to silence ourselves. Music can ease the discomfort we feel in silence, but for this reason it can also undermine the very purpose for the prelude. In a culture of amusement, it is difficult to find a way for music to function so that it conducts us into the presence of the holy. We are so accustomed to the background music we constantly hear in restaurants and elevators, in our cars and places of work, that we may miss the theological significance of music in worship.[4] But in spite of this potential problem with how we understand and engage music, it has a profound power to transport us into the presence of God, to evoke our religious affections and orient them reverently toward God. For many people, music offers the most powerful experience of the presence of God in worship. The musical prelude can be as powerful as silence in assisting us to silence ourselves and to be open to the love of God that relentlessly seeks us out, even as a woman searches for a lost coin.

Quieting ourselves and our concerns does not mean that we and they are unimportant; it means that we and they are not of first importance. We were made to worship God, and this means all of our highest hopes and deepest fears need to be ordered theocentrically with reference to the purposes of God. The simple act of preparing oneself for worship, then, cultivates the religious affection of humility because when we ready ourselves to do what we were made to do—to worship God—we must first locate ourselves within the broader context of God's designs. Opening ourselves to the presence of God through movement, music, and silence helps us to locate our value and purpose within the total context of a cosmos that sings the glory of its Creator. Practices of gathering, then, both evoke our sense of humility and direct that humility toward God as the one from whom all value and meaning flow.

Sometimes, as we gather for worship, we will feel humble. We may sense strongly how vast is God's creative activity, and this will evoke a sense of our own small but significant place in the creation. At other times we will come into the church building, busy ourselves with greeting friends, wrestling children out of bulky winter coats, and finding our accustomed pews as a matter of routine that hardly warrants reflection at all. On these days we will not listen attentively to the prelude, letting it float over and around us, lifting us up, and moving us toward union with God. We will not let ourselves settle into the silence, allowing it to drown out our busy thoughts and plans. Instead, we will sit in our places, perhaps locate the hymns for the day in the hymnal, read announcements from the bulletin, look around to see who is present, and simply wait until the prelude or silence ends so that we can move ahead with the service. But even on these distracted days, because we are engaging in liturgical acts that call for humility, we are developing a habit of humility that orders and shapes our lives in distinctively Christian ways. Even on the days when we do not feel humbled to gather in the presence of God, God is training us in humility through repeated liturgical acts. God is gradually making us people of humility, people who meet the world with a readiness to value ourselves in a way that does not diminish others. The feeling of humility might wax and wane, but the affection is nonetheless sustained by practices of gathering.

Eventually, practices of gathering that evoke, shape, sustain, and direct our humility will order our identities is such a way that we will sense something amiss on the days when we enter the worship space with distraction. A discomfort will accompany us throughout our gathering activities. Our acts of gathering through movement, music, and silence will feel somehow wrong. This feeling of wrongness is partly good because it indicates how deeply we have been shaped in humility. When we fail to express humility at times when we ought, such as the time of gathering, we will sense a diminishment of self. We will sense that we are not yet fully what God has made us to be. But we will also sense that we are on our way toward that goal, or else we would not be attuned to the "wrongness" at all.

The Service of Worship: The Call to Worship

Liturgist: Ascribe to the LORD, you gods, ascribe to the LORD glory and strength.

People: Ascribe to the LORD the glory that is due the holy name; worship the LORD in the beauty of holiness.

L: The voice of the LORD is upon the waters; the God of glory thunders; the LORD is upon the mighty waters.

P: The voice of the LORD is a powerful voice; the voice of the LORD is a voice of splendor.

L: The voice of the LORD breaks the cedar trees; the LORD breaks the cedars of Lebanon;

P: The voice of the LORD splits the flames of fire; the voice of the LORD shakes the wilderness.

L: The voice of the LORD makes the oak trees writhe and strips the forests bare.

All: The LORD sits enthroned as Sovereign forevermore. (Ps. 29:1–5, 7–8a, 9a, 10b; adapted from *Book of Common Worship*, 641–42)

O come, let us sing to the LORD; let us make joyful noise to the rock of our salvation! Let us come into [God's] presence with thanksgiving; let us make a joyful noise to [God] with songs of praise. (Ps. 95:1–2)

As the prelude or silence ends, we move from preparing for worship into the service itself. When we gather for worship, we "come into [God's] presence," and this coming together is accompanied by glad shouts of joy. We call ourselves into worship by praising God with delight and gratitude. The time of gathering in worship begins with ascriptions of praise that point to our awe and reverence before God, and for Christians this awe and reverence are good news that prompt the religious affections of delight and gratitude. We greet one another in the name of the Lord; we call ourselves into worship, often with the responsive reading of a psalm of thanksgiving; we sing ourselves into worship, using a hymn of praise and adoration. The service begins with the affections of awe, delight, and gratitude because it is indeed good to be in the house of the Lord. It is delightful to stand before the presence of God, because the God who makes us quake with awe is always also the God who brings us good news in Jesus Christ. And so it is right to begin worship by expressing the religious affections of awe, delight, and gratitude.

We often call ourselves into worship with the responsive reading of a psalm, such as Psalm 95. A collective call to worship is theologically significant for at least two reasons. First, the collective nature of the call to worship beckons us to our true identity as members of that covenant community called into existence at God's gracious initiative. When we call ourselves into worship, we are remembering who we are and who we are called to be through participation in the covenant community. We are not, first and foremost, individuals who come together to form a community of worship. Rather, we come into our identities as redeemed individuals through the formative power of the Holy Spirit at work in the church.

Second, the Psalms provide the earliest liturgical material for both Jewish and Christian worship. When we use these ancient liturgical texts to call ourselves into worship, we join our voices to the voices of members of the covenant community throughout history. We praise God in the company of a great cloud of witnesses. As our individual voices merge together in the collective recitation of the psalm, we are reminded that God calls a community into covenant and calls us as individuals into relationship with God through that community. The collective call to worship cultivates religious affections within individuals who are essentially social selves.

When we use the words of the Psalms to call ourselves into worship, we recline in the long history of the church as a confessing community. We rest on the tradition that has shaped us and our community from apostolic times. We set aside our own words, and the cognitive control that they embody, to take up the words of the age-old community that brought us into being. Using the words of others requires that we let their words shape our linguistic selves. Rather than using our words to name and interpret the tradition, we use the words of the tradition to form and direct our individual lives. We learn to "come into God's presence with thanksgiving" because we have been shaped as persons of gratitude, and we were shaped for gratitude by expressing thanksgiving through words given to us by the tradition. We learn to offer "joyful songs of praise" because we have been formed to meet the world with a readiness to experience delight, and we were ordered for delight by expressing that affection in words we inherited from the children of Israel. We learn to "ascribe to the LORD the glory that is due the holy name" because we have been linguistically formed for awe through the words of the community that confesses Jesus Christ, and our awe has been directed to God in Christ through use of the words of an ancient community.

Because we are social selves set within a covenant community and linguistic selves set within a confessing community, the words of the Psalms can call us to be what God made us to be, creatures who worship. As the Psalms call us into our true identities, they form in us religious affections. In the remainder of this section, we explore how the call to worship forms three religious affections: awe, gratitude, and delight.

Since awe is the gateway religious affection, it is appropriate that we begin with a call to worship and a hymn of praise and adoration that express and evoke this affection. Awe is that religious affection that we experience when we are both drawn to and repelled by the power and glory of God. The capacity of the call to worship to express, evoke, and shape awe is closely connected to the imagery and metaphors that it uses. We "worship the Lord in the beauty of holiness," but this is a beauty that both attracts and disturbs us, whose danger we feel all the more acutely the closer it draws us in. The peculiar mix of beauty and danger, of attraction and repulsion, suspends our normal way of engaging our world. In awe, God disorients us in order to reorient us. The content of the beauty of God is glory that "thunders," a voice that "breaks" cedar trees, that "splits the flames of fire," that "shakes the wilderness," and that "makes the oak trees writhe." When we call ourselves into worship with imagery and metaphors such as these, we awaken and invigorate the religious imagination. Such imagery and metaphors convey dimensions of who God is that cannot easily be captured or ever exhausted by our everyday speech. In the call to worship, we do not *explain* God; rather we *revere* God, who is profoundly other than us and who meets us in metaphors and images that resist our drive to manage God for our own ends.

Through the play of imagery and metaphor on our religious imagination, the psalm shapes our generic capacity for awe into *Christian* reverence because God is that awe-full one worthy of our worship. The call to worship shapes our generic awe into Christian reverence by providing it with theological content. The most basic affirmation of our monotheistic faith is that all the things of the world are creatures belonging to one Creator; the one God who creates the world is not to be confused with the things of the world. We may stand in awe before the great sequoia, but we do not worship it. Nevertheless, awe is still appropriate before the great sequoia because the glory of its Creator shines through it, thus allowing it to become an icon, a window onto the power and beauty of the God we worship. We find ourselves suspended in awe before the great sequoia and reverent toward God, who creates and sustains it at the same time. Awe ordered as reverence suspends our normal way of engaging our world. It disorients us in order to reorient us, and this disorientation purifies us of our false valuation of the creation and disrupts our fallen tendency to reduce all others to mere "its" that serve our narrow ends. In awe, we are opened through participatory knowledge to relate as "thous" to God and to the creation that betokens God's glory. Using such a psalm to call us to worship both evokes awe and shapes it into Christian reverence, and such reverence ensures that we neither worship the creation as idol nor devalue it as mere "it."

Because there is a logic or pattern to the religious affections that binds them all together, we should not be surprised that the awe evoked and shaped by the call to worship is often accompanied by and closely related to a second religious affection, gratitude. When we are called to worship the creator God "who sits enthroned as sovereign forevermore," we are reminded that all things come to us as gifts, as that which we have not earned and do not deserve. Recognizing in awe that the world belongs to God means recognizing with gratitude that it does not belong to us and that we receive it as gift. The call to worship and hymn of praise and adoration often give voice to our gratitude. When, for example, we use Psalm 95 to call ourselves into worship, we "come into God's presence with thanksgiving." And we express this thanksgiving even when we may not feel it. Doing so has the capacity to sustain us in gratitude. While the call to worship may not always generate an immediately felt, emotional experience of gratitude, it nonetheless sustains us as people of gratitude by nourishing the religious affection that over time will blossom into felt experiences of gratitude.

The call to worship is but one activity of worship that sustains our religious affections in this way. We recite the creed even when our faith and understanding are weak. We confess our sins even when we do not feel contrite. We sing our gratitude even when we are not feeling grateful. We express our awe even when our sense of the majesty of God is dull. This is very similar to the way that children learn their manners. We require them to say "thank you," when they are not grateful, with the expectation that they will be schooled in gratitude through the repeated linguistic practice and eventually come to experience the emotion of gratitude when it is appropriate. Likewise, when we hear, "This is the Word of God for the people of God," we respond, "Thanks be to God," even when we do not feel grateful. Why? We respond this way because that linguistic practice, through constant repetition, can pass over from being a phrase we have memorized to a response we know by heart. It becomes a lens through which we view reality so that we become people who meet the world with a readiness to acknowledge with gratitude our dependence. When we are repeatedly invited "to come into God's presence with thanksgiving," we expect that eventually we will respond with heartfelt thanksgiving.

The call to worship, like the entire liturgy, does not depend on our emotions, which we sometimes feel and sometimes do not feel. It works at the deeper affectional level. The call to worship gives us work to do (*leitourgia*) and words to say, regardless of how we feel. It gives us permission to rest on the faith of the confessing community when our own faith is weak. The power of the call to worship, and indeed that of the whole liturgy, does not depend upon occasional "mountaintop" experiences; it gives us food to sustain us for the journey through the valleys and plains of life. Christian identity is primarily formed in worship over the long course of a lifetime, rather than through sporadic moments of intense feeling.

The third religious affection that is closely connected to the call to worship is delight. The redirecting of our affectional desire is especially visible in delight. Delight is the joy and pleasure we take in experiencing the goodness and integrity of another without subtracting from that goodness and integrity. Such delight arises from our participatory knowing of that other as thou. In delight, we are caught up in celebrating the intrinsic goodness of that thou, seeing such goodness as deriving from that being's relation to God. We know another in a participatory way that calls for delight when we join our acknowledgment of the intrinsic goodness of that other with an affective response to that intrinsic goodness. To return to the example offered by Jonathan Edwards, when we delight in honey, we do more than simply examine it in its jar; we taste its sweetness and take pleasure in it. When we call ourselves to worship by "shout[ing] with joy to the rock of our salvation," our joy signifies a delight in the presence of God that is grounded in an objective acknowledgment of the goodness of God and a subjective engagement with and affective response to that goodness. The call to worship directs our delight toward God, who is the source of all that is good and pleasurable in the creation.

ABIDING: MUTUALITY AND INTERDEPENDENCE

May the peace of Christ be with you.
And also with you.

In the ordering of Christian worship, most of our time is spent abiding together in peace, and the time of abiding together revolves around Word and sacrament. Abiding around Word and sacrament reflects the church's incarnational life because the church extends and continues the ministry of Jesus Christ, who is Word made flesh, the Word of God become human. Appropriately, then, our worship involves both linguistic acts, centered primarily in the proclamation of the Word, and material acts, centered primarily in the sacraments. Both Word and sacrament come to us as means of grace by which God enables us to enter into God's life-giving and life-sustaining presence. Through the service of Christian worship, the Holy Spirit focuses us on the glory of God, but it is crucial to Christian worship that the God into whose presence we come is the God who meets us and who is revealed to us in the person of Jesus Christ.

Since we will discuss the worship of God through Word and sacrament at much greater length in chapters 8 and 9, here we want to focus on an important act of worship that moves us into the time of abiding: the passing of the peace, which follows the assurance of pardon. Many Protestant worship services have only recently recovered the passing of the peace, and sometimes it is difficult to understand why it is part of our worship of God and what function it serves within the broader ordering of worship. In some churches, it is simply an informal time of greeting one another that takes place somewhere in the middle of the service. Though members of the congregation may be glad enough for the opportunity to chat briefly with one another, the casual nature of the greeting can seem out of place in an otherwise more orderly service. In other congregations, the passing of the peace is a more ritualistic greeting with members greeting one another solemnly, "May the peace of Christ be with you," and responding, "And also with you." This method of passing the peace of Christ better conveys the sense that worship transforms our everyday ways of relating to one another, but it can still remain unclear why we are greeting one another in this way.

This ancient practice of greeting one another with the peace of Christ serves a crucial function in worship; it allows us to enter into a deeper fellowship with one another and opens us for a more genuine worship of God. To understand why this is so, we need to attend to the place that the passing of the peace occupies in the order of worship. Following the assurance of pardon, it indicates that those who greet one another with the peace of Christ do so as flawed and frail creatures who have received the unmerited mercy of God. We greet one another just after what is perhaps our most vulnerable time in worship, when we honestly admit our failings, repent of our brokenness, and plea for the mercy of God. We gather in worship with all of our flaws and failings in full view, and we continue in worship as those who have been accepted by God in spite of this brokenness. We exchange the peace of Christ with fellow Christians who are just as broken and wounded as we are. We greet one another as those who know that "there is a balm in Gilead to make the wounded whole" and who trust that God will grant us peace.

The peace of Christ provides the means through which we move from the time of gathering in worship to the time of abiding in worship. If the time of gathering focuses primarily on the purifying function of worship, then the time of abiding focuses primarily on illumination, that is, on how, through the corrective power of Word and sacrament, we are made able to see the presence of God shining through creatures. When through Word and sacrament the creation ceases to be idol and instead becomes icon, we are enabled to recognize the presence and power of God in all things, to value all things accordingly, and to relate to all creatures as those who belong to God. Through the gathering acts of worship, perhaps especially through the prayer of confession, we have put aside a false valuation of ourselves and of the creation, and now we can greet one another with a hospitality that is rooted in a theocentric reordering of ourselves and of our social relationships. Purification does not lead us to reject the creation. Instead, it reorients us so that we can be illuminated by the creation, so that other creatures can mediate the presence of God to us.

Once we have set aside our tendency to deify ourselves, reducing our fellow creatures to a means to our ends, or to negate ourselves, refusing to recognize our own capacity to be full partners in social relationships, we can greet each other with real hospitality that reflects the openness and love with which Christ greeted all children of God. He ate and drank with sinners; he conversed with both social elites and social outcasts. When we exchange the peace of Christ with one another, we express the openness and love of Christ. Exchanging the peace of Christ inducts us into a service of worship in which we also converse, eat, and drink together. In hearing and responding to the Word, we enter into a conversation with the people of the Bible whom God called into covenant community. In partaking of the Lord's Supper, we eat and drink together. In exchanging the peace of Christ, we anticipate and live into the renewal of our humanity that God is effecting through the proclamation of the Word and the celebration of the Lord's Supper. The passing of the peace indicates that our honest confession of sin has truly been met with the mercy of God, and that through Word and sacrament, God continues to renew and transform us and all the relationships that make us who we are.

Sin fragments both our inner lives and our ability to enter into relationships with other creatures, but the redemption offered through the incarnation restores harmony and wholeness to both our inner lives and our social lives. The passing of the peace ritualistically enacts this transformation. We revisit our brokenness in the prayer of confession; we revisit our redemption in the assurance of pardon; and we enact the reordering of self and social relationships entailed in that redemption when we exchange the peace of Christ with one another. In a sense, the order of worship reenacts the mortification and renewal of our baptism. In baptism, we die in Christ, and we rise in Christ. Likewise, the weekly service of worship invites us to continue this dying and rising in Christ through confession and assurance. And weekly we are invited to live out our baptism in relationships with one another as we exchange the peace of Christ.

This reordering of the self and its social relationships flows into and reinforces the renewal of the religious affections, especially our sense of mutuality and interdependence. Mutuality and interdependence constitute the religious affection through which we sense that our capacity to flourish depends upon relationships that respect the integrity and enhance the goodness of others. Our lives are deeply connected to the lives of others. They are dependent on us, and we are dependent on them. Such relationships of interdependence and reciprocity are not simply an accidental feature of who we are; rather, we are who we are as individuals only through the network of relationships in which our lives are embedded. Mutuality and interdependence entail a proper valuation of ourselves and other creatures. To relate with mutuality to others requires that we abandon both the impulse toward self-negation that would encourage us to lose our identities in service of others and the pride that would simply exploit others in our drive for self-deification. Our sense of mutuality and interdependence requires that we affirm the integrity and value of both ourselves and others. Only then can the relationships between ourselves and other creatures be life-giving for all. In the passing of the peace, our sense of mutuality and interdependence is ritually enacted and enhanced. Relationships of domination and exploitation that require us to objectify others give way to relationships marked by mutual empowerment that grow out of knowing other creatures as "thous." Finally, we should note that we do not simply "pass the peace"; rather, we "pass the peace *of Christ*" to one another and thus affirm that the renewal of our sense of mutuality and interdependence, which overcomes the inner and outer fragmentation of the fall, is accomplished through the life, death, and resurrection of Jesus Christ—the one who "has broken down the dividing wall [of hostility]" and "entrusted the ministry of reconciliation to us" (Eph. 2:14; 2 Cor. 5:18).

SENDING: OBLIGATION, SELF-SACRIFICIAL LOVE, HOPE, AND DIRECTION

> Go out into the world in peace; have courage; hold on to what is good; return no one evil for evil; strengthen the fainthearted; support the weak, and help the suffering; honor all people; love and serve the Lord, rejoicing in the power of the Holy Spirit.[5]

> The grace of the Lord Jesus Christ, the love of God, and the communion of the Holy Spirit be with all of you. (2 Cor. 13:13)

Worship calls us together as the body of Christ to abide in peace and sends us out as renewed and transformed persons. The acts of sending in worship include the charge and benediction. We conclude worship by being charged to live in ways that extend our worship of God by enhancing the flourishing of God's creation. We are charged with very specific tasks. We are to "strengthen the fainthearted" and "help the suffering." The charge calls attention to the fact that the ugliness and fragmentation of our world violate the beautiful vision that worship reveals to us; and we are charged to meet that ugliness and fragmentation with peace, courage, goodness, and love. The benediction—the "good word" of God's blessing—assures us that the grace, love, and communion of the Holy Trinity accompany and empower us as we meet the ugliness and fragmentation of the world with God's renewing grace.

Both the charge and the benediction point us to the ethical dimension of Christian worship. Christian worship forms us for the moral life, giving us a vision of the good grounded in a renewed sense of God's sovereign purposes for the world and a heightened sense of the sinful distortions that remain in our world. Worship shapes us as moral agents and strengthens us for moral action. Christian worship helps us to see the presence of God's kingdom already in our midst. It offers us a glimpse of the beauty of God's unfolding plan. It reveals to us the ugliness and fragmentation that still await God's sovereign and reconciling love and grace. Christian worship forms us to be agents of God's reconciling love, invites us to participate in the expansion of God's kingdom, charges us to seek goodness and beauty wherever we find evil and ugliness, and blesses us to these ends. In other words, our worshipful encounter with the attracting beauty of Christ disturbs us when it calls our attention to the ugliness of injustice, and it changes us as it impels us to work for the beauty of justice.

While Christian worship flows into the moral life, worship is not subordinate to the moral life. At least since the eighteenth-century Enlightenment, Christians have been tempted to reduce the value of worship to its function in cultivating public morality. Immanuel Kant, for example, argued that belief in God is important because that belief provides motivation for moral living. For Kant, the entire value of faith is subordinate to the ethical enterprise of humanity. If there were no God and no afterlife of accountability, reasoned Kant, there would be no ultimate motivation for struggling to be moral. Moreover, the singular function of worship with its rituals and sacred words is to promote rational morality. Kant even longed for a day in which humanity would outgrow the need for such worship and would instead achieve a public morality based on reason alone.[6]

Though few contemporary Christians would formulate the relationship between worship and morality in such an explicitly reductionistic way, we do sometimes assume in practice that the primary purpose of worship is to make us moral. This practical reductionism has consequences for how we think about worship. Parents take their children to church so that they will be "good people," and political leaders invoke the generic faith of American civil religion to promote "family values." While it is appropriate to want our children to be formed in the moral life and to allow our faith to shape our public values and policies, faith and worship cannot be reduced to these functions. The chief end of worship is not to make human beings moral. The chief end of worship is to glorify and enjoy God forever. We do not worship so that our religious affections will be formed for moral living. Rather, we worship to glorify God, acknowledging that when we offer true worship the providence of God ensures that it has the derivative effect of forming our religious affections so that we are equipped for moral living. God does not exist to make us moral. We live moral lives to glorify God, whose beauty and truth we celebrate in worship. So worship is neither disconnected from the moral life nor reducible to it.

Worship forms us as moral agents because it shapes, sustains, and directs the religious affections that underlie our capacity for moral action. Christian moral action grows out of and is sustained by the religious affections, and the moment of sending in Christian worship is crucial for this process because it highlights four religious affections closely associated with the moral life: the sense of obligation, self-sacrificial love, hope, and the sense of direction.

The words of the charge help us to see in a more expansive way the scope of our moral obligations. Often the specific obligations with which we are charged will reflect themes highlighted in the sermon. The charge included above offers but one example of how the sending moment of worship enumerates our obligations and expands their scope. Regardless of the particular words used in the charge, it should sensitize us to the ugliness and fragmentation that remain in the broader world around us, thus joining our sense of obligation with a more expansive vision of those others to whom we have these obligations. Because our sense of obligation grows out of our sense of mutuality and interdependence, the charge embeds the obligations it enumerates within the context of our relationships with other creatures. Our sense of mutuality and interdependence is evoked by the passing of the peace, and the charge connects that sense to our concrete obligations to others, thus reflecting the broader ordering of our religious affections. In the charge, we are reminded that our obligations extend beyond ourselves, our families, and those in our confined social circle, and we come to see those who might otherwise be invisible to us and with whom we have little social interaction. We are charged to "strengthen the fainthearted; support the weak, and help the suffering," and in so doing to "honor all people." The charge expands our sense of obligation by directing it beyond our immediate circle to those on the margins of our individual and communal life.

The moment of sending not only directs our sense of obligation toward an ever-expanding circle of creatures; it also shapes that sense of obligation in a distinctively Christian way. The charge reminds us that in loving and serving others, we are "lov[ing] and serv[ing] the Lord." We love and serve God by loving and serving other creatures. The charge recognizes that in carrying out our moral obligations we are continuing that pattern of the incarnation in which God's love and grace are incomplete until they become real, concrete, and particular in the lives of all creatures. The Christian's sense of obligation is rooted in the theological awareness that in loving and caring for those on the margins, we are extending and continuing the pattern of love and grace found in the incarnation. Such love calls us to imitate the self-sacrificial love of Christ, who in the incarnation "did not regard equality with God as something to be exploited, but emptied himself, taking the form of a slave, being born in human likeness. And being found in human form, he humbled himself and became obedient to the point of death—even death on a cross" (Phil. 2:6b–8). In shaping our sense of obligation, the sending moment of worship also evokes in us the religious affection of self-sacrificial love. The benediction further shapes our generic sense of obligation into Christian obligation and self-sacrificial love by granting to us the grace, love, and communion of the triune God that is necessary if we are to continue the incarnational pattern of Christian obligation. The charge and benediction shape our generic sense of obligation into a Christian sense of obligation by grounding it in the incarnation and extending to us the presence and power of the triune God that is necessary for fulfilling that obligation.

Since there is a logic or pattern to properly ordered religious affections, it is not surprising that the sense of obligation in the moment of sending is closely connected to the religious affection of hope. Obligation and hope are woven together by a common longing for the kingdom of God. Our deepest desire, expressed in the Lord's Prayer, is that God's kingdom will come on earth. Just as that desire for the justice of God's kingdom generates in us a sense of obligation, especially toward the marginalized, it also evokes, expresses, and sustains our sense of hope. We hope for the day when the fainthearted are strengthened, when all people honor one another, when all things exist to "love and serve the Lord," and when all the world exists in peace. Even as the charge reminds us of our obligations, it beckons us toward the possibilities and newness opened in Christ, the ground of our hope.

The charge and benediction together shape hope by giving it specifically Christian content. On the one hand, the charge gives us hope-filled work to do, developing and expanding the goodness and new possibilities opened by the inbreaking of God's kingdom in the incarnation. The gift of a new task and the call to participate with God in carrying it out overcome that fallen impulse toward self-negation in which we allow ourselves to be defined by resignation in the face of the fragmentation of our world. On the other hand, the benediction assures us that this is not our work alone and that we are utterly dependent on the grace, love, and communion of the Holy Trinity in the carrying out of our obligations. Our dependence on the power of God for initiating and fulfilling the kingdom of God overcomes that fallen impulse toward prideful self-deification in which we identify our self-interest with the kingdom of God and arrogate to ourselves the power to establish that kingdom on earth. Sending in worship, then, roots our senses of hope and obligation in a deep and humble sense of our place in God's world.

Finally, the sense of obligation and hope ingredient in the sending acts of worship are also closely connected with another religious affection, our sense of direction. Even in the midst of our fragmentation and brokenness, we have a natural sense that our lives are ordered to some end, that we exist for some purpose. As worship reorients us theocentrically, it directs us toward our true end. We discover again the true purpose and meaning of our lives and those of other creatures. Worship grants us "a foretaste of glory divine."[7] It invites us to anticipate and to participate in the new creation. If only for an hour on Sunday morning, we can glimpse and live into the harmony and wholeness that God intends for our world. The acts of sending that conclude worship turn us outward toward God's creation with a renewed sense that we and it exist for the glory of God, and that our common end and our common good are found through relationships of mutuality and interdependence. Our sense of direction is given Christian content when we acknowledge that the whole creation conspires toward the one end of celebrating God's glory. In seeking this one end, we discover that the glory of God entails the flourishing and harmony of all God's creatures. The acts of sending charge and bless us to seek the good of all creatures because they belong to God. The sending acts of worship bring full circle the process that begins as we gather for worship. In being sent, we move back out through the narthex into a broken and fragmented world, but we do so as people who have experienced the grace, love, and communion of God, who seeks such communion with all creatures.

When we reflect on the age-old pattern of gathering, abiding, and sending in Christian worship, we find that through it God meets us in particular times and places, to purify and illuminate us, to renew and restore our religious affections through the words and embodied acts of the liturgy. By examining particular acts of worship, such as the call to worship, the passing of the peace, and the charge, we discover that each moment of worship expresses, evokes, sustains, directs, and shapes certain religious affections. By examining the broader pattern and movement of the liturgy, we discover that God renews and transforms not only our individual religious affections, but also the whole order, pattern, and logic of them. This comprehensive repatterning of the affections generates in us a theocentric posture in which we come to see, value, and relate to other creatures in a manner that honors their intrinsic beauty as beings that belong to and glorify God.

7

Prayer

"Pray then in this way: Our Father in heaven, hallowed be your name. Your kingdom come. Your will be done, on earth as it is in heaven. Give us this day our daily bread. And forgive us our debts, as we also have forgiven our debtors. And do not bring us to the time of trial, but rescue us from the evil one." (Matt. 6:9–13)

We learn to pray. If we are raised in Christian households, then from earliest childhood we learn to pray at mealtimes and at bedtime. Our parents give us words to pray, and with time those words become our words. The church, too, teaches us to pray. In Sunday school and worship we learn the Lord's Prayer, the very one that Jesus taught his disciples. He gave them instruction in how to pray and words that they should offer as their own prayer. Across the centuries of Christian worship, the words of the Lord's Prayer have served as a paradigm for how we ought to address God.

The Christian church sometimes simply repeats the Lord's Prayer in its worship. But we also elaborate on it, isolating some of its themes and expanding them into prayers of their own. We expand "hallowed be your name," when we offer prayers of adoration and thanksgiving. We expand "forgive us our debts," when we offer prayers of confession. And we expand "give us this day our daily bread," when we offer prayers of intercession. Throughout this chapter, we explore the relationship between the religious affections and prayer as it is offered in the public worship of the Christian church. We begin with a general theological discussion of the nature of prayer, first as speech and then as silence. Next, we turn to a discussion of prayers of adoration, confession, thanksgiving, and intercession.

PRAYER AS SPEECH AND SILENCE

We develop the theological meaning of the speech of prayer with five themes. First, the speech of prayer is *generative and creative*, rather than merely descriptive. In this regard, our speech is a finite reflection of the speech of God that creates the world and becomes incarnate in Christ the living Word. In chapter 5 we discussed the fact that we are linguistic selves who use language not merely to point to reality but to make things happen, and this is especially true of the language of prayer. We use language not simply as a static stand-in for reality, but to order, categorize, and arrange reality. Likewise, the speech of prayer orders the world for us as the arena of God's creative and redemptive activity and locates us within that world as those made to glorify God and to rejoice in God's activity. Through the language of prayer that we inherit and use, we construe the world in a particular way, and this construal affects how we relate to others, how we act in the world, and how we generate meaning in our lives. Our speech in prayer, that is, construes the world as the place where God's kingdom is coming and thus orders our actions and relationships so that they anticipate the time when God's will prevails on earth.

In prayer we reflect God's generative speech as we speak into greater reality our redemptive relationship with God. In prayers of adoration, for example, our speech reorders our world around the sovereign beauty of God, and such prayers locate us, with humility and delight, within that world. In prayers of confession, our speech names the fragmentation of our condition and moves us toward reconciliation with God and others. In prayers of intercession, we remember our dependence on God and express our desire that the world come more fully to reflect the conditions of creaturely flourishing. In prayers of thanksgiving, as we speak our gratitude for the good gifts of life, we learn to regard those good gifts as grounded in the goodness of God and to give up our tendency to regard all things as commodities to be valued merely according to how they serve our purposes. The speech of prayer is generative and creative. Through it we enact new meaning that demands from us a new way of being in the world and forms us for that new life.

Second, the speech of prayer must be *rooted in the biblical narrative* as the shared story of the church. The metaphors, images, and words of public prayer arise from Scripture and generate a world of meaning that links the community at prayer with the church across the ages. The generative power of the speech of public prayer derives from its rootage in the revelation of God as it comes to us in the words of Scripture. All language shapes our capacity to see the world in certain ways, but the language of the Bible, as the unique and authoritative witness to God's self-revelation in history, has a special, normative capacity to do so. In appropriating the symbols, narratives, images, and metaphors of the Bible in our public prayers, we are immersed in a biblical-linguistic world of meaning that is at once familiar and foreign to us. As the covenant community, the church's identity is grounded in the old and familiar stories, symbols, metaphors, and teaching of Scripture, and yet because these old and familiar things derive from the living Word of the living God who meets us afresh in the Holy Spirit, these old and familiar things become foreign again and in their foreignness speak afresh to disorient and reorient us. When in prayer we appropriate the ancient words of Scripture, we are entering what Karl Barth called "the strange, new world [of] the Bible" that "sets a question mark against" many of our common assumptions about the meaning and purpose of our lives.[1] When we pray the Lord's Prayer, for example, we pray not to an impersonal force of nature, but to "our Father." We pray not for riches and personal advance, but for "daily bread" and for a "kingdom" in which God's will is accomplished on earth as it already is in heaven. We petition for forgiveness from the "debt" of sin. These age-old images teach us to interpret our God, our world, and our place in that world in new ways.

When in prayer we draw on the images, metaphors, symbols, and stories of Scripture, we experience a reversal of interpretive power. We do not interpret the text, but instead we allow God's self-revelation to interpret us and our world. While it can certainly be appropriate to pray using our own words, when we pray with the words of Scripture and tradition, we can be more intentional about setting aside our cognitive mastery and control of our environment. We let *our* world again become *God's* world. In appropriating the words of Scripture in its public prayer, the church across the ages has found the shared story that establishes and preserves its identity in a world of competing stories about who we are, to whom we belong, and what our purpose is. The words of the tradition play on our religious imagination, opening fresh interpretive possibilities so that we see the world differently, value other creatures differently, and find our place in God's plan with a new humility and delight. Without these resources, we tend to fall back on our own words, mired as they are in the competing narratives of our time—narratives of nationalism, consumerism, and amusement, among others. As a result, we approach God in prayer with a closed set of assumptions that do not allow the Word of God to break in and illumine our world with its corrective power. But when we pray through the time-tested words of the tradition, we deliberately open ourselves to the new possibilities made available through the living Word of the Ancient of Days.

Third, public prayer should be offered in *the voice of the community* rather than in the voice of the individual. Public worship must reflect the covenantal nature of the church, especially in the prayers offered to God in worship. Part of the theological significance of affirming that the church is a covenant community, rather than merely a voluntary society of individuals, lies in recognizing that the collective body of Christ precedes individual faith and is the primary recipient of God's call to faith. Accordingly the worship of the church is first and foremost the worship of the community and not that of individuals. The prayers of worship, like all of the acts of public worship, should reflect the communal nature of the church as a covenant community. Sometimes this will involve unison prayers, but at other times prayers will be offered by one individual on behalf of the whole congregation. When public prayers are offered by an individual, they should be spoken in ways that faithfully reflect the voice of the community at worship. For instance, the pronouns chosen should be collective in nature. The individual praying is praying not *for* the congregation but *on behalf of* the congregation, and this should be reflected by the use of "we," "us," and "our," rather than "I," "me," and "my" in public prayers. The public prayers of worship are the prayers of the people, not the prayers of the pastor or liturgist. Moreover, allowing an entire congregation to join in the prayer offered through the voice of one individual means the prayer must be both well-ordered and delivered at a pace that allows it to gather up the hearts and minds of the entire congregation, so that while it is spoken by one, it is offered by all.

Fourth, the speech of prayer is *offered to God.* The immediate function of public prayer is not to provide information *about* God or the community, but to *address* God and, in so doing, to lift the community at prayer into sanctifying fellowship with God. While it may seem obvious that prayer should be directed to God, it is not always so in practice. When we remember the needs of the community before God in prayer, we sometimes find ourselves using prayer as the venue for offering to the congregation information about those needs. We may do this with the best of intentions, believing that it is easier to pray for the restoration of health if we know, for example, that Jack's bypass surgery is scheduled for Thursday. It may very well be important for the congregation to receive this information, but venues other than prayer are more appropriate for disseminating it. At other times, with similarly good intentions, worship leaders use prayer to teach or reinforce theological truths. While our prayers to God ought to reflect faithfully our theological tradition (*lex orandi, lex credendi*), the purpose of the prayer is not to teach such truths. In prayer the presence of theological truths serves to speak appropriately to God, rather than to speak didactically to the congregation. When public prayer is addressed to God rather than to one another, it becomes the occasion for lifting the hearts and minds of the congregation into person-forming fellowship with the triune God. Coming into God's presence in a sustained way through prayer opens us to what Calvin called "mystical union"—an affection-forming communion with God in which the Holy Spirit works the mystery of sanctifying grace in our lives. According to Calvin, "as we must turn keenness of mind toward God, so affection of heart has to follow." He continues, "God gives us the Spirit as our teacher in prayer to tell us what is right and temper our emotions."[2]

Fifth, the speech of prayer aims to *remember collectively the creaturely condition* before God and, in so doing, to locate creaturely existence within the broader theocentric purposes of the sovereign God.[3] When we discussed the fragmentation of the fallen religious affections in chapter 3, we noted that our self-deification leads us to value not only other creatures, but even God, according to how they serve our purposes. This impulse to enlist God for our purposes can manifest itself in prayer, perhaps especially in prayers of intercession. We may come to believe that our prayers prompt or cause God to do our bidding and that the chief function of prayer is, as Schleiermacher put it, "to throw some additional weight into the scale" so as to tip God's benevolence into the service of our self-interested visions of the good.[4] But prayers that emerge from, reflect, and cultivate redeemed religious affections are ordered to the glory of God and locate human purpose and value within the broader economy of God's sovereign plan. In prayer, we name our condition and seek God's purifying and illuminating grace, which promises to restore all things, and we are opened for a theocentric transformation of perspective that corrects our self-serving impulse to seek God for what we can get from God.

Public prayer, however, is not only about our speech to God. It is also about our silence before God. Coming into the presence of God in prayer involves a reciprocity that not only allows us to address God but also allows God to address us. Speech often entails a degree of control; silence in prayer allows us to relinquish that control in a way that generates affective receptivity to the presence of God in our lives. In the silence of prayer, we do not expect to hear audibly or even immediately the word of God to us; instead we deliberately suspend our drive for cognitive mastery of our world and discipline ourselves for receptivity to the transforming word of God, wherever it may encounter us. The transforming word of God may come to us in moments of insight but more often it comes to us over time as the receptivity signaled by silence settles across the whole of our lives so that we come to hear the word of God in the sustained reflection and measured judgments that occur over the course of a lifetime. The prayers of public worship must accordingly include and make time for silence that honors receptivity to God's transforming presence. This can include not only silent prayers, but also silent periods within spoken prayers that create a space for receptivity to the word of God.

Public prayer, then, is about both speech to God and silence before God that bring us into the divine presence, where God purifies and illumines us, renewing our affectional lives and reorienting us theocentrically toward the purposes and glory of God. In the remainder of this chapter, we will explore this understanding of prayer as it comes to expression in prayers of adoration, confession, thanksgiving, and intercession.

PRAYERS OF ADORATION: AWE, DELIGHT, AND HUMILITY

> It is truly right to glorify you, Father, and to give you thanks, for you alone are God, living and true, dwelling in light inaccessible from before time and forever. Fountain of all life and source of all goodness, you made all things and fill them with your blessing; you created them to rejoice in the splendor of your radiance. Countless throngs of angels stand before you to serve you night and day, and, beholding the glory of your presence, they offer you unceasing praise. Joining with them, and giving voice to every creature under heaven, we glorify your name and lift our voices in joyful praise.[5]

This prayer, adapted from the Alexandrian Liturgy and attributed to a fourth-century bishop, Basil the Great, is intended for use at the beginning of the Prayer of Great Thanksgiving that precedes the Lord's Supper. But it also serves as a good model of a prayer of adoration that might be used at the beginning of a service of worship during the time of gathering. Like all good prayers of adoration, it prompts us to ascribe praise and glory to God and, in so doing, focuses us on the majesty of God. Prayers of adoration often emphasize the transcendence of God. When we speak of the transcendence of God, we are referring to the ways in which God is different from and stands over against the creation. God is the Holy One of Israel, who is not subject to the limitations of time or space, whose being does not derive from or depend upon another, and who "dwells in light inaccessible." God's transcendence, of course, is always balanced by God's immanence—the fact that God is present in and accessible through creation. While other types of prayer may emphasize God's immanence, prayers of adoration rightly call attention to the distance between God and creatures and function to cultivate the religious affections of awe, delight, and humility.

In the prayer of adoration above, the community at prayer draws on rich biblical imagery and metaphors that work on the religious imagination of worshipers, enabling them to direct speech of praise and celebration to God in a way that simultaneously generates in them a new affectional posture of awe and reverence before the transcendent God. The biblical imagery appropriated in this prayer functions to awaken our sense of dependence on and desire for God. We are utterly dependent on the One who "alone is God," who is the "fountain of all life," who "made all things," and whom the angels "serve . . . night and day." Yet we also deeply yearn for and desire this same One, for the one who "alone" is God, is also "living and true." The one who is the "fountain of all life" is also the "source of all goodness." The one who "made all things" also "filled them with . . . blessing." And the one whom the angels "serve . . . night and day" also receives their "unceasing praise." This imagery at once attracts us and causes us to pull back in godly fear, and the tangle of these two countervailing impulses lies at the heart of awe. In awe, we are drawn forward into union with the One who is supremely majestic and beautiful, even as we recoil and cover our eyes in the face of the overwhelming brightness of that One who dwells in a light so inaccessible that we might be overwhelmed by it.

In evoking the sense of awe, prayers of adoration disorient us by suspending our normal familiarity with God. In doing so, they awaken in us a godly fear that is akin to wonderment rather than cowering. Prayers of adoration place us in the position of Moses standing before the burning bush—attracted to it, curious about it, and yet aware of its danger (Exod. 3:1–4:17). In prayers of adoration, we, like Moses, stand before the God who refuses to be named, whom we cannot capture or control with our cognitive categories and everyday naming of our world. We stand on holy ground and must remove our sandals, and this is disorienting for us. We meet God not on our ground, but on *holy* ground— ground set aside from normal use for God's use. In prayers of adoration, we meet God not on our familiar turf, but in the unfamiliar, strange desert of holy ground. We sense that our normal ways of behaving in the world are not appropriate while standing on holy ground, and we must be instructed by God on how to relate properly to God. We are so accustomed to naming the creation and to using it as a means to achieve our purposes that we are disoriented when in prayers of adoration we meet God, not as one who can be named and who exists to serve our purposes, but as the One for whose purposes we exist.

Speaking of the awe and godly fear involved in the adoration of God, though, has not always been easy for the Christian church. For many, speaking of "godly fear" evokes powerful images of an angry, wrathful, judgmental God before whom we must cower in terror and abject submission if we are to avoid the fire and brimstone of hell. Some in the church want to lift up and valorize this mode of approaching God because of its power to drive us to repentance. But portraying God in this manner can lead to a destructive and manipulative tendency to undervalue our goodness and to equate salvation with an otherworldly escape. Others, wishing to reject this image of God, have opted to avoid all language of the judgment of God or of the majesty and holiness of God, focusing instead on how God is immanent in the creation and lovingly cares for all creatures. But failing to appreciate the transcendence and otherness of God can lead to an excessive familiarity and a sentimental form of false intimacy with God.

Both those who evoke the image of a wrathful God and those who avoid speaking at all of the transcendence of God falsely assume that "godly fear" means that we must cower in terror before God. Both groups reduce transcendence to wrath, forgetting that God's transcendence also includes God's endless grace, unconditional love, and superlative beauty. God is other than us in part because of God's bottomless capacity to love, a love that calls into question our own tendency to love in an exclusive and partial way. When we enrich our conception of God's transcendence to include these other dimensions of God's otherness, we discover that "godly fear" refers to the awe that we experience in the presence of divine beauty; it points to the ways in which that beauty is both attractive and disruptive. Our awe of God is not cowering terror or abject submission, but neither is our relationship with God akin to our common creaturely friendships. Instead, awe lures us toward God, reminds us that we are not God, and invites us into lives of expansive love.

In prayers of adoration, we acknowledge and express our rightful place as creatures of God who exist to glorify God. We are drawn toward the One who created us "to rejoice in the splendor of [God's] radiance," but this attraction is always commingled with holy fear and reverence before the One who alone is God "dwelling in light inaccessible." The awe and reverence evoked and nourished by prayers of adoration "set a question mark against" our assumption that God exists for us. Such reverence, sustained through the regular practice of offering prayers of adoration, disrupts our tendency to instrumentalize God and reorients us by granting us a new, theocentric vision of our place in God's world.

This new vision of our place in God's world prompts both humility and delight. On the one hand, remembering our creaturely condition before God reminds us that we are not God and that all things do not exist to serve our ends, and in humility we rediscover our utter dependence on God and our interdependence with other creatures. On the other hand, when we recognize our creaturely condition, we are liberated from the need to be God. We are free again to be finite beings, to be creatures. Such new freedom also carries with it the delight that comes from living in mutuality with all God's creatures, experiencing pleasure in the ways that they show forth divine majesty and beauty.

In adoring God, we are reminded that although we are not God, neither are we insignificant. We are not "the fountain of all life" or the "source of all goodness." God is, but we along with "all things" are the recipients of that life and goodness. In shaping humility and delight, prayers of adoration are the occasion through which God not only purifies us of our self-deification but also corrects our self-negation. When through the regular offering of prayers of adoration we humbly find our rightful place in God's world, we delightfully discover that we are not insignificant. We are the creatures who "give voice to every creature under heaven." We speak for them. We give voice to the mountains and trees that offer their praise in silence. We speak for the oceans and stars as we "lift our voices in joyful praise." Prayers of adoration thus reawaken a proper sense of our agency before God and other creatures and require us to become the beings that God created us to be—those who are responsible for speaking forth the praise of the creation for its God and living out this new reality in the world.

PRAYERS OF CONFESSION: CONTRITION AND HOPE

> Merciful God, we confess that we have sinned against you in thought, word, and deed, by what we have done, and by what we have left undone. We have not loved you with our whole heart and mind and strength. We have not loved our neighbors as ourselves. In your mercy forgive what we have been, help us amend what we are, and direct what we shall be, so that we may delight in your will and walk in your ways, to the glory of your holy name.[6]

The prayer of adoration lifts us to the lofty heights where we praise God, who dwells in light inaccessible, and give voice to every creature under heaven. In the next moment of worship, however, we find ourselves plunged back into the gritty reality of the brokenness and fragmentation of daily life. As one call to confession, drawn from 1 John, reminds us, "If we say we have no sin, we deceive ourselves, and the truth is not in us" (1 John 1:8–9). But why does the liturgy carry us so quickly from the heights of adoration to the depths of confession? It does so because as prayers of adoration draw our attention to the transcendence of God, we also become aware of God's moral distance from us. To proclaim the transcendence of God is not only to proclaim that God is different from us in terms of God's metaphysical attributes; it is also to proclaim that God is different from us in terms of God's moral attributes. The transcendent God is not only sovereign but also holy.

God's holiness comes to expression in the harmonious and morally perfect ways God relates to all things. This perfect, harmonious way of relating first shows itself in the inviolable love among the Father, Son, and Holy Spirit, in which each person of the Godhead completes and sustains the others. The perfect mutuality and hospitality that characterize the relationships among the three persons of the Trinity spill forth in the perfect way that God relates to all creatures. The principal quality of God's relational holiness is sovereign and inclusive love. We experience God's holiness most acutely when we sense our own unholiness, when we are aware of the fragmented and distorted relationships that diminish our lives and alienate us from God. Experiencing the disjunction between God's perfect holiness and our unholiness awakens in us the religious affection of contrition and drives us to confess our sins. We stand before God as persons who, in the distortion of sin, have violated others and in doing so have diminished ourselves before God.

God's sovereign and inclusive love reaches to every creature, whereas our own restrictive love would exclude those who do not serve us or who are different from us. Persons and institutions that perpetuate poverty, prejudice, and injustices of all kinds stand under the judgment of God, whose holiness would cleanse, sanctify, and claim all creatures. And this is what we confess: that we have not been what God made us to be, those who love and serve God and neighbor; that we have, by "thought, word, and deed" failed to love; that, by our actions and by our failures to act, we have not loved as broadly or as deeply as we might. And so, with true contrition, with sorrow and remorse, we confess our sins before God and one another.

The contrition that we express in the prayer of confession includes sorrow and remorse for the wounds we inflict on others, humiliation for the ways that these acts diminish ourselves, a sense of guilt, defilement, and unworthiness for having profaned the sacred things mediated to us through other creatures, and a mournfulness over the realization that at least some of the goodness and beauty that we have corrupted may be lost to us forever. In the contrition that accompanies the prayer of confession, we realize that our sinfulness radiates out simultaneously to distort our relationship with God, others, and ourselves. Our sin, then, is never private but always social, for it entails not simply a distortion of our inner heart, but also destructiveness toward God and others. The inner fragmentation of our hearts is related in complex ways to the outer fragmentation of our relationships with others. It is important, therefore, that our prayers of confession be offered publicly and corporately in the liturgy.

If our sinfulness always encompasses ourselves, other creatures, and God, so must the prayer of confession. Accordingly, the prayer of confession above begins with the realization that "we have sinned against [God]" by not having "loved [God] with our whole heart and mind and strength" but moves immediately to confess that "we have not loved our neighbors as ourselves," and concludes by seeking forgiveness for "what we have been" and strength for amending our being and actions. Because our sinfulness and contrition always have this triadic structure, it is fitting that our acts and prayers of confession also reflect it. Our sinfulness has resulted in the violation of other creatures and God as well as ourselves. Our prayers of confession should accordingly be public and corporate, for this best reflects and acknowledges the full scope and ramification of our sinfulness.

Prayers of confession in public worship are offered with pronouns that reflect the corporate and public dimensions of our sinfulness. It is "we" who confess, rather than simply an aggregation of "I's" whose sinfulness is private and confined to the inner recesses of the individual heart. In prayers of confession, we recognize that we have not simply failed to be the individuals God wants us to be; as the church we have failed to live into our new identity as a covenant community. In confessing our sin together, publicly and corporately, we are bearing witness to the necessarily triadic structure of our sinfulness and acknowledging honestly and openly the full scope of our fragmentation and alienation. We are simultaneously opening ourselves and the covenant community to the amending power and grace of God, who calls us to be not simply new creatures in Christ but also "a holy nation, God's own people" (1 Pet. 1:9).

The prayer of confession, although it grows out of our awareness of God's holiness and our unholiness, invites us to "approach the throne of grace with boldness" because the God before whom we confess, under whose judgment we stand, is also the God who always forgives (Heb. 4:16). We confess our sin with the expectation that the God of grace will forgive us and meet us with endless mercy. The prayer of confession is thus not designed to be a form of self-flagellation; its purpose is not to denigrate us or undermine the integrity of our lives. It is instead a moment of honesty about the human condition in all of its brokenness and tragedy, and a moment of hope in the God who meets us amidst such brokenness for healing, wholeness, and restoration. The God who meets us in the prayer of confession is the God whose holiness does indeed stand in judgment on us, but this very holiness already includes the perfect love and forgiveness brought in Christ.

For this reason, genuine contrition is always accompanied by hope, and the prayer of confession included above offers this vision of new possibilities when it concludes with the hopeful expectation that God's mercy will order our lives "so that we may delight in [God's] will and walk in [God's] ways, to the glory of [God's] holy name." Christian hope sees possibilities for delightful obedience to the will of God even in the midst of our confession that we have not loved God and neighbor as we ought. Even in the midst of our brokenness, we see real ground for hope that relationships may be reconciled and the goodness of creation restored and expanded. Because our hope is always commingled with contrition that involves an honest assessment of our brokenness and limitation and that seeks God's mercy to forgive, amend, and direct our lives, it does not degenerate into self-deceived, wishful thinking that pridefully assumes that human effort and ingenuity alone can set the world aright. But because our contrition is always commingled with hope, it does not degenerate into self-hatred or fuel the fallen impulse toward self-negation.

The liturgy reinforces the inseparability of contrition and hope by concluding the prayer of confession with the plea for mercy ("Lord, have mercy upon us") and the assurance of pardon. The plea for mercy involves the honest admission of our utter inability to heal the wounds of our souls. It joins the sorrow and remorse of contrition to a deeper awareness of our utter dependence on God's sovereign grace and our deepest desire for a reconciliation that only God can effect. The ritual of confession does not conclude until we are offered the hope contained in the assurance that God does pardon. Our confession is not complete until we receive this good news of the gospel, that in Jesus Christ we are already forgiven. The plea for mercy is always followed by an assurance of pardon. Between the plea for mercy and the assurance of pardon, between contrition and hope, nothing is ever interposed. There are no requirements listed in order to gain or merit God's mercy, no suggestions for self-improvement, no chastisement for having failed once again. Nothing comes between the plea and the promise of God's grace; nothing uncouples contrition and hope in the Christian life.

PRAYERS OF THANKSGIVING: GRATITUDE, RIGHTNESS, AND WELL-BEING

> Accept, O Lord, our thanks and praise for all that you have done for us. We thank you for the splendor of the whole creation, for the beauty of this world, for the wonder of life, and for the mystery of love. We thank you for the blessing of family and friends, and for the loving care which surrounds us on every side. We thank you for setting us at tasks which demand our best efforts, and for leading us to accomplishments which satisfy and delight us. We thank you also for those disappointments and failures that lead us to acknowledge our dependence on you alone. Above all, we thank you for your Son Jesus Christ; for the truth of his Word and the example of his life; for his steadfast obedience, by which he overcame temptation; for his dying, through which he overcame death; and for his rising to life again, in which we are raised to the life of your kingdom. Grant us the gift of your Spirit, that we may know Christ and make him known; and through him, at all times and in all places, may give thanks to you in all things. Amen.[7]

Prayers of thanksgiving are offered to God throughout the service of worship. Anytime we address speech to God that expresses our gratitude, we offer one. Even our set response of "thanks be to God" following the assurance of pardon, the reading of Scripture, or the acceptance of bread and cup in the Lord's Supper is a prayer of thanksgiving. Such prayers may be included in the prayer of adoration, as part of the prayers of the people, during the prayer of

dedication following the taking up of the offering, in the singing of the doxology when we acknowledge God as the one "from whom all blessings flow,"
and are always a central part of the Prayer of Great Thanksgiving that precedes the words of institution during the sacrament of the Lord's Supper. We
speak our gratitude to God at almost every turn of the service of worship,
because thankfulness to God is called for as we gather in adoration and confession, as we abide together to be illuminated by the service of Word and
Table, and as we are sent out in peace.

The prayers of thanksgiving that we offer express our gratitude in a way
that calls attention to the object-oriented nature of that religious affection.
When we pray, "Thanks be to God," we are expressing gratitude for something specific: for the pardon God grants us, for the illuminating truth and
beauty of Scripture, and for the bread of life and the cup of salvation. In the
prayer of thanksgiving above we do not offer generic thanks to God; we offer
thanks specifically for the "splendor," "beauty," "wonder," and "mystery" of
creation, life, and love; for family and friends; for meaningful work; and even
for the hardships we encounter, insofar as they provide us with opportunities
to deepen our relationship with God. Our gratitude takes on a specific form
in response to a particular object as we affirm that the glory of God shines
through it. Our gratitude gestures toward the presence of God within the
"dazzling theatre" of creation.[8] Our prayers of thanksgiving, then, must be
specific; they must identify in particular that for which we are thankful.

Prayers of thanksgiving not only express gratitude; they also train us in it.
The repeated linguistic practice of offering thanks attunes our hearts to the
giftedness of life, to the beauty and goodness of creation that come to us
unearned and undeserved, and to our utter dependence on God and our interdependence with all creatures. Prayers of thanksgiving channel our desire and
sense of dependence toward God, who is the source of all goodness and beauty
within the creation. Just as the repeated practice of saying "please" and "thank
you" schools a child in the social graces that facilitate respectful interactions,
so the constant practice of offering thanks, even when we do not feel grateful,
trains us in the religious affection of gratitude.

Over the course of a lifetime, as we speak gratitude that we may or may not
feel in any given moment, the Holy Spirit infuses our linguistic practice with
purifying and illuminating grace, and slowly but certainly turns our hearts
toward the glory of God. This slow turning toward divine glory, this certain
reshaping of our hearts, forms us as people of gratitude, people who meet the
world with a readiness to acknowledge that it comes to us not as an entitlement, but as a gift. And this acknowledgment of the fundamental giftedness of
life is bedrock to Christian identity. Don Saliers explains the relationship
between prayer and gratitude in this way:

> It is irreligious to take the world for granted, and to remain unaffected
> by its grandeur and misery. . . . Coming to have the capacity for grat-
> itude for those things truly worthy . . . is essential to our humanity.
> Human maturity is bound up with a capability for gratitude. This link
> between a central feature of Christian prayer and a trait of human
> moral maturity must not be taken lightly. So far as prayer is first and
> last speaking God's name in praise and gratitude, it is part of the dis-
> covery of our humanity as well.[9]

Praying our gratitude is a central part of our religious identity because being
Christian entails being affected by the "grandeur and misery" of the world,
being attentive to the "things truly worthy," and "speaking God's name in
praise and gratitude."

Because the creation mediates the presence of God to us, our gratitude to
God is always also gratitude for the world that God has made and for our place
in that world; gratitude points to and situates us within a world that is rightly
ordered and hospitable to our flourishing, a world that evokes in us two additional religious affections: a sense of rightness and a sense of well-being. Our
sense of rightness is our sense that the world is not haphazard but ordered
according to God's intention. Our sense of well-being is our sense that this
order of the world is hospitable to us, that it allows for our flourishing; we
sense that the structures of the world are not fundamentally aligned against us,
but that we belong here and that our well-being within this order has been
taken account of by God, who generates that right order. The natural order is
a place of splendor, beauty, wonder, and mystery because all of its parts con-
spire to glorify God. Our sense of the rightness of the natural order involves
acknowledging not simply that the world is ordered to God's glory, but that it
is right, good, and fitting that it is ordered this way. Our sense of well-being
grows naturally out of this sense of the good and fitting nature of the order of
the world as we find our place within it. We may acknowledge distortions
within the natural order of the world—cancers that destroy healthy tissue and
organs, natural disasters that bring untold suffering—but we can recognize
them as distortions precisely because they violate our sense of the fundamental goodness and rightness of the world. It is fitting, then, that we offer prayers
of thanksgiving for the goodness of the natural world, even in the midst of its
distortions.

Our sense that the world is ordered in a fitting way, that there is a rightness
about it, extends not only to the natural order, but also to the social order, to
the "blessing of family and friends." We sense that we were made for community and that our well-being is rooted in it. We do not simply find ourselves
within social and familial contexts of care and nurture; we also sense that we
were made to live in these relationships, that our identities are rightly shaped

within them. We may acknowledge and lament sinful distortions in our social lives—governments that ignore and perpetuate poverty and injustice, families that are abusive, churches that are indifferent to suffering and intolerant of difference—but again we recognize these as distortions, precisely because they disrupt our sense that there is a basic rightness about how our social lives are ordered and that this rightness is made in part to ensure our well-being. It is fitting, then, that we give thanks for the communities that care for and nurture us, even in the midst of the brokenness that plagues all human institutions.

These senses of rightness and well-being rooted in our relationship to the natural and social orders mean that we affirm, for example, that our embodiment is good and not merely some unfortunate and accidental feature of our identities that we hope to escape when we get to our real home in heaven. God made us for this world; it is right that we are here, that we find our meaning and purpose, our well-being, within the context of this earthly order, that we are ultimately redeemed within this world, and that the kingdom of God comes when this world is made new and all of the current distortions of God's good order are set right. We sense that the world is ordered as it ought to be, that we belong here, and that this belonging beckons us to offer thanksgiving to God.

PRAYERS OF INTERCESSION: AFFECTIONAL DESIRE AND DEPENDENCE

"Father, if you are willing, remove this cup from me; yet, not my will but yours be done" (Luke 22:42).

Grant, Almighty God, that all who confess your Name may be united in your truth, live together in your love, and reveal your glory in the world. [*Silence*] Lord, in your mercy hear our prayer.

Guide the people of this land, and of all the nations, in the ways of justice and peace; that we may honor one another and serve the common good. [*Silence*] Lord, in your mercy hear our prayer.

Give us all a reverence for the earth as your own creation, that we may use its resources rightly in the service of others and to your honor and glory. [*Silence*] Lord, in your mercy hear our prayer.

Bless all whose lives are closely linked with ours, and grant that we may serve Christ in them, and love one another as he loves us. [*Silence*] Lord, in your mercy hear our prayer.

Comfort and heal all those who suffer in body, mind, or spirit; give them courage and hope in their troubles, and bring them the joy of your salvation. [*Silence*] Lord, in your mercy hear our prayer.

We commend to your mercy all who have died, that your will for them may be fulfilled; and we pray that we may share with all your saints in your eternal kingdom. [*Silence*] Lord, in your mercy hear our prayer.

Almighty and eternal God, ruler of all things in heaven and earth: Mercifully accept the prayers of your people, and strengthen us to do your will; through Jesus Christ our Lord. Amen.[10]

There is probably no time of prayer when it is more difficult to locate creaturely existence within the broader context of God's sovereign will than when we offer prayers of intercession. There is perhaps no form of prayer in which it is more difficult to maintain a theocentric orientation than when we give voice to our deepest needs and ask for God's healing love and restoring grace. In prayers of intercession we speak to God of the broken places in our lives. We express our anguish over illness and tragedy. We give voice to our frustration and anger over continuing poverty, injustice, and sin in our world. We ask God to intervene, to set the world right, to bring peace where we are mired in conflict, to bring justice where we are complicit in the oppression of others, and to heal where our bodies and minds are broken and have failed us. We bring to God petitions that God will bring goodness and beauty to our broken and distorted lives, and this is dangerously close to asking God to do our will. Prayers of intercession present us with a great opportunity and with a great temptation. The great opportunity is to present to God our deepest needs; the great temptation is to imagine that our prayers "throw some additional weight" onto the scales and influence God to do what God might otherwise refrain from doing. We are tempted, in short, to reorder God's will around our own.

We begin by thinking about this great temptation and then turn to the great opportunity that prayers of intercession offer us. Behind the temptation to reorder God's will around our own is a flawed conception of God's love for us. We imagine that God's love for us is conditional, that God does not will our good and will not act for our well-being unless we ask God to do so in just the right way. Because we know that God already knows our deepest needs, we imagine that the point of prayer is not to inform God, but to prompt God to action. As one misguided church sign once announced, "prayer is the nerve that moves the muscle of God." We provide the brains; God provides the brawn. But at bottom, this way of thinking is flawed and even destructive. It implies that God is smug and capricious, that God knows what is good but will not pursue the good unless we say the magic word. What kind of God would that be? Certainly a God worthy of our worship will not make certain that our checking account shows a positive balance at the end of each month because we have asked for "my daily bread," while allowing a starving child to die in agony because she does not know how to pray. This is perhaps the central pastoral problem related to intercessory prayer. Certainly, this smug and capricious God is not the one we have in mind when we pray that God will "guide the people of this land," "give us all a reverence for the earth," and "comfort and heal" those who suffer.

So, then, if we are not trying to "throw some additional weight" onto the scale prompting God to act for our good, what are we doing in intercessory prayer? Jesus' own prayer in the garden of Gethsemane, offered on the night of his betrayal, offers us an excellent model of intercessory prayer (Luke 22:39–46). Jesus prayed, "Father, if you are willing, remove this cup from me; yet, not my will but yours be done" (Luke 22:42). In a sermon entitled "On the Power of Prayer in Relation to Outward Circumstances," Friedrich Schleiermacher examines this prayer and discovers in it important principles that ought to inform our own intercessory prayers.[11] Throughout the remainder of this section, we will draw on his insights in our own exploration of three aspects of intercessory prayer.

The first feature that Schleiermacher notes is simply that Jesus did indeed lay his petition before God. He came to God in his time of anguish and near-despair, asking that God would lift from him the burden of suffering and death. Jesus wished deeply to be released from the agony that awaited him, and he asked God to grant him that release. We too have the privilege to bring before God our deepest needs. We too may ask God to grant our heart's desire. It is perfectly appropriate and legitimate to lay our petitions before God. When we speak our petitions, we highlight our deepest desires and highest loyalties. We bring those desires and loyalties intentionally into the presence of God, where the grace of God may shed light on them and transform them.

Second, in intercessory prayer, we encounter the sovereign grace of God, and this encounter is life-changing. Jesus did not simply bring to God his desire for release from suffering; he also submitted that desire to the will of God, accepting that ultimately God's will, and not his own, must be done. The function of the intercessory prayer was to transform Jesus' desires. God did not release him from suffering, but did give him strength to face the challenges that awaited him. Jesus' desire to avoid suffering was transformed into a desire to obey the will of God, come what may. Intercessory prayer functions in a similar way for us. We bring to God our heart's desire and submit that desire to the sovereign will of God so that God may redirect that desire and, in so doing, reorient all of the religious affections through which it courses. Intercessory prayer, animated by the Holy Spirit, has the power to effect a theocentric reorientation of our perspective. We may come in prayer seeking our own will but discover, through that prayer, the will of God. We may come speaking our own desires but, through prayer, find those desires redirected. We may come in prayer with the expectation that we know what God wants of us and for us and find ourselves instead willing to depend more deeply on the mercy of God. When the Holy Spirit uses intercessory prayer to redirect our desires and reorient our sense of dependence, when the logic and order that binds the religious affections together is renewed and restored, then we may discover new directions for our lives and a new strength and resolve to take our place within God's broad and gracious plan.

In prayer we come into a communion with God that we cannot fully explain and the meaning of which cannot be exhausted with words. Prayer has the mysterious power to work on the one who prays, effecting a new way of knowing and being related to God and to other creatures. We honor this mysterious communion when we allow space for silence in our intercessions. We signal with this silence that we not only want the prayer to allow us to speak our desires but that we also want to be opened to the transforming power of the Holy Spirit working through that prayer. We want as much to hear God's desires as we want to speak our own, and we want the speaking of our desires to become the occasion for aligning ourselves with the desires of God. We want "my will" to become "thy will."

Finally, the theocentric transformation of our religious affections occasioned by intercessory prayer has consequences for our knowing and doing. Jesus not only came to know the will of God and accept it; he also found strength, courage, and vision to act on that will. He came to know, accept, and find peace in the role that his suffering and death would play in human redemption. He actively worked in ways that he knew would ultimately lead to his death. He did not refuse to work on behalf of the suffering, the poor, and the outcast. He did not shy away from challenging those in power. He continued to live a disruptively redemptive life even though he knew that it would lead to suffering and death.

Our own intercessory prayer has similar consequences for our knowing and doing. Through prayer we may glimpse a vision of God's will for all creation and find strength to pursue that vision actively. Our prayer that God will relieve the suffering of those in poverty is not complete until we engage in action to bring economic justice for all people. Our prayer that God will comfort the bereaved and welcome the outcast is not complete until it flows into our lives so that we become God's agents of comfort and hospitality. Our prayers and our moral lives are deeply connected. We do indeed pray what we believe, believe what we pray, and live what we pray and believe. *Lex orandi, lex credendi, lex bene operandi.*

Throughout this chapter we have explored the relationship between the public prayers of worship and the religious affections. We discovered that the speech of prayer is generative and creative rather than merely descriptive; is rooted in the biblical narrative as the shared story of the church; is offered in the voice of the community rather than the individual; is offered *to* God; and aims to remember collectively the creaturely condition before God and to locate creaturely existence within the broader theocentric purposes of the sovereign God. When we explored prayer as silence, we discovered that it generates affective receptivity to the divine presence and opens us afresh to the purifying and illuminating work of Christ. Finally, an exploration of prayers of adoration, confession, thanksgiving, and intercession has revealed their mysterious capacity to bring us into the presence of God and thereby to express, evoke, sustain, direct, and shape religious affections such as awe, contrition, gratitude, and the desire and dependence that run through them all.

8

The Service of the Word

Telling stories is a powerful and primal human activity. When we meet someone new and strike up a friendship, we invite that person to come to know us by telling the stories of our lives. We learn to know others by listening to their stories. Likewise, every family has its own stock set of stories, and to be a member of that family, to share its identity, is to know these common stories. As a family grows and changes, as new family members are born or join by marriage, each new member grows into the identity of the family by learning its stories. And the family identity itself changes as the new members add their own stories. We even "remember" stories that occurred long before our membership in the family. We remember how the great-grandmother we never knew always left her pies to cool on the windowsill. We remember how Granddad's tomatoes were never bigger than they were the summer after the garden flooded. This remembering and retelling of the stories of the family helps to maintain the identity of the family and of its individual members. Clans, tribes, communities, and nations also tell identity-making and identity-shaping stories. Early human communities gathered in common places to hear minstrels sing the stories of the group, to hear the elders tell of the great deeds of ancient heroes, and to pass on these stories to new generations who would retell them and add tales of their own great deeds. Learning to hear the stories of a friend, a family, or a community, and learning to retell these stories well, are the central acts that allow us to build friendships, join a family, or become a member of a community. Listening to and telling stories are basic to our humanity.

Preaching is, at least in part, an effort to tell us who we are by telling the story of who we have been as a community of faith. It starts with the biblical story and attempts to find in it indicators of the meaning of our life stories, the end toward which they are ordered, and the key that brings coherence and order to them. But, as we have already seen, there are competing stories vying to shape our identities. The cultural contexts of amusement, consumerism, and nationalism are but three examples of competing identity-forming narratives. When preaching acknowledges that we were made for order, that our individual and common lives may be ordered to some end, it runs contrary especially to the culture of consumerism and amusement in which we find ourselves. Such a culture encourages us to lose ourselves in the moment and not to search for meaning beyond the instant. Such a culture can offer us only the momentary pleasure of a purchase or the fleeting feeling of mild amusement that accompanies a particular encounter. But we find no meaningful narrative that binds together all of those moments into a coherent story that moves us in any particular direction. At most, a life defined by consumerism and amusement will consist of a series of thirty-second commercials strung together into some semblance of a life; at most, such a culture can bring the thinnest of meanings to that life, a spare expectation that there is some singular "right" path that a life should follow.

The strong forces of social formation emerging from this culture encourage and exacerbate our fragmentation. The culture of consumerism presents us with seemingly endless products that generate endless desires and then attempt to sate them. But those products never satisfy our deepest longing, and they never bring unity and coherence to our multiple desires. The multiplicity of our longing results in an inner fragmentation that disrupts the underlying order of the religious affections. In chapter 3 we saw how affections such as hope, direction, delight, and self-sacrificial love become distorted as a result of our misdirected desire. Our inner fragmentation inevitably results in the broken relationships of outer fragmentation.

Through its proclamation, the church presents us with an alternate community of social formation, one in which God works providentially to reorient our religious affections through the retelling and rehearing of our sacred stories. Remembering and retelling the sacred story of Scripture engages us in a participatory form of knowing that reorients our religious affections as it reconstitutes our Christian identity. Such remembering is never merely about the past. Memory is also about the present and future, who we are and who we will become. In the remainder of this chapter, we will discuss the relationship between preaching and the cultivation of the religious affections under three rubrics. First, preaching cultivates particular religious affections by inviting us into participatory knowledge of particular biblical narratives. Second, we explain how preaching invites us into such affection-forming, participatory knowledge through an active engagement with the religious imagination.

Third, we explore the effect of restored affections on our lives as we are called into new patterns of living that anticipate the fullness of the reign of God.

PREACHING BIBLICAL NARRATIVES AND THE CULTIVATION OF PARTICULAR RELIGIOUS AFFECTIONS

Preaching allows us to appropriate the biblical narratives because it brings us into participatory knowledge of them. When we retell the sacred stories of Scripture and extend their interpretive power over the present from the pulpit in public worship, we are engaging in a powerful form of participatory knowing in which God's grace purifies and illumines the deepest affectional structures of our identities as the covenant people. When we hear the sacred stories retold and extended in sermons, we are never simply receiving information in a purely objective, disinterested way. Instead, we are drawn into the stories; we feel their conflict and drama; we yearn for their resolution; and we identify with the characters. We grieve with David over the death of his son Absalom, we share Amos's outrage at the subordination of faith to nationalism, and we rejoice with the woman at the well who finds forgiveness and acceptance from Jesus. When we hear and extend the sacred stories that make us who we are as the covenant people, the rigid boundary between the knower and the known partly dissolves, the chasm of centuries that separates us from these ancient biblical characters and conflicts is spanned, and we enter "the strange new world [of] the Bible" to be transformed by it. The stories of this strange new world become the interpretive lens through which we view our lives. We make sense out of the elements of our autobiography and everyday experiences by interpreting them through the categories and concepts found in the Bible. The words, images, plots, and metaphors of Scripture become the vocabulary that we use to tell our own stories. The meaning of standing before the great sequoia is recast in light of the psalmist's declaration that all creatures sing the praises of God. We begin to recognize that the wounding of our friend and all the broken relationships in our lives merely repeat the pattern established by Adam and Eve, by Cain and Abel. We learn to receive the good things in life as gifts when we recognize that "the earth is the LORD's" (Ps. 24:1).

At the heart of this participatory knowing is an act of appropriation in which the ancient stories of the Bible become *our* stories. When we hear again the ancient stories of creation and fall, of God's call to Abraham and Sarah, of bondage in and exodus from Egypt, of wandering in the wilderness, of Ruth's faithfulness, of King David's weeping for the loss of Absalom his son, of the prophet Amos's ejection from the temple at Bethel, of John baptizing in the desert, of Jesus' healings and miracles, and of the missionary journeys of Paul, we are remembering the grand, sweeping narrative of *our* community. These ancient stories, once foreign and alien to us, have become our stories, the source of our identity in the present. The little stories of our lives are intersected by the grand narrative drama of Scripture, and this point of intersection makes the disconnected events of our past meaningful by locating them within the framework of God's purposes and activities as recorded in Scripture and proclaimed from the pulpit. In the weekly retelling and hearing of the episodes of Scripture, we are opening ourselves to the identity-forming power of God's revelation. Preaching, as Fred Craddock reminds us, involves "making present and appropriate to the hearers the revelation of God."[1] In the sermons, we extend these identity-forming stories into the present, where they function to gather up and interpret properly the meaning and significance of the fragmented, disconnected episodes of our daily experience. Sermons ensure that remembering the stories of Scripture is never simply about the past; they extend remembering into the present by illuminating, interpreting, and weaving the meaning and significance of our experience into the grand biblical story of God's redemptive self-revelation.

In earlier chapters we noted how participatory knowledge of the natural world attunes us to the beauty of the whole creation by making us aware of our interdependence with all creatures, and how participatory knowledge of the attractive power of the beauty of Christ reorients our desires and sense of dependence. Likewise, participatory knowing of the sacred narratives has an affection-forming power. Scripture points us to God as the ultimate object of our desiring; it draws us to God as the one on whom we are utterly dependent. Scripture calls us out of our idolatry and into participatory knowledge of the God of Abraham and Sarah, Isaac and Rachel, and Israel and Rebekah, and it does so precisely through the stories of these founders of the faith, who themselves learned to put aside their idols so that they could desire and depend upon God. The biblical narrative forms our affections, then, because it reorients our desires and dependence, and when it does so, it cultivates in us the full range of appropriate religious affections. Biblical stories take us through awe at God's mighty deeds in freeing the children of Israel from bondage in Egypt, contrition over their and our choice of the golden calf over the God who has redeemed us, gratitude for the gift of the law at Mount Sinai, delight in the beauty of creation expressed in the Psalms, and hope in the vision of God's final restoration of all things offered in Isaiah and the Revelation of John. The proclamation of Scripture is a means of grace through which God reorders our religious affections.

This reordering of the religious affections often happens when preaching highlights a particular religious affection embedded within a particular biblical narrative, and we appropriate that religious affection for ourselves. We consider three examples, beginning with the account of the prophet Amos castigating the Israelites for their indifference to the plight of the poor. Amos's prophetic outrage is rooted in his deep sense of mutuality and interdependence, which is utterly violated by the self-satisfied affluence of the wealthy who "lie on beds of ivory, and lounge on their couches, and eat lambs from the flock, and calves from the stall," while they "trample on the needy, and bring to ruin the poor of the land" (Amos 6:4; 8:4). Amos contends that the wealthy have "turned justice into poison" and calls out for a reversal in which the wealthy go into exile, the poor are raised up, "justice roll[s] down like waters, and righteousness like an ever-flowing stream" (Amos 6:12; 5:24). This vision of justice and righteousness given to him by God demands conditions that allow for the flourishing of all, for a renewed and rich set of relationships in which neighbors depend upon one another, provide for the good of one another, and live in mutuality and hospitality. As we appropriate the story, Amos's sense of mutuality and interdependence becomes our own, and this heightened religious affection makes us increasingly aware of the self-satisfied affluence of our own age. We begin actively seeking creative ways to use our resources to extend the circle of privilege to include those who are marginalized, so that Amos's God-given vision of mutuality and interdependence may be more fully realized and so that the conditions of the world may increasingly come to conform to our sense of how they ought to be, a sense rooted in our religious affections. Appropriating the story of Amos not only heightens our sense of mutuality and interdependence, it also spills over into heightened senses of obligation and well-being as we become increasingly aware of our ability to meet the needs of others so that they may experience a renewed sense of well-being.

The account of Jesus' affirmation that the Sabbath was made for humanity provides a second example of how appropriating a biblical narrative reorders our religious affections, in this case the religious affections of delight and rightness. When the Pharisees criticize Jesus because he allows his disciples to pluck heads of grain as they walk through a field on the Sabbath, he responds that God did not make humanity for the sake of keeping the Sabbath, but made the Sabbath so that we might have a day to rest and delight in God's good creation (Mark 2:23–28). Jesus' reinterpretation of Sabbath-keeping rests in his sense of delight. When he rejects the legalistic restrictions of the Pharisees, Jesus affirms that Sabbath is ultimately about resting from the routines of work so that we may delight in the work of God in creation. When the rules of Sabbath-keeping, which are subordinate to this greater end, interfere with our ability to delight, they must be set aside. A rhythm of time that allows for enjoyment and delight is part of the structure of creation itself. Sabbath-keeping is intended to honor this structure of creation. Human life, like all of creation, has a right rhythm of work and relaxation. This is how God has ordered the world, and it is right for it to be this way. Sabbath is about recognizing and honoring this rightness. When we appropriate this story, then, not only does Jesus' delight become our delight, but also his sense of rightness becomes ours.

The account in the Second Epistle to the Corinthians (5:16–21) of how our ministry of reconciliation grows out of Christ's reconciling work provides a third example of how appropriating a biblical narrative reorders our religious affections, in this case the religious affection of direction. Paul reminds the Corinthians that because they have been reconciled to God in Christ, they have been given a new identity and a new purpose; they are to be "ambassadors for Christ" who exercise his "ministry of reconciliation" in the world (2 Cor. 5:20, 18). To have a Christian identity means to have a particular purpose and direction for one's life. Like the Christians at Corinth, we are directed toward the reconciling righteousness of God. When we appropriate this sense of direction for ourselves, we are charged, as the Corinthians were, to order our lives in such a way as to encourage relationships of harmony, to overcome the barriers that divide people, to seek opportunities to make peace where there is conflict, and to invite outcasts into the inclusive love of Christ. Paul's sense of direction, when we appropriate this passage, becomes our sense of direction.

To ensure that the full story of the canon is told, remembered, and extended and that the full range of properly ordered religious affections is cultivated through preaching, we encourage the use of a lectionary. The Revised Common Lectionary, for example, prescribes biblical selections to be read on appointed Sundays across a three-year cycle. Those who attend church regularly will hear nearly the full counsel of Scripture over the course of those three years. Because the lectionary covers every kind of biblical literature and includes all of the central stories that compose that grand narrative of salvation, it calls our attention to themes and stories we might otherwise overlook in favor of old standbys, and it encourages pastors to make broad and expansive use of biblical materials. As a result, use of the lectionary helps preachers to attend to the full range of religious affections. It assists in achieving one of preaching's central tasks—participation in the theocentric reorientation of the people of God by presenting Christ afresh for the redemptive encounter that trusts God to evoke, sustain, shape, order, express, and direct our religious affections.

This focus on reorientation of the religious affections as a central task of preaching should alert us to two possible abuses of the preaching office. First, we may psychologize the text by projecting onto it or reading into it our own psychic states. This abuse of the preaching office fails to trust the ancient narrative to speak in relevant ways to the modern world. It also represents a kind of exegetical laziness that refuses to honor and enter into the world of the Bible and seek its meaning on foreign soil. Second, some emotionally manipulative preaching seeks to force to the surface particular emotional expressions in particular moments that can be harnessed for the preacher's interests and agenda. This abuse rests in a fundamental failure to distinguish between an emotion and an affection. It also domesticates the biblical narrative so that it cannot speak in surprising and prophetic ways to us. Focusing attention on the affection-reorienting function of preaching instead requires that we honor the text of Scripture with careful and deliberate exegesis, sustained attention to the literary and cultural context of the passage under consideration, and humble and well-planned rhetoric that lets the Bible speak to us on its own terms, trusting that over time the stories have their own integrity and power to interpret our lives and to reorient them theocentrically.

When we appropriate biblical narratives, they reorder our religious affections and render our lives more intelligible because such appropriation allows us to locate the episodes of our individual and communal lives within the larger narrative of God's work in history. In preaching, we appropriate a common memory as the people of God, and this shared memory serves as the interpretive lens that makes the meaning of our individual and social lives visible. God's self-disclosure as we find it in Scripture and proclaim it in sermons illuminates our lives by revealing to us their true meaning and by pointing us to the coherence, pattern, and purpose that bind together all the individual episodes of our personal and communal histories in a meaningful way. When preaching retells and extends the stories of Scripture from week to week, it works to gather up the isolated threads of our past and weave them together with the threads of the biblical narrative to produce a comprehensive fabric of meaning for our lives. The stories of our lives are contextualized within the grand story of God's self-disclosure in history, and we are enabled to see, understand, and embrace our place and purpose within this grand story. H. Richard Niebuhr characterized revelation as that "which brings rationality and wholeness into the confused joys and sorrows of personal existence and allows us to discern order in the brawl of communal histories."[2] Part of what God reveals to us is the meaning of our own lives and the purpose of our own history. Our knowledge of ourselves and our knowledge of God, as Calvin so emphatically reminds us at the beginning of his *Institutes*, are deeply interconnected.[3] To know God is to apprehend our own place within God's order. When our personal and communal histories are grafted onto the common memory of the grand narrative of Scripture, what had been chaotic and fragmented now becomes ordered and coherent. Our individual and communal lives acquire purpose and direction when preaching lifts them into the broader context of God's revelatory activity in history.

Appropriation also renders our lives intelligible because it prompts us to remember episodes of our individual and communal lives that we would prefer to forget. Niebuhr pointed out that divine revelation not only serves the illuminating function of bringing meaning and coherence to our lives, but that it also serves a purifying function. Purification is that process through which we identify and let go of our idols. Through contact with God's self-disclosure in Scripture, he explained, "the heart not only understands what it remembers but is enabled and driven to remember what it had forgotten." We prefer to create and hold onto idolatrous images of ourselves and our communities that leave out our failures and frailties, our bias and ignorance. We suppress and push aside those memories that violate our perfectly constructed self-image. But Niebuhr warns that "we do not destroy this past of ours; it is indestructible. We carry it with us; its record is written deep into our lives. We only refuse to acknowledge it as our true past and try to make it an alien thing— something that did not happen to our true selves. . . . Our buried past is mighty; the ghosts of our fathers and of the selves that we have been haunt our days and nights though we refuse to acknowledge their presence."[4]

Preaching extends this purifying function of Scripture by drawing attention to the very honest portrayal of the failings and frailties, biases and ignorance, of the founders of our faith offered in the Bible. Scripture does not shy away from portraying either the mighty deeds of faithful King David or his betrayal and adultery. Scripture unflinchingly shows us the earnest truthfulness of Peter as he confesses Jesus to be the Son of the living God and the shattering moment of his denial of Christ. It shows us the rapid growth of the early church and the sometimes bitter infighting of the newly founded congregations. The Bible refuses to allow us to suppress the flaws of our past; it shatters our carefully constructed but false image of a perfectly faithful tradition. The Bible presents us with memories that we would just as soon forget.

Good sermons extend that purifying function of Scripture when they help us to remember what we would prefer to forget. They help us to locate the larger, coherent story of our lives within the seemingly incoherent jumble of our memories, by including all of the little stories of our lives, our best and worst moments, our faithfulness and our faithlessness, our earnest honesty and our cowardly denials. In so doing, preaching delivers us from the idolatry of our past, from the temptation to portray ourselves as so perfect that we are virtual gods. When preaching helps us to identify with the biblical narratives of failure, when it helps us to see that this mottled history is *our* history, it extends the prophetic function of Scripture that unmasks the idolatries of individuals and societies by exposing their failings before God. When we hear again Jesus' statement to the rich young ruler that "it is easier for a camel to go through the eye of a needle than for someone who is rich to enter the kingdom of God," we are reminded of our lingering faith in wealth as our ultimate source of security (Matt. 19:24). When we hear that after being healed by Jesus only one of ten lepers—the Samaritan among them, no less—returned to express delight and gratitude to God, we are reminded of our own joyless and casual ingratitude toward God for the gifts of life, health, and new possibilities (Luke 17:11–19). When we hear again the parable of laborers who each received the same payment despite having worked different amounts of time, our narrowed sense of justice that would deny to the economically marginalized the senses of rightness and well-being is laid bare (Matt. 20:1–16). And when we hear again Paul's affirmation that in Christ "there is no longer Jew or Greek, there is no longer slave or free, there is no longer male and female," we see again the forces of racism, sexism, and other forms of discrimination that linger on in our hearts and religious institutions where they undermine a genuine sense of mutuality and interdependence (Gal. 3:28).

This purifying function of preaching offers an alternative narrative to the prevailing cultural narrative of nationalism. Niebuhr explained that "our national histories do not recall to the consciousness of citizens the crimes and absurdities of past social conduct, as our written and unwritten autobiographies fail to mention our shame."[5] Nationalism not only co-opts genuine religion for demonic ends; it often constructs a sanitized national narrative that conveniently omits those episodes of history that would demystify nationalism's spellbinding power and appeal. We remember a Thomas Jefferson whose principles of liberty strum the inner chords of our patriotism, even as we forget the ugly truth that he endorsed slavery and owned other human beings. We speak triumphantly of America as a Christian nation, forgetting that the demonic distortion of this national faith sacralized slavery, racism, and sexism. We proudly invoke the rhetoric of liberty, democracy, and civil rights for all, even as we conceal and forget our covert funding of dictators, death squads, and regimes of political repression when it serves our short-term, strategic interests. The faithful proclamation of Scripture will not allow such sanitized narratives of nationalism to go unchallenged. When we hear again Amos condemning King Ahab for co-opting the religion of Israel and subtly remaking it to serve the interest of king, court, and nation, we are forced to confront again the same impulse in our own individual and national life. When we hear the book of Revelation speak of Rome as the apocalyptic beast, we are reminded how the jaws of tyrannical governments—even democratic governments—inflict suffering, bloodshed, and injustice, sometimes under the battle flag of liberty. When we hear again the first commandment, "You shall have no other gods before me," delivered to Moses even as the Israelites shaped their golden calf at the foot of Mount Sinai, we are reminded of our allegiance to the constructed god of the nation rather than to the sovereign God "who rules over the nations" (Exod. 20:3; Ps. 22:28).

Preaching has the power to purify us by exposing the conveniently con-
cealed and easily forgotten episodes of our lives, and when it does, it is a means
of grace whereby God liberates us to relate properly to God and other creatures. Preaching mediates the purifying grace of God that works to reorganize
the distorted pattern of dependence and desire that runs through the fallen
religious affections. Such grace redirects awe and reverence from nation to
God, grounds hope not in the triumph of armies and economies but in the
inbreaking kingdom of God, delights in the well-being of all people rather
than merely in the well-being of one's fellow patriots, and understands that the
obligation of citizenship entails not blind allegiance to nation but an allegiance
to the truth of the God before whom all "the nations tremble" (Hab. 3:6).

PREACHING AND THE RELIGIOUS IMAGINATION

The power of preaching to cultivate and reorder particular religious affections
rests in its ability to bring us into participatory knowing of particular biblical
narratives. But how does it do so? In this section, we propose that the religious
imagination provides the means by which preaching brings us into the presence of Christ through participatory knowing of God's self-disclosure in
Scripture. Through preaching, the Holy Spirit makes Christ present to our
imaginations for an affection-transforming, redemptive encounter with the
Word of God. When we preach sermons, we do more than offer information
about Christ, and we do more than offer exhortation to live moral lives in
Christ. In sermons we engage in a means of grace wherein the Holy Spirit
continues to open the hearts and imaginations of the people of God to the
affection-transforming presence of Jesus Christ. In preaching we do not
merely *learn about* Christ; we *meet* Christ. And in meeting Christ as "thou," we
are opened for the continuing transformation of the deepest affectional structures of our identities. The Word of God, read and proclaimed through the
power of the Holy Spirit, brings us into communion with the incarnate Word
who, over the course of our lifetimes, restores God's image in us.

We meet Christ for a redemptive encounter in part when we are made able
to see Christ present in other people and are attuned to the continuing creative work of the Logos sustaining the world, but our meeting of Christ goes
far beyond this basic attunement to Christ's presence in the creation. Preaching opens us for a redemptive, affection-forming encounter with Christ that
is mystical and mysterious. Christ is present in the power of the Holy Spirit,
here in this service of worship where two or three are gathered. Christ is present in the power of the Holy Spirit, *now* in these words that are spoken. In an
almost sacramental way, the words formed in the material working of lungs,

lips, tongue, and ears serve as signs of an inward, spiritual grace that lifts us up into the presence of God and transforms us inwardly so that we relate to all things "here below" as creatures who belong to God. In ways that we cannot fully explain, but sense in the very depths of our being, Christ comes to dwell within us. In this encounter with the Word of God read and proclaimed, the Holy Spirit assures us not simply that there is a God "out there in the darkness and void of human life," but also that our lives are lived out within and made meaningful by a relationship with this God. Niebuhr explains that "what this means for us cannot be expressed in the impersonal way of creeds or other propositions but only in the responsive acts of a personal character. We acknowledge revelation by no third-person proposition, such as that there is a God, but only in the direct confession of the heart, 'Thou art my God.'"[6]

Christ becomes present to us in preaching through the work of what Garrett Green calls the "faithful imagination." In his work *Imagining God: Theology and the Religious Imagination*, Green explains that "imagination re-presents what is absent; it makes present through images what is inaccessible to direct experience."[7] Christ, who is absent from us and seated at the right hand of God the Father, may become present to us again, may be "re-presented," through the metaphors, symbols, and narratives given in Scripture for the faithful working of our religious imagination. We are accustomed to thinking of the imagination as a tool for generating fiction, but Green proposes that the imagination may make accessible for us not only that which is "imaginary," but also that which is real but difficult to grasp. The Christian religious imagination makes use of the metaphors, symbols, images, and narratives of Scripture to organize our experience of the world properly. Green maintains that we ought to "regard the imagination as . . . the ability of human beings to recognize in accessible exemplars the constitutive organizing patterns of other, less accessible and more complex objects of cognition."[8] When we say that Christ becomes present to us for an affection-forming, redemptive encounter through the religious imagination, we do not mean that we merely conjure up an imaginary encounter with Christ the way a child conjures up an imaginary encounter with Santa Claus. Rather, we mean that Christ, who is really, objectively present to us in the power of the Holy Spirit, becomes known and accessible to us when our faithful religious imagination is lifted into the world of biblical metaphors, symbols, and narratives. When Christ becomes present through preaching, we are transformed because in Christ our faithful religious imaginations allow us to see "the ultimate 'shape,' the organizing pattern, of reality itself, thereby illumining the meaning and value of human life."[9] Our imaginative encounter with the metaphors, symbols, and narratives of Scripture through preaching provides the "normative paradigm" for understanding properly God and the world around us.[10] Through faithful preaching, Scripture becomes, to borrow an image from Calvin, the indispensable pair of spectacles that "[gather] up the otherwise confused knowledge of God in our minds, [disperse] our dullness, clearly showing us the true God."[11]

The affection-forming power of Christ comes to us here and now in the play of biblical metaphor, symbol, and narrative on the faithful religious imagination, and this means that preaching must be as evocative as it is didactic. We often think of sermons as providing information or exhorting us to Christian living, and sermons do these things. The church has always valued preaching as part of the teaching office. But the educative and hortatory functions of preaching occur within the affection-forming liturgical role played by the sermon. The sermon is not a brief break from the service of worship that focuses on teaching; it is not a short lecture. It is, instead, teaching that is woven into a service that offers praise and thanksgiving to God. The entire service of worship invites us to come intentionally into the presence of God so that we may offer God our worship and be opened, through that worship, to the person-forming power of God's presence. The sermon too invites and escorts us into the presence of God, who cannot ultimately be named or exhaustively explained, but can be approached only by way of broken and approximate language that gestures in the right direction. Metaphors and images that leave room for the work of the religious imagination provide language that is appropriately humble, that does not pretend to name God univocally or to explain God without remainder.

There is a complex relationship between language, the religious imagination, and the religious affections, and our understanding of preaching can be deepened by attending to it.[12] Metaphor, symbol, and narrative offer modes of discourse the meaning of which cannot be exhausted by translating them into more abstract, literal, or propositional forms of speech. We may be able to translate some of the basic meaning of a metaphor or symbol into a more literal, propositional mode of communication, but the full, exhaustive meaning of that symbol or metaphor ultimately eludes such translation. Something gets lost in the translation. Important dimensions of meaning that work on the religious imagination and affections are lost when we move from symbol, metaphor, and narrative to abstract concept or literal proposition. Preaching does involve the use and explication of abstract concepts and does indeed expound upon the propositions to which we assent as people of faith, but these concepts and propositions are never the whole of preaching. The symbols, metaphors, and narratives from which these concepts and propositions derive and to which they point always have a "surplus of meaning" that is more evocative than denotative, more suggestive than exhaustive.[13] Our encounter with these metaphors, symbols, and narratives is often more intuitive and poetic than syllogistic and prosaic. When we hear Scripture speak of God as "the rock of our salvation," "the Lion of the tribe of Judah," and "our Father in heaven," our religious imagination is piqued and energized in a way that reinterprets our present experience (Ps. 95:1; Rev. 5:5; Matt. 6:9). While important theological propositions are surely embedded in such metaphors and symbols and will often naturally emerge in preaching, such propositions are always in service of the powerful work of the primary symbols and metaphors upon the faithful religious imagination and religious affections. Preaching honors this "surplus of meaning" by moving us intentionally into the world of biblical metaphor, symbol, and narrative, trusting that in this world we meet Christ afresh in a participatory, affection-forming way through the power of the faithful religious imagination.

Scripture provides the preacher with a rich stock of metaphors, symbols, and narratives that can be extended creatively as we interpret our own lives in the present, but it also provides a model of language that opens a wide range of imaginative possibilities for the preacher. In other words, we are not confined to repeating and reworking biblical metaphors, symbols, and narratives. We may also draw on our own experience and on the model of language provided by the Bible in order to generate new metaphors, symbols, and narratives that nonetheless remain faithful to God's self-revelation in Scripture. When Gerard Manley Hopkins says that the grandeur of God "will flame out, like shining from shook foil," he moves beyond biblical images of God, but does so in a way that both opens us to a new perspective on the presence of God in the world and grounds us in the fundamental truths about God conveyed in Scripture.[14] Good poetry and literature enliven our imaginations and affections and provide us with fresh perspectives on the work of God in the world. In his *Preaching*, Fred Craddock argues that "reading good literature enlarges one's capacities as a creative human being and has a cumulative effect on one's vocabulary, use of language, and powers of imagination."[15] Craddock insists that the reason for such reading is not to plunder literature for sermon illustrations, but to hone one's own skills in using language to invite the people of God into a deeper awareness of the meaning of Scripture and of the continuing work of God in their midst.

Much of the power of metaphor, symbol, and narrative resides in their special capacity to work on the total structures of the human heart, especially the religious affections. The metaphors, symbols, and narratives of Scripture made available through the regular proclamation of the Word in public worship engage the totality of who we are; they organize our understanding of the world and locate our particular experiences within the framework of God's broader activity and purposes, and in so doing they simultaneously evoke deep and immediate affective responses in us. They touch the nerve of desire and dependence that sensitizes us to our place in the world, and their power and meaning radiates out to transform our religious affections. When preaching conducts congregants into the rich world of biblical metaphor, symbol, and narrative and allows them to linger imaginatively in this inexhaustible world of meaning, it functions as a means of grace for the cultivation of appropriate religious affections.

When we hear from the pulpit that "the Lord is my shepherd" who "makes me lie down in green pastures" and who "leads me beside still waters" and when we hear that this shepherd will guide us safely "through the darkest valley" to dine at "a table . . . in the presence of my enemies" where our "cup overflows," we are not merely receiving information for our cool powers of ratiocination. These words of Psalm 23 move us across the terrain of the ancient Near East and draw us into the rich, imaginative world of its metaphor and symbols; when this world is explored in sermons that honor and extend its metaphoric and symbolic nature, we experience the power of revelatory truth to express, evoke, shape, direct, sustain, and order properly our religious affections. When with the psalmist the sermon takes us into the valley of the shadow of death and enables us to find that valley in our own day, we experience the hope that the psalmist experienced, the sense of direction provided by the guidance of the good shepherd, the senses of rightness and well-being that accompany rest in green pastures and beside still waters, and the delight and gratitude that spill out from our cup at God's table.

When preaching draws the faithful imagination of the people of God into the normative world of biblical metaphor, symbol, and narrative, it cultivates in them well-ordered religious affections grounded in a proper understanding of God and the world. Biblical metaphors, symbols, and narratives are deeply connected with truth, including the creedal and confessional affirmations of the church. Religious imagination and doctrine are not antithetical to one another, but are mutually reinforcing. Christian preaching honors not only the role that biblical metaphor, symbol, and narrative play in cultivating a faithful Christian imagination, but also the creedal, confessional, and doctrinal truths of the church that naturally emerge from, reflect, and anchor the church's ongoing imaginative engagement with these metaphors, symbols, and narratives. Preaching does, indeed, teach the creedal, confessional, and doctrinal truths of the church, confident that such teaching does not supplant the cultivation of the faithful Christian imagination and religious affections but rather nurtures, sustains, and enriches them. Thus preaching is always also the teaching office of the church. Preaching gathers up the truths of the church as a confessional community and enlists them in service of a faithful affection-forming, imaginative engagement with the God who meets us afresh in Jesus Christ through the power of the Holy Spirit.

This relationship between doctrinal truth and the religious imagination is crucial for the proper formation of the religious affections because the faith that we confess, that we seek to articulate through creeds and confessions, includes specific beliefs and cognitive content that shape our religious affections. When we affirm that the church is a confessional community, we indicate that it is a community of belief, and that the specific content of its beliefs is inextricably bound up with the affectional lives of its members. Preaching works because of the intricate interplay of our affectional, cognitive, and volitional capacities. When we address the minds of the congregation, providing them with "something to think about," we are also addressing their hearts. When we bear witness to the grace and majesty of God unfolding in the world, we open ourselves for a redemptive encounter with Christ, who reshapes and illuminates the total structure of our identities, including our minds, hearts, and wills.

Sermons that invite our faithful imaginations to linger in the metaphors, symbols, and narratives of Scripture participate in our illumination. They make Christ present to us in a way that allows us to see the true meaning and value of our lives, but they also participate in our purification. When the narrative of Scripture is evocatively explored in sermons, we find our individual and community life stories woven into the biblical narrative. The biblical narrative acts as the norm against which our own narratives are judged. Preaching, then, becomes an act of pastoral care that relates the life of the community to the revelation of God available to us in Scripture.

But that act of pastoral care is not always comfortable or comforting, for sometimes it calls into question the expectations of our contemporary life. Purification is that process through which we identify and let go of our idols, and preaching serves an important purifying function when it helps us to see clearly and to question deeply what we truly value. Preaching participates in our purification by pushing back against our insistence on meeting the Bible on our terms and against our temptation to assume that our context is the normative one and that the Bible must be made relevant to it. Such an attitude takes certain assumptions of the modern world as unchangeably given, then goes to the Bible seeking to extract from it insights and truths that fit with those assumptions. We assume a culture of consumerism, for example, and then go to Scripture seeking advice about how to be good and responsible consumers, expecting the Bible to offer us advice about how to balance our spending priorities so that we may dress fashionably and still give adequately to the poor. We assume a culture of nationalism and then go to Scripture seeking validation of our national policies. We assume a culture of individualism and then go to Scripture seeking a model of salvation that provides us with everlasting amusement.

The proper question is not how the Bible might be made relevant to our lives, but whether our lives and values might not have become irrelevant to the disruptively redemptive, liberating truth of the gospel. Good preaching can help us to recognize that God's self-revelation in Scripture provides the norm for our lives and values, rather than assuming that our lives and values provide the norm against which biblical relevance is measured. Preaching can help us to identify with the brokenness of the people of God in Scripture and to see, through their stories, our own brokenness. Preaching is purifying when it helps us to reweave the limited, fragmented story of our lives into the grand, normative narrative of Scripture.

PREACHING AND ANTICIPATORY PARTICIPATION IN THE REIGN OF GOD

When preaching participates in the reordering of our religious affections by awakening our religious imaginations so that we can come into a participatory knowing of God's self-disclosure in Scripture, it sheds the light of God's grace on our lives, inviting us into participation in the coming reign of God and into a prophetic critique of the broken structures of our world. So far, we have argued that preaching participates in the restoration of our religious affections and that it does so through an engagement with the faithful religious imagination. In this section, we explore how preaching—and indeed the entire service of the Word—calls for a response in the form of new life patterns that anticipate the fullness of the reign of God. Sermons describe that coming reign of God with such richness and depth that we begin to lean into the reality of God's reign even now. When enlivened by the Holy Spirit, sermons partly effect the new life patterns for which they call.

Jesus' sermons serve an important illuminating function as they draw our present lives into the coming reign of God. He often taught in parables that offered rich images to describe what the reign of God is like. Jesus' own mode of preaching was evocative, provocative, and descriptive. Jesus simply described what the reign of God looked like, and those descriptions were so powerful that they pulled his listeners into a deep knowledge of the ways of God, a knowledge that actually participated in the kingdom he described. He taught that God is like a woman who searches for a single lost coin, and this description calls us into the reign of God as a place where no one is insignificant or unworthy of God's searching, redeeming attention (Luke 15:8–10). Jesus proclaimed that the reign of God is like finding a treasure hidden in a field and selling everything that you own to acquire that field (Matt. 13:44). In doing so, Jesus invites us to see that the world as God would have it is so overwhelmingly attractive that we will reorder our whole lives to pursue our desire for it. Jesus preached that God is like a vineyard owner who pays workers what they need, regardless of what they have earned, and this description invites us into a kingdom where everyone will have work and daily bread (Matt. 20:1–16).

We would do well to model our own sermons on Jesus' example. His parables are rich with the images of everyday life, and he uses those familiar images as a window to the strange and beautiful world of God's coming reign. He uses those images to play on our imaginations, to cultivate our religious affections, and to illuminate the ways that our present lives participate already in the coming reign of God. We come to participate in it even now as we lean into God's promises. When our own sermons follow Jesus' example, they are richly descriptive, drawing on the familiar to reveal the mysterious. They illumine and celebrate the presence of God working in our midst even now. The Holy Spirit uses the "moving power of living speech" in sermons to offer us a "foretaste of glory divine."[16]

Jesus' parables also served an important purifying function. He drew on familiar images to illuminate a glorious future, but he often used those very images in a way that upset the expectations of his listeners. His sermons were not only evocative; they were also provocative. He compared the kingdom of God to leaven that a woman puts into three measures of flour (Matt. 13:33). Gordon Lathrop points out that leaven is a symbol of unholiness for Jesus' listeners.[17] Jesus, then, uses the familiar image and utterly reverses its meaning. Now the presence of the profane in the midst of the holy symbolizes God's inclusive love for all humanity, Jew and Gentile alike. When Jesus likens God to a generous vineyard owner, he implicitly calls into question the social structures that leave laborers without sufficient work to provide for their material needs. His vision of God's glorious future sheds light on the inglorious present. His invitation to participate in the justice and hospitality of the coming reign of God calls attention to the injustice and inhospitality of the present order. His prayer that God's will be done on earth as it is in heaven, highlights the great distance between the goodness for which God made us and the fragmentation we have made for ourselves.

When our own sermons offer rich descriptions of the peace, justice, hospitality, and delight of God's coming reign, they also inevitably call attention to the conflict, unfairness, and lack of mutuality and interdependence that characterize our present situation. Sermons that invite us into God's future also invite us to critique our present and to respond to the Word of God read and proclaimed with action that grows out of gratitude for all that God has provided us. Sermons that awaken in us participatory knowledge of God's coming reign prompt us to take action in the present that anticipates that coming reign. For this reason, preaching serves an important ethical function. In preaching, the doxological and the moral intersect. As sermons call us to worship God—to offer praise and thanksgiving to God—they also call us into good works consonant with our confession of faith. Sermons call us into lives of grateful service (*lex bene operandi*) that reflect what we believe (*lex credendi*) and how we worship (*lex orandi*).

As they constantly move us between purification and illumination, sermons reorient all of our religious affections. We lean with hope into God's future, and that hope is given a distinctively Christian shape by our participatory knowledge of the nature of God's reign. We glimpse a vision of God's work in the world, and our sense of direction is evoked and ordered so that we move purposively into action that accords with God's will. We anticipate the mutuality and interdependence of all things and seek relationships that reflect that goodness even now. As we acknowledge that God initiates and completes the final restoration of all things, we also acknowledge that our participation in that future depends on God's grace, not on our merit, and we are grateful. The image of all things existing in harmony evokes delight in us. Preaching participates in the restoration of all our religious affections because it calls us by way of the religious imagination into participatory knowledge of God's coming reign.

Throughout this chapter we have explored the ways in which remembering and retelling the sacred stories of Scripture as we read and proclaim the Word of God participates in the reorientation of our religious affections. We have focused on the ways in which sustained exposure to the proclamation of the Word of God repatterns our affectional identities. First, we noted that preaching reorders particular religious affections by helping us to appropriate particular biblical narratives in which those affections are highlighted. Preaching, moreover, brings intelligibility to our lives by locating our individual narratives within the broader context of God's work in the world and by enabling us to remember what we would prefer to forget. Second, we explored the ways in which preaching works through the religious imagination to present Christ afresh in our time and to open us to the redemptive power of the incarnation. In doing so it purifies us by reworking and reweaving the limited, fragmented story of our lives into the grand, normative narrative of Scripture. Finally, preaching illuminates us by inviting us to participate proleptically in the coming reign of God, and it purifies us because that eschatological hope and the vision of God's kingdom offer a prophetic critique of the brokenness and injustice that prevail in the present world.

9

Sacraments

As they were going along the road, they came to some water; and the eunuch said, "Look, here is water! What is to prevent me from being baptized?" He commanded the chariot to stop, and both of them, Philip and the eunuch, went down into the water, and Philip baptized him. (Acts 8:36–38)

When [Jesus] was at the table with them, he took bread, blessed and broke it, and gave it to them. Then their eyes were opened, and they recognized him. (Luke 24:30–31)

Words alone are never enough in the Christian faith. Whether it is Philip's proclamation of the gospel to the Ethiopian eunuch in Acts or Jesus' explanation of the Scriptures to two disciples on the road to Emmaus, the faith proclaimed in words is completed and sealed with a sacramental act. For the Ethiopian eunuch, the gift of faith inevitably led him into the waters of baptism. For the two disciples on the road to Emmaus, the breaking and blessing of bread at the hands of Jesus finally allowed them to recognize him and realize that he was the fulfillment of the very Scriptures he had earlier been explaining. Water, bread, and wine, no less than the proclaimed Word, make Christ available to people of faith. In these material substances that are basic to human life, we meet God. In fact, our faith, proclaimed and received in words, is incomplete until it is sealed to us in sacramental signs in which material elements—water, bread, and wine—are indispensable. Word and sacrament belong together as means of grace in Christian faith and worship.

The use of water, bread, and wine in the sacramental life of the church points back to two important theological affirmations: the goodness of the material order in which human life is embedded and the centrality of the incarnation in the Christian faith. In the creation stories of Genesis, after creating the material world, God declares that it is good. It is good in all of its physicality. We hear in these same stories that "the LORD God formed man from the dust of the ground, and breathed into his nostrils the breath of life; and the man became a living being. And the LORD God planted a garden in Eden, in the east; and there he put the man whom he had formed" (Gen. 2:7–8). Human beings come from the dust of the earth; we are formed by God from the dirt and placed by God in a garden where the very dirt from which we were formed continues to provide for our nourishment and flourishing. God intended human existence to be an embodied existence, and this is in fundamental continuity with the material nature of the broader, good creation. Because the creation is good, because it embodies the very speech of God, the particular creatures included within it mediate God's presence to us. Sacraments arise out of and reflect the goodness of the whole created order, including the goodness of our embodiment within this order. Embodied beings need embodied means of grace. The capacity of water, bread, and wine to serve as vehicles of divine grace that lift us as embodied beings into the presence of spiritual grace is grounded in God's prior declaration that the whole of the material world is good and expressive of God's sovereign purposes.

The sacraments also point to a second important theological affirmation, the centrality of the incarnation in the Christian faith. God not only created us for embodiment but also redeems us through embodiment. In the incarnation God becomes human, becomes embodied, for our redemption. In the incarnation God enters our fragmentation, becoming broken for us, so that we might be restored to unity and harmony. The unity of God and humanity in Jesus Christ provides our desire and sense of dependence with a new object and orientation. The incarnation mediates the purifying and illuminating grace of God to us through the material of Christ's humanity as it draws us toward the attracting, disrupting, and transforming beauty of Christ. The sacraments participate in this incarnational mediation of the grace of God. Through them, God continues to make use of the good creation to draw us in, disrupt our idolatries, and transform our affectional lives.

While the whole of creation mediates the presence of God to us, the Christian church has assigned a special place to water, bread, and wine in its public worship. Across the ages, Christians have acknowledged that in the sacramental use of water, bread, and wine in public Christian worship, we meet God in a unique and especially concentrated way.[1] In baptism and the Lord's Supper, water, bread, and wine are joined to the power of the Holy Spirit and become, by this union, special "ordinances" of God that mediate God's purifying and illuminating grace to worshipers. The material signs of water, bread, and wine are taken up by the Holy Spirit, who, through their sacramental use, "seals" us in faith. According to Calvin, sacraments "are like seals of the good will that [God] feels toward us, which by attesting that good will to us, sustain, nourish, confirm, and increase our faith."[2] Sacraments are both "signs and seals" of the promise and grace of God. While various strands of the Christian tradition have articulated differently the precise relationship between the material sign (i.e., water, bread, and wine) and the seal (i.e., the power and grace of God at work in the sacraments), all Christians have affirmed that the material signs and God's sealing activity must not—indeed cannot—be separated from each other. The material signs, without the activity and grace of God sealing them to our hearts in worship, are not sacraments; and the sealing activity whereby the Holy Spirit nourishes, cultivates, and strengthens our faith, without the presence and use of the material signs of water, bread, and wine, is not a sacrament either. Sacraments are sacraments by virtue of the inseparable union of the sign and seal.

As signs and seals, sacraments mediate the grace of God that purifies and illuminates our affectional lives as we worship, cultivating, restoring, and ordering our religious affections in a theocentric way. When Calvin argued that the sacraments are made effective through the presence and power of the Holy Spirit, he drew attention especially to the way that through the power of the Holy Spirit "our hearts are penetrated and affections moved and our souls opened for the sacraments to enter in."[3] In the sacraments the Holy Spirit penetrates our hearts and moves our affections. In sealing the material signs of water, bread, and wine to us in worship, the Holy Spirit reorders the sense of dependence and the pattern of desire that run through and bind together our religious affections and identities. Along the way, the sacraments also cultivate particular religious affections.

The power of the sacraments to cultivate and shape our religious affections is inseparably connected to the materiality of the signs of water, bread, and wine. Earlier, we discussed how our religious affections are object-oriented. We always experience a religious affection in relation to a created object that calls that affection forth in us. We never feel a generic sense of awe, but only awe evoked, sustained, and occasioned by the great sequoia, for example. The object-oriented nature of the affections partly accounts for the power of water, bread, and wine to cultivate and transform our affectional lives. Because we are embodied beings, our religious affections are always cultivated and occasioned by our encounter with the material world of our senses. In the sacraments, God works the mystery of grace in a manner consistent with and affirmative of our embodiment as affectional beings. Water, bread, and wine are the created, material objects that occasion the cultivation and reshaping of our religious affections. They are the material means whereby we are raised into the presence of God's transforming grace. Without these material signs in the sacraments, our religious affections have no object to call them forth and into the presence of God's gracious, sealing work.

Just as the signs and seal of the sacraments cannot be separated from each other, neither can the power of the sacraments be separated from the institutional church as the body of Christ. Just as God's grace is mediated through our embodied nature, so too is it mediated through our social nature. An essentially embodied and social self needs the essentially material and communal means of grace that the sacraments provide. God calls the church into existence and sustains its covenantal life through the Holy Spirit, who dwells in its midst. The Holy Spirit who seals our faith in the sacraments is the same Holy Spirit who dwells within the covenant community, nurturing individual faith and shaping the religious affections of individuals through its common life and worship. The sacraments are God's gift to the church and only through the church to individuals. The Holy Spirit as the agent of power in the sacraments and source of ecclesial life secures the inseparability of the sacraments and the institutional church. Because the sacraments are given to the church, not to private individuals, the public worship life of the church is the appropriate context for their celebration. The communal life of the church is an essential dimension of the power of the sacraments. When an infant is baptized into the church, baptismal vows are spoken not only by the parents but by the congregation as well, and when we celebrate the Lord's Supper, we do so as a shared meal, a meal of fellowship. It is in the public, communal context of worship that the sacraments work to cultivate and transform our religious affections.

The social dimension of the sacraments intersects the church's identity as a community of memory and hope. In the celebration of the Lord's Supper, for example, we remember that on the night in which our Lord was betrayed he shared a meal of bread and wine with his disciples. As we likewise share the bread and cup, we are invited into anticipatory participation in the heavenly banquet, and our community is called to embody even now the hospitality and delight that will be made complete only in God's time. In baptism we remember and participate in the dying and rising of Christ, and we are joined to and hope for the resurrection life of the eschatological community. The common meal and sacred washing connect us to memories of all the common meals of Scripture and to all of God's mighty works involving water. The sacraments are enmeshed in the sacred narratives that give the community its identity. They enact bodily central narratives of the faith. But likewise, the sacramental meal and bath grant us a vision of God's coming reign. Through them we find ourselves rooted in salvation history and leaning into God's future. The sacraments draw our desire toward God, whose goodness we can "taste and see" (Ps. 34:8), and they secure our sense of dependence on God, who claims and seals us in faith. Through the sacraments we are drawn toward God, and our identities are reshaped in the embodied interplay of memory and hope as our affections are drawn toward this new object, the superlatively beautiful presence of God. We devote the remainder of this chapter to an exploration of how baptism and the Lord's Supper act as means of grace that reorder particular religious affections.

BAPTISM

Baptism is the sacrament that initiates us into the Christian community; it is a "divine birth" through which we are marked as members of the body of Christ.[4] Already in the New Testament we are commanded to make new disciples, baptizing them in the name of the Father, Son, and Holy Spirit. The heart of the rite is simply the washing of a candidate in water while the name of the Holy Trinity is pronounced. There are, of course, disputes about this simple form at the heart of the rite. Who is eligible for baptism, professing believers alone or also their children? What form ought the washing to take, full immersion, pouring, or sprinkling? But the simple act of baptizing with water in the name of the triune God has marked the beginning of the life of faith since the earliest days of the Christian church.[5] The implicit themes of this simple sacramental act have been made explicit in the expanded rite that surrounds baptism. Candidates for baptism are presented by representatives of the congregation; they or their sponsors renounce the power of evil and affirm their faith, often in creedal form; a prayer of thanksgiving is offered over the water; the candidate is then baptized, blessed, and welcomed to the life of the church.

In this section we explore three theological themes, noting how this sacrament of new birth that marks us as members of the body of Christ also forms particular religious affections. First, we explore the root metaphor of baptism, dying and rising with Christ, and how it is linked to the purification and illumination of our religious affections, especially contrition and hope. Second, we highlight how baptism reorients our sense of dependence and thereby reshapes our religious affections, especially gratitude and humility. Finally, we discuss the covenantal and communal context of baptism in relation to the religious affections, especially our sense of mutuality and interdependence and our sense of obligation.

Dying and Rising in Christ: Contrition and Hope

Baptism initiates us into a life of dying and rising with Christ. In Romans, Paul asks, "Do you not know that all of us who have been baptized into Christ Jesus were baptized into his death? Therefore we have been buried with him by baptism into death, so that, just as Christ was raised from the dead by the glory of the Father, so we too might walk in newness of life" (Rom. 6:2–4). As we descend into the waters of baptism, our sinful selves descend into the tomb with Christ. As we rise from those waters, we emerge into resurrection life, a life in which the Holy Spirit brings order, purpose, and harmony out of the chaotic, feckless fragmentation of our sin. We are baptized once, perhaps in a moment of life before we can even remember, but that singular, unrepeatable act seals us in a life of faith in which we are constantly dying and rising with Christ. We are initiated into a Christian life that daily repeats the pattern of mortification and renewal, that daily calls us to put off the brokenness of sin and to rise up in the power of the Holy Spirit to a life of beauty.

The baptized life of mortification and renewal signals our constant need of purification and illumination. To die in Christ is to put away our idolatrous tendency to invest the finite creation with infinite significance. Our misdirected desire and disoriented sense of dependence seek in creation the meaning, purpose, and security that only God can provide. In our self-negation, we measure our value and worth by the products that we can consume and, in so doing, make idols of those products. Or else, in our prideful self-deification, we measure the value and worth of all other things according to how well they serve our self-interest and, in so doing, we make idols of ourselves. But the mortification of baptismal life prompts purification as it redirects us toward God as the proper object of our longing and as the one on whom we ultimately depend. The act of washing in baptism powerfully symbolizes this purification; as the water cleanses us bodily, it also initiates us into a life in which our sinful idolatry can be washed away. Baptized life invites us to put away our idols as we are purified by the Holy Spirit. At the same time, to rise in Christ is to be illuminated, to discover the creation as icon, as a window to the beauty and glory of God. As we give up our false valuation of other creatures, we are enabled to value them both for their intrinsic worth and as those who may mediate the presence of God to us. The baptized life of mortification and renewal is a life in which we are always being purified and always being illuminated, a life in which we are always exchanging idols for icons.

Because baptism involves identification with Christ, it initiates us into the attracting, disturbing, and transforming beauty of his life. Baptism attracts us to Christ; it beckons us into a way of living that embodies his beauty. But the quality of that attractive beauty is such that it involves dying to the false beauties offered by consumerism, amusement, and nationalism. Divine beauty disrupts these idols. Baptized living in the beauty of Christ also involves rising with Christ in a way that transforms us and how we engage our world. Baptized life is life in which we actively work for the beautification of the world; we work to bring harmony in the midst of fragmentation by resisting the urge to transform all creatures into commodities, seeking conditions of economic justice that enable all people to flourish, celebrating sexual intimacy in lifelong covenantal relationships that honor and enhance the well-being of our beloved, and overcoming political conflict and the divisiveness of racism with acts of reconciliation grounded in justice. This disruptive and transforming engagement with the world grows out of our attraction to and identification with the life, death, and resurrection of Christ. When we are drawn into the attracting, disrupting, and transforming beauty of Christ through baptism, such beauty slowly but certainly, over the course of a lifetime, overcomes the fragmentation and distortion of the deepest affectional structures of our being.

The mortification and purification of baptism express, shape, and sustain the religious affection of contrition. In the baptismal liturgy we renounce "all evil, and powers in the world which defy God's righteousness and love" and "the ways of sin that separate [us] from the love of God."[6] Implicit in our renunciation of sin is the recognition that we have defied God's righteousness, that we have been complicit in evil and the powers of the world that perpetuate injustice and alienation between us, other creatures, and God. In speaking forth our repudiation of the fragmentation in which our lives are entangled, we are expressing our sorrow for having diminished the lives of others as well as our own lives. Speaking the renunciations aloud—or having them spoken on our behalf in the case of infant baptism—is crucial because our expressed contrition needs to be witnessed by a community of faith that receives us through baptism and that promises to sustain us in our baptismal life of mortification and renewal.

The sacrament of baptism also shapes our contrition because it gives specific, Christian theological content to our interpretation of the brokenness of our lives. We may sense vaguely that our lives are fragmented, but the Christian faith shapes our ability to interpret that brokenness in terms of idolatry, self-deification, and self-negation. The baptismal liturgy, rooted in the metaphor of dying and rising, further suggests that what is wrong with us penetrates beneath the surface level of individual bad actions on our part to the original fragmentation that funds those broken acts. It is not simply our individual transgressions that are put to death; our very selves, the very heart of who we are, must be given up and given over to Christ. Baptism shapes contrition both because it names our brokenness as idolatry and because it reveals the full scope and depth of our brokenness.

Finally, the sacrament of baptism sustains our contrition because we are baptized into a covenantal community of faith. As members of that community we become witnesses and sponsors as others make their baptismal renunciations, expressing their contrition. We "promise to guide and nurture [them] . . . by word and deed, with love and prayer, encouraging them to know and follow Christ and to be faithful members of his church."[7] The vocation of our own dying and rising encompasses guiding and nurturing the dying and rising of others. As we witness and sponsor others who are baptized, our own sense of contrition is renewed. The baptized life of mortification and renewal also sustains the religious affection of contrition, because we are baptized into a community that remembers its dying in Christ every week as we publicly confess our sins. The contrition that we express in our baptismal renunciations and that is shaped by the mortification of the self included in that baptism is sustained through our participation in a community of the baptized that regularly receives new members and that publicly confesses its fragmentation.

The renewal and illumination of baptism direct, evoke, and order the religious affection of hope. Baptism directs the religious affection of hope toward its proper object, God, who is the source of all goodness and the ground of all hope. If our dying in Christ prompts contrition, then rising in Christ is cause for hope, and the prayer of thanksgiving offered over the water evokes such hope. As the prayer evokes memories of God's great acts involving water—the Spirit of God hovering over the waters at creation, the destructive waters of the flood, the parting of the Red Sea—it also points us with hope to the ways in which God will use these waters of baptism to bring forth new possibilities and new life. We pray that God will "move over this water that it may be a fountain of deliverance and rebirth. . . . [that God will] raise . . . to new life [all who are cleansed by it], and graft them to the body of Christ."[8] We pray that God will renew us in this life and seal us for life everlasting. We invest the work of God in the waters of baptism with great hope, hope that we will rise with Christ to renew and restore the world now and hope that we will rise with Christ when God's reign is fully realized. Such hope is grounded in the work of the Holy Spirit in baptism. We are marked as members of the body of Christ, indwelt and illuminated by the Holy Spirit that we may see the presence of God at work in the world now and ultimately witness God's final restoration of all things.

Baptism also participates in the ordering of hope in relation to the other religious affections. Earlier we noted that in the constellation of well-ordered religious affections, contrition and hope emerge simultaneously out of the humility and gratitude prompted by the religious affection of awe. Standing in awe before the face of God calls us to be humble about our place in God's world and grateful for the goodness and beauty of the lives that God has given us. When we acknowledge that awe calls for humility and gratitude, we become aware that we have failed to respond in these ways, and we experience contrition. But that contrition is always accompanied in the Christian life by a sense of hope, a sense that we are called to participate in God's work of expanding and developing the goodness of the creation. Baptism participates in the ordering of hope in its relationship to humility, gratitude, and especially contrition precisely by evoking it in a rite that moves us from the contrition implicit in the renunciations, through the thanksgiving over the waters, into the hope of life everlasting.

Because we are baptized into a life of mortification and renewal, of purification and illumination, hope is always deeply connected to contrition. The inseparability of purification and illumination, of contrition and hope, means that our contrition never becomes despair and our hope never becomes naive optimism. Baptism seals us in a faith that is played out over the course of a lifetime as we learn to destroy idols and to seek out icons on a daily basis. The hope that is cultivated through this life of mortification and renewal radiates across the full spectrum of the religious affections as each one is purified and illuminated. The eschatological renewal of all things for which we hope, for example, heightens our sense of obligation to work in ways that extend the ground of hope to others. The hope that emerges from baptized living permeates our sense of mutuality and interdependence because that which is hoped for is found in our midst even now as we realize relationships of equality and hospitality. The baptismal liturgy itself reflects this as the congregation vows to take on obligations to its new members and as new members are blessed with the peace of Christ that promises a new life of gracious acceptance for all. The sacrament of baptism, then, cultivates contrition and hope as it prompts our purification and illumination and as it engrafts us into the attracting, disrupting, and transforming beauty of Christ.

Baptism and Our Sense of Dependence: Gratitude and Humility

No moment in the life of faith bears witness more fully to our utter dependence on God than the moment of baptism. Whether the one being baptized is an infant or adult, baptism is something *received*, something done *to us* and *for us* by God through the ministry of the church.[9] In baptism we passively receive the grace of God. In baptism we sense acutely that through the application of water, God is initiating a new relationship with us. Baptism is thus not first and foremost something that we do, something that we initiate; it is not primarily a ritual in which we act or give testimony to our faith, though in time these may follow as response. Rather, God acts in baptism to initiate a new relationship with us; in baptism God claims us as children of the covenant and in claiming us inducts us into the covenant community where we will be nurtured in faith through the life and worship of the church. The profession of faith included in the baptismal liturgy is not so much a declaration of our faith as it is a joyful acknowledgment of the faith that has first claimed us. In baptism we are passive; we receive. Baptism points to our utter dependence on God

Baptized life takes the moment of baptism, the moment in which we passively receive divine grace, as paradigmatic of the Christian life. To be baptized is to enter the Christian life with its constant, pervasive attunement to our continuing utter dependence on God. In pointing to our continued utter dependence on God, baptism erodes the foundations of our idolatries, in which we seek ultimate security from the finite objects of our world. As broken and fragmented creatures, we are prone to misidentify the basis of our dependence and to seek security from other creatures, which leads us into lives of anxiety and frustration when creatures are ultimately unable to provide us with the meaning and security we seek. But our baptism stands in prophetic criticism over this anxious searching for security. Baptized living calls us constantly to turn again to God as the one to whom all of our relative dependencies point and as the one on whom we are ultimately dependent. Just as in baptism we passively receive God's active claim on our lives, so in baptized living we affirm and celebrate our continuing dependence on God's goodness. Paradoxically, this prophetic moment of baptism becomes the liberating moment that sets us free to be finite, dependent creatures and to accept this finitude and dependence as gifts from God.

The baptismal reorientation of our sense of dependence has consequences for all of our religious affections, but here we focus on gratitude and humility. When we take baptism as paradigmatic for the whole of the Christian life, we are reminded that life comes to us as sheer gift. We receive the good things of this world passively; we do not generate them or earn them; we are not entitled to them. The good things of life come to us as sheer, unmerited grace from the sovereign, loving God upon whom we utterly depend. Baptism opens us to gratitude, to thankfulness to God for the giftedness of all that we are and have. In cultivating gratitude, baptism awakens in us what consumerism had lulled to sleep. Consumerism teaches us to mark our world with price tags and to assign value to other creatures according to the standard of human utility. Other creatures come to us not as gifts but as products purchased with the income we have earned through the labor of our hands. Our baptism shatters the illusion that we make our way in the world solely through our own labor and merit. Baptism attunes us afresh to the fact "that [we] belong—body and soul, in life and in death—not to [ourselves] but to [our] faithful Savior, Jesus Christ."[10] Baptism teaches us to accept our dependence with gratitude and creates in us a spirit of generativity that prompts us to increase and multiply on behalf of others the good gifts of this world. We are enabled to give freely and generously without expecting payment of any kind. We can give freely as we have received freely. The gratitude that baptized life sustains thus begins to open us for self-sacrificial love and genuine delight in the well-being of others. When we experience the world as gift, we no longer need to imagine our fellow creatures simply as competitors in a zero-sum game. Instead, we may expend ourselves on behalf of others, even as God has given so freely to us.

The reorientation of our sense of dependence engendered by baptism also purifies and illumines the religious affection of humility. Humility is that religious affection through which we learn to find our place in God's creation, neither overestimating nor underestimating our significance. Baptism evokes and sustains humility because, on the one hand, we passively accept redemption that we cannot accomplish on our own and, on the other hand, in this passive acceptance we are marked as those whom God cares for, loves, and claims as God's own. We are not of first importance, but neither are we unimportant. The sacrament of baptism that stands at the beginning of the Christian life serves as a paradigm for baptismal living in which we increasingly overcome our tendencies to self-deification and self-negation. Awareness of our utter dependence is, at the same time, awareness that we are not God and that it is good to be what we are, finite creatures of a loving, giving God. Baptism generates awareness that genuine meaning and purpose are found not in the reorientation of all things around ourselves, but in their and our orientation around the purposes of the sovereign God. Likewise, baptismal humility includes the awareness that in baptism we are marked with a new identity, empowered by the Holy Spirit to be new creatures in Christ. Baptism marks the birth of a new self that is worthy of the infinite care and love of God and that is called to a new sense of agency and responsibility as we work toward and lean into God's new creation.

Baptism and the Covenant Community: The Sense of Mutuality and Interdependence and the Sense of Obligation

While baptism is a rite in which God initiates a new relationship with the person being baptized, God's gracious initiative is mediated to us through the covenantal community that is the church. Since we are social beings, God's grace comes to us in a manner that reflects our social natures. Because baptism is initiation into the Christian life, it is simultaneously initiation into the church as the proper context for the nurturance of that life. Accordingly, baptism is never a private rite but always a public one in which the one baptized is surrounded by the covenant community. We witness this communal, covenantal context of baptism when, in the case of infants, promises are spoken on behalf of the infant by parents or sponsors who vow "through prayer and example, to support and encourage [the baptized person] to be a faithful

Christian." Moreover, whether the one baptized is an adult or infant, the con-gregation promises "as members of the church of Jesus Christ, . . . to guide and nurture [the one baptized] by word and deed, with love and prayer, encouraging [this one] to know and follow Christ and to be [a] faithful mem-ber of his church."[11] Baptism is thick with communal obligations and covenan-tal ties; it is precisely through these that God initiates, nurtures, and sustains faith in the one receiving baptism. The shared life of the church becomes the vehicle whereby God cultivates our religious affections and attunes us prop-erly toward God and the world.

The covenantal and communal nature of baptism cultivates two religious affections: the sense of mutuality and interdependence and the sense of obliga-tion. The covenant community into which baptism initiates us is a community whose shared obligations and identity grow out of a renewed sense of mutu-ality and interdependence. It is a community in which our lives as individuals are enriched by participation in the community and contribute to the well-being and flourishing of others within that community. The mutuality and interdependence of the covenant community beckon us toward a new under-standing of the nature of social power that ultimately works to overcome our sinful impulses toward both self-negation and prideful self-deification.

Feminist and other liberation theologians have drawn attention to the fun-damentally different model of social power found at the heart of the gospel. From the perspective of privilege, power is often construed as "power over." Power is thought of as the capacity for control and domination, for managing and coercing other people, sometimes subtly and at other times overtly, to achieve the ends and aims of those who possess power. Social power so con-ceived is a zero-sum game in which there is only a limited amount of it to go around, so that if you have power, I do not. Because power is conceived of as a limited commodity, the goal is to get as much of it as we can and to prevent others from getting as much as they can, so that we can work our will in the world.[12] But the gospel vision of social power expressed in our renewed sense of mutuality and interdependence is radically different. Exercising social power is construed not as exercising "power over" others but instead as working for the empowerment of others. Power is not a limited commodity—a "thing"—to be grasped at in a zero-sum game; instead, power is a relational reality that no single individual possesses, but that can be realized only when it configures communal life in ways that enhance and enable all members of the community to realize their agency and vocation in God's new creation.

Our renewed sense of mutuality and interdependence requires a fundamen-tal reconception of the nature of social power, so that power is construed as a capacity to contribute to the well-being of all by empowering others to become the beings that God has called them to be, enabling them to realize their full identity, agency, and vocation as those claimed by God in baptism. The new vision of social power ingredient in our renewed sense of mutuality and interdependence thus undermines our fallen impulses toward both self-deification and self-negation. In dying to the model of social power as "power over," which funds our fallen drive toward self-deification, we are rising in Christ to a new model of social power, in which we not only contribute to the empowerment of others but are ourselves empowered by others in the covenantal community to become the selves that God calls us to be—selves with a renewed sense of integrity, agency, purpose, and vocation in God's world.

When we lay down our impulse to exercise power as domination and take up a baptismal life of empowering others, we discover the native link between mutuality and interdependence, on the one hand, and a heightened sense of obligation, on the other. We are baptized into a rich nexus of obligations. In the community of the baptized we give up a conception of power in which we work to "get" from others so that they may not "have" and take up, instead, a model of power in which we are embedded in relationships of obligation through which we both give and receive love, care, respect, and hospitality.

THE LORD'S SUPPER

If baptism is the sacrament that initiates us into the Christian life, then the Lord's Supper is the sacrament that sustains us in that life. Just as there are words and material acts at the heart of the baptismal rite—baptizing in the name of the Trinity and washing with water—so also there are words and material acts at the heart of the eucharistic rite—the words of institution and a common meal. The meal begins as we are invited to a common table and continues with a prayer of thanksgiving, a story that recalls to our memories the significance of the meal, and then the sharing of a common loaf of bread and a common cup that anticipate the eschatological banquet. The Lord's Supper is a Eucharist, a meal of thanksgiving for the redemptive life, death, and resurrection of Jesus Christ. It is a meal that calls us to active responses of gratitude that grow out of our passive acceptance of God's grace as it was sealed to us in baptism. Beyond this connection to gratitude, though, the meal is thick with theological meaning, and in this section we develop just two of those themes as they relate to the religious affections. First, we highlight the dynamic of memory and hope present in the Lord's Supper and link it to the religious affections of a sense of direction and delight. Second, we develop the connection between the Lord's Supper and the redirection of our desire, a redirection that opens us to individual, communal, and even cosmic communion that shapes and directs our senses of rightness and well-being.

Memory and Hope:
The Sense of Direction and Delight

The dynamic of memory and hope in the Lord's Supper is embedded in the words of institution and the invitation to the table. We begin the words of institution by directing our memories to the night of Christ's betrayal, recalling how he gave thanks over bread and cup, shared them with his disciples, and exhorted them to remember him. The invitation to the table often includes an eschatological description of a table where people come from every compass point to gather for a common meal and concludes, "Behold, all things are made ready," an allusion to Jesus' parable of the great banquet (Luke 14:17). So, the Lord's Supper points at once back to the ministry of Jesus and forward to the realization of the kingdom that was initiated in that ministry.

Both the remembering and the anticipation call us into an active, participatory knowledge. We do not simply recall facts from the distant past; we remember and retell the stories of our faith in an identity-constituting way. To remember the night on which Christ was betrayed is to participate once again in the central drama of the faith, to be pulled afresh into the foundational story of our identities. To come to the Communion table to partake of a common loaf and cup in hopeful anticipation of the day when people will come from east and west, from north and south, to sit at table in the kingdom of God, is already to participate in that kingdom now. In the Lord's Supper we share a common meal in which we remember and hope and, in doing so, discover the direction for our lives and the delight of tasting and seeing the goodness of God.

But what, specifically, do we remember? And for what do we hope? We remember the disruptively redemptive life of Jesus, a life so disruptive that it led to his betrayal, arrest, and execution. If we remember that Christ died for us but forget the quality of life that led to that death, we circumvent the profoundest meaning of the crucifixion and evacuate the reign of God in which it participates of its specific content. We remember, then, that Jesus ate and drank with sinners and tax collectors; we remember that he preached a kingdom in which the last are first and the first are last; we remember that he challenged the hypocrisy of those with economic, political, and religious power; we remember that he conversed with women, that he blessed the poor and the outcast, that he subverted conventional hierarchies and set aside his own place of privilege as a man and a rabbi to accept a shameful death; we remember that he gave his life—and not just "gave up" his life—to spread the good news of the expansive and inclusive love of God for all people.

This expansive love of God sets the conditions of our hope. What we hope for is precisely the day when the reign of God is fully come, when we gather as equals at the banquet table, when the mountains are made low and the valleys are raised up. We hope for the day when inclusive love and the end of hierarchical domination are no longer seen as subversive, when we can no longer distinguish between those in the center and those on the margins of society, when nations shall "beat their swords into plowshares, and their spears into pruning hooks," and when "nation shall not lift up sword against nation, [or] learn war any more" (Isa. 2:4). What we hope for has already begun in the resurrection of Jesus from death. In accepting the cross, Jesus bears the consequences of his disruptive life. On the cross, he enters fully even into our suffering and death, even into our alienation from God. If the cross represents our ultimate rejection of Jesus' expansive love and our ultimate failure to accept others, then the empty tomb represents God's ultimate rejection of our intolerance and ultimate acceptance of us in spite of it. When we come to the Table, we remember something specific, and we hope for something in particular: the reign of God as it is initiated in the life, death, and resurrection of Christ and as it comes to fulfillment in God's beautiful future.

Through our active remembering and hoping in the Lord's Supper, God restores our affectional sense of direction. The sacrament sets before us an attractive vision of a new creation grounded in the peace, justice, and righteousness of Jesus Christ. In setting this vision before us, the Lord's Supper shapes our sense of direction, giving it specifically Christian content. We are restored not to a generic sense that we must have *some* direction in life, but to a specific sense of which direction we ought to go. The content of the life of Christ as it shapes our memories and the specificity of the coming reign of God for which we hope fill out our sense of direction. If the fallen human heart is, as the old hymn says, "prone to wander," then in the Lord's Supper we encounter purifying and redemptive grace that "like a fetter, bind[s our] wandering heart to" God and "seal[s] it for [God's] courts above."[13] The fallen heart, prone to wander among its idols, dividing its attention among them, encounters the divine grace that reorients and redirects it toward its proper end. The purpose we pursue is nothing other than the expansion and development of the beauty unleashed in the world by the incarnation, a beauty that attracts us, disrupts our idolatries, and invites us to become agents of beautification in the world.

In restoring our sense of direction through the Lord's Supper, God also renews our sense of delight. Prayers of Great Thanksgiving embed us within a cosmic context in which our "highest joy" is to join our voices with the voices of all the creatures of the earth and with the heavenly chorus of angels to sing God's praises.[14] To find new direction, to be grounded in a renewed sense of God's cosmic purposes made known in Christ, to be singularly focused on that disruptively redemptive vision of God's reign initiated by Jesus "tune[s our] heart[s] to sing [God's] grace."[15] It is delightful to come together around a table where all the pretensions of privilege and merit have fallen away, where no one is marginalized, because only God is at the center, and where the hospitality born of mutuality and interdependence is ever expanding to include the least of these. When through the sacrament of the Lord's Supper we enter into what Orestes Brownson called "life by communion," we enter into a new way of being in our world that colors all of our common life in the hues of gracious, hospitable delight.[16] To live "life by communion" is to be trained into the religious affection of delight so that we become people who are dispositionally ready to meet the creation as a place that properly calls for delight and to notice with acute anguish when continued sin and evil prevent it from being so.

The eucharistic restoration of our sense of direction and delight has the power to expose the idolatry of nationalism. In directing us toward Jesus' vision of an eschatological banquet in which "they will come from east and west, from north and south, and sit at table in the kingdom of God" and in cultivating in us delight in the sheer goodness of God and flourishing of all creatures in the new creation, the Lord's Supper indicts the narrowness and distortion of nationalistic religion. Having dined at the Lord's Table and having glimpsed a vision of God's expansive, inclusive love, we are made able to see how nationalism intentionally excludes the "foreigners" who come from east and west, north and south; we see the vanity of false delight that revels not in the intrinsic goodness of God but instead in the instrumental use of God for distorted human ends. We see the bankruptcy of false delight that revels not in the flourishing of all creatures in a new heaven and new earth but instead in the triumph of national interests, in a blind inattention to the well-being of "outsiders," and in the sweet intoxicant of "power over" that swells the patriot heart to vanquish all competing interests. The grace of the Lord's Supper, as it restores and renews our senses of direction and delight, calls us to remember the resurrection of Jesus Christ as God's "no" to human violence, and it calls us in hope toward the ever-expansive love of the kingdom of God that liberates us from enslavement to the false god of the nation.

The Lord's Supper and the Redirection of Desire: The Senses of Rightness and Well-Being

In the Lord's Supper we enter into communion with God in Christ, and this union with Christ affects our hearts. After we have been invited to come to the Lord's Table, we join together in a prayer of thanksgiving that often begins with the Sursum Corda, a dialogue between the liturgist and the congregation in which we are exhorted, "Lift up your hearts," and we respond, "We lift them to the Lord." Communion, then, is about being lifted into the presence of God so that we may "give thanks to the Lord our God." As our hearts rise up, Christ meets us through the bread and the wine, and we are mystically united with him so that our hearts sing forth the glory of God.[17] In this communion, we encounter Christ as "thou," as one who is known not simply as a truthful proposition to which our minds assent, but as a person before whom our hearts are opened and in whose presence our religious affections are graciously renewed. It is only because Christ is really, objectively present to us in the sacrament that we are opened for such affection formation. This is no mere memorial meal; it is a living, vital encounter with the resurrected Christ, who is present in our midst, and not only in our memories, even now.

When we come into communion with Christ in the Lord's Supper, we come to know him in an affection-forming, participatory way that graciously reorients the deepest chords of desire that run through our affectional lives. The Christ whom we meet in the Lord's Supper meets us in all of his attractive, disruptive, and transforming beauty. As incarnate beauty, Christ meets us mystically in the bread and wine and by divine grace becomes for us the new object of that current of yearning, attraction, and desire that courses through our religious affections. In the broken body and bread, in the blood and wine poured out for us, we are drawn into participation in the beauty of a life lived, lost, and resurrected again. When Christ's body is broken and fragmented for us and we come to touch, taste, and consume the broken bread and wine of the communion meal, we come by this participation to desire Christ, to desire what Christ desired, to yearn and long for the eschatological beautification of the world that first began in the incarnation. When we tear bread from the loaf, when we pour wine into the cup, when we taste the broken bread of Christ's broken body, when we drink the wine of his spilled blood, we come to participate mystically in the redemptive fragmentation of Christ that paradoxically brings new wholeness, harmony, and unity to the world. This mystical and tactile experience of the Lord's Supper mediates to us the purifying and illumining grace of the gospel. In this rite, the fragmented, divided desire that runs through our affectional lives is reunified and singularly focused on the supreme beauty of the Christ who meets us in the sacred meal. The confused yearning of the fallen human heart that led it to wander aimlessly among its idols is gradually purified by God's grace. This same grace also gradually illuminates for us the supreme beauty of Christ, who becomes the singular object of our affectional desire.

Just as baptism reorients the sense of dependence that runs through all of our religious affections, so the Lord's Supper redirects the deepest chords of desire that orient the human heart. As the desire that courses through our religious affections is redirected away from its multiple idols and toward the singular beauty of Christ, it draws together the fragmented pieces not only of our individual lives but also of the communal and cosmic context in which those lives are embedded. In sin, our inner fragmentation generates distorted behaviors that result in broken relationships, and that outer fragmentation acts back upon and exacerbates our broken inner lives. But the Lord's Supper, as it participates in the grace of the incarnation, works to draw our fragmented lives together so that we can live into reconciling relationships that further enhance our individual healing. But the meal itself is always already a social event, which means that the healing of our outer fragmentation does not simply follow from the healing of our individual fragmentation; instead, our individual and communal lives are always working alongside one another, through the grace of Christ, to lead us into harmony and wholeness. Finally, the "balm in Gilead" that makes our wounded individual and communal lives whole ultimately gestures toward a restoration of the entire created order. As we come into communion with Christ through the bread and wine of the Eucharist, we anticipate the cosmic communion of all things when the reign of God fully comes.

The eucharistic redirection of our desire renews our sense of well-being, our sense that the world is ordered in a way that allows for our flourishing. Our sense of well-being depends upon an awareness that there is a place for us in the creation and a purpose for our lives within God's plan. This sense of well-being is sustained through our participation in the sacramental meal as we discover our place within a community that gathers around a common table, is fed by the fruits of the good earth, and is drawn out of the fragmentation of sin into reconciliation. We discover that neither the material order nor the social order in which our lives are embedded is hostile to our existence. We discover instead that, by divine grace, they may once again set the conditions of our flourishing. We discover a community that, at our baptism, vowed to guide and nurture us and that now is sustained and strengthened through the grace mediated by the Lord's Supper. We discover good things of the earth —food as common and nourishing as bread, drink as simple and delightful as wine—that come together to sustain our lives and to delight our senses. We discover in the Lord's Supper a renewed sense of well-being that extends to both our communal and our creational, cosmic contexts. Through this common meal we find ourselves drawn into communion with Christ, and through Christ with one another and indeed the whole, good creation.

The eucharistic redirection of our desire also restores our affectional sense of rightness, our sense that the world is supposed to be as it is and that the broken places in the world represent aberrations. This sense of rightness is as simple as our affirmation of the goodness of the material world, our deep sense that creatures are not meant to live autonomously, but in relationships of interdependence with one another, and our awareness that we were meant to live as social creatures. The sense of rightness includes an awareness that all things have a place in the creation, that the world displays an order that is good. The

Lord's Supper directs our sense of rightness, in part, by pointing us to our proper place in that right ordering of the creation. The Alexandrine Liturgy of St. Basil that begins when we join the heavenly chorus and give "voice to every creature under heaven" to glorify God, continues by locating us within the created order, not only as those who speak for the creatures who do not have language, but also as those who "rule and serve all [God's] creatures." It goes on to note that when, through sin, we turned from the purposes to which God had set us, Christ "destroyed death and made the whole creation new."[18] When we come to the Lord's Table through a prayer such as this, we become acutely aware of how sin distorts our sense of rightness and carves out a place for us in the created order that sets us in opposition to our divinely ordained role as the creatures who speak for the voiceless and care for the vulnerable. That awareness of the broken places in the world prompts us to relocate ourselves in the place fitted for us, to find our place in God's good and right ordering of the world. In the prayer, we again join our voices to those of the angels and sing God's glory on behalf of all material creatures. We come to the table with a restored sense of the rightness of the world and with a renewed commitment to order our lives to that rightness. When we live out our eucharistic sense of rightness, we become intentional about speaking for the voiceless and caring for the vulnerable. In short, we participate by anticipation in cosmic communion even as we come together through table fellowship into communion with Christ and one another.

Throughout this chapter we have explored the ways in which the signs of the sacraments seal us in the faith of Christ, renewing and restoring our religious affections. We have noted that in baptism we are initiated into a life of continually dying and rising with Christ that restores the religious affections of contrition and hope. Such a life also reorients our sense of dependence and renews the religious affections of gratitude and humility. And because baptism is an act of the covenant community, it also cultivates our sense of mutuality and interdependence and our sense of obligation. We have also described how the sacrament of the Lord's Supper sustains us in the Christian life by prompting the identity-forming acts of remembering and hoping, and that this memory and hope renew our senses of direction and delight. Finally, we have also highlighted how the Lord's Supper redirects our desire and restores our senses of well-being and rightness.

Epilogue

Some Concluding
Reflections on Music

I realize that when they are sung, these sacred words stir my mind to greater religious fervor and kindle in me a more ardent flame of piety than they would if they were not sung; and I also know that there are particular modes in song and in the voice, corresponding to my various emotions and able to stimulate them because of the mysterious relationship between the two.[1]

We do not condemn speaking and singing but rather strongly commend them, provided they are associated with the heart's affection.[2]

There is scarcely anything in the world which is more able to turn or bend this way and that the morals of [humankind than music]. . . . And in fact, we find that it has a secret and almost incredible power to move hearts in one way or another.[3]

Throughout this book, we have explored the relationship between worship and the religious affections, focusing on the relationship between particular religious affections and various acts of worship, such as the call to worship, the passing of the peace, the charge and benediction, prayer, preaching, and the sacraments. And while we have sometimes noted how hymns and service music such as the doxology are woven into these elements of worship, we have not treated music as a subject in itself. This is in part because music is not a separate act of worship so much as it is a different mode of worship within other moments of the liturgy. We often come into the sanctuary to prepare ourselves for worship as the prelude is offered; we may offer our prayers through song; Scripture, especially the Psalms, may be proclaimed in hymns; we often conclude our prayers of confession with the singing of the Kyrie; and during the

Lord's Supper we may sing the Sanctus and the memorial acclamation. Music, both instrumental and vocal, is an integral part of most Christian worship services. It is woven into nearly every act of worship, and it has a profound power to move us into reverence and to enhance our sense of the presence of God.

As Paul Westermeyer points out, it was precisely their awareness of music's profound power to move our religious affections that left Augustine and Calvin somewhat uneasy about it.[4] Augustine was keenly aware of the power of music in worship to "kindle . . . a more ardent flame of piety" by stimulating "various emotions" through "the mysterious relationship" between the lyrics and the melody. Calvin too recognized in music an unparalleled power to "bend this way and that" human morals, and he approved of the use of music in worship only insofar as it cultivated the "heart's affection" for genuine piety. For Augustine and Calvin this affection-forming power of music made it potentially threatening and required that it always be accompanied by careful theological consideration and guidance. Music, left unguided by theological reflection, could function to exacerbate the brokenness and infidelity of the human heart. In the context of public worship, both Augustine and Calvin feared that music could be used not to praise God but to entertain and amuse congregants. There is an important insight to be gleaned from Augustine and Calvin: music is a powerful mode of communication, and when we use it in the worship of the church, we must be intentional about insuring that it functions to draw us toward genuine reverence before God, rather than allowing it to reinforce the culture of amusement.

In these concluding reflections, we explore three themes that help to ensure that our understanding of the nature and function of music in worship receives appropriate theological guidance. First, music in worship ought to anchor our emotions in our religious affections. Second, the delicate interplay between lyrics and melody ought to draw the congregation into participation in the disruptively redemptive life of Christ. And finally, music in worship ought to order and express the full range of religious affections. Because these three themes are central to the broader understanding of Christian worship already developed in this book, they will also serve as a conclusion for the entire work.

MUSIC ANCHORS EMOTIONS IN THE RELIGIOUS AFFECTIONS

We gather on Sunday not to be entertained but to *worship*. We meet not as an audience but as a *congregation*. We come not as spectators of an event but as *participants* to engage in the worshipful work of the people of God. Such theological affirmations serve to remind us that when we listen to music or sing during worship, we are doing something different from what we do when we attend a concert and sing along or even when we go to the symphony and listen attentively. Concerts and symphonies are worthwhile and meaningful human activities, and with the whole creation they ultimately glorify God. But they are not the worship of the gathered body of Christ. Music in worship, as Westermeyer says, "is broken to word and sacrament."[5] It is immediately ordered to the glory of God and functions in the context of the means of grace to reorder our religious affections and orient us theocentrically.

The proper function of music in worship is to cultivate the religious affections, rather than simply to excite and immediately discharge evanescent emotions. This is not to say that music cannot or should not touch our emotions; thankfully, it often does. However, when music functions properly in Christian worship, it does more than touch our emotions. It also tunnels down through these emotions to the deeper, abiding religious affections that ground the most basic and enduring features of our identities. The problem with music is not that it moves us emotionally, but that it may do so in a casual and fleeting way that does not penetrate to the underlying dispositional structures of our identities that are grounded in the religious affections. When music stimulates and discharges emotions apart from any enduring connection to our religious affections, it is functioning not as worship but as entertainment. The use of music for entertainment is often good and edifying in human experience, but in worship we are asking for more from music. We are asking music to mediate divine grace; we are enlisting it in service of the purifying and illuminating grace of God that shapes us into the kinds of people that God would have us be; we are asking of music that it not merely swirl about in the surface eddies of emotion but, instead, train our affections over a lifetime. We are asking of music that it redirect the underlying affectional current of dependence and desire so as to move us from the fragmentation of sin to the new wholeness of our redemption.

Westermeyer points out that as the church has increasingly accommodated its worship to a market-driven model that seeks to "hook" consumers and sell them a "product," it has lost patience with the slow work that music ought to do in shaping Christian identity over the course of a lifetime. "The temptation," he explains, "has been to substitute superficial praise choruses or poorly crafted attempts to tell God how we feel [for more traditional hymnody and Psalter singing]. That the church might have a message and a schooling responsibility has often escaped its recent gaze."[6] The proper role of music in worship resides in its capacity to school our religious affections over time and, by so doing, to renew and transform our total identities as the beloved children of the sovereign God.

When we do turn our gaze to music's role in schooling the religious affections, we discover that the power of music to touch our emotions provides it with a natural entryway into the realm of the religious affections. The enduring quality of affections partly distinguishes them from emotions that come and go, but the two are not utterly separate either. To become a person of gratitude, a person who is dispositionally ready and constitutionally open to respond to the world as a place that properly calls for thankfulness, we must first have experienced the emotion of gratitude on numerous occasions. When that emotion settles down and becomes an enduring feature of our basic temperament, it has become an affection. And when that affection finds its ultimate object in the sovereign God, it has become a religious affection. Because of the "mysterious relationship" between music and emotions, music is one of the most powerful and natural ways to evoke emotional experiences so that they may be trained on the glory of God and may begin to settle down in us and become permanent features of our identities. But emotional experiences do not cease to be important once they have settled into affections because we gain access to those deep affectional structures of our identities only when we tunnel down to them through corresponding emotions. Because music has an "incredible power to move hearts," then, it also serves as a natural gateway for training the affections that underlie our emotions. Music helps to anchor our emotions in the religious affections.

Because of the deep connection between emotions and affections, and because of the inherent emotional power of music, music in worship offers one of the most potent means through which the Holy Spirit may work to form us for the Christian life. Music does this not only because it evokes and expresses our religious affections; it also directs them toward God as their proper object, shapes them in a peculiarly Christian way through the theological guidance offered by the words of hymns and Psalms, sustains them as the melodies and harmonies of these hymns work their way into our hearts through our memories, and orders them with reference to other affections cultivated elsewhere in the liturgy. Although we are most likely to notice its power to evoke and express the affections, we must not lose sight of the other powerful ways in which music cultivates our religious affections. In fact, music can cultivate our affections in all of the same ways that the rest of the liturgy does.

METAPHOR, MUSIC, AND PARTICIPATION

When considering the power of music in worship, we may attend to the words of hymns, to how those words are set to music, and to the power of music without words. Consider how the lyrics of hymns cultivate the religious affections. Throughout this book, we have maintained that human beings are linguistic beings—beings whose identities and ways of perceiving and engaging the world are shaped by the linguistic practices in which we are embedded. We have also explored how the language of metaphor, image, and symbol are especially powerfully in shaping our religious imaginations and religious affections. Metaphors, images, and symbols, especially those drawn from or developed out of Scripture, contain rich deposits of meaning that cannot be exhausted by translation into more everyday, literal forms of speech. The metaphors, symbols, and images of the Christian faith arouse our religious imagination and by God's grace enable us to gain access to that which otherwise would be inaccessible to us. Biblical and liturgical metaphors, symbols, and images draw us into a different world of meaning—the world of normative meaning in which we are enabled to construe properly God, the world, and our place in relation to both. The words of the church's hymns, whether sung by the congregation, a choir, or an individual, are words that draw on, elaborate, or extend the metaphors, symbols, images, and narratives of Scripture, and much of the power of these sung words resides in their capacity to draw us imaginatively into the world of proper meaning grounded in God's self-revelation. The lyrics of our hymns energize our religious imagination, opening up for us richer, more complex ways of understanding and engaging our world. When we sing the lyrics of hymns, replete as they are with symbol, metaphor, and image, we are drawn into a form of participatory knowing that involves the totality of who we are. Our religious imagination is gradually and graciously vivified, and as it is, the root complex of dependence and desire that courses through our religious affections is purified and illumined, distorted affections give way to restored affections, and fragmentation, pride, and self-negation yield to the wholeness modeled on and made possible by the redemptive beauty of the incarnate Christ. When we sing the words of our hymns, we are participating in Christ's new world of meaning that is at once attractive, disruptive, and transformative.

But as Augustine himself noticed, though the words of hymns are powerful, there is something about setting those words to music that imbues them with a more intense affection-forming power than they might otherwise have. When the words of hymns are joined to a musical setting, Augustine notes, they "kindle in [us] a more ardent flame of piety than they would if they were not sung." The sense of the words is powerful, but when that sense is joined to the sound of musical notes, hymns become potent shapers of the religious affections. When the religious affections are lifted into the symphonic play of sound and sense, they become especially malleable to purifying and illuminating grace. Much of the affection-forming power of music in worship resides in this fittedness between sound and sense. When sound and sense work together effectively in worship, we experience their harmony in a pleasing way. We have a sense that *these* words go well with *that* tune. When we sing Luther's "A Mighty

Fortress Is Our God," for example, the images, symbols, and metaphors of the verses fit with the slow, heavy, and deliberate tempo of the music. "O Sacred Head, Now Wounded" requires a soulful, mournful sound, and "O for a Thousand Tongues to Sing" calls for a major key. This relationship between sound and sense is experienced most acutely perhaps when there is a lack of fit. Although "Amazing Grace" can be sung to the tune of the theme song from the old television comedy *Gilligan's Island*, it simply does not communicate the same message when it is. Such significant dissonance between sound and sense can undermine the affection-forming capacity of music in worship.

While much of the affection-forming power of music in worship resides in the fittedness between sound and sense, still another dimension contributes to its power, namely, the embodied and social nature of singing in public worship. When we sing in worship, we are participating in an activity that demands more than our minds alone. Singing demands our bodies. It demands our lungs, lips, tongues, ears, eyes, and legs. We sit or stand, contract our vocal chords to match words with notes, fill our lungs to carry us without interruption through a portion of a verse, view the words and notes in our hymnals, and hear the voices of our fellow congregants as well as our own voices; and we do all this together as a congregation. Singing in worship is a deeply social and embodied activity, and an important part of its affection-forming power resides in its sensuous and social character. For this reason, therefore, while Christian worship may include music by choirs, quartets, soloists, and so forth, congregational singing should remain primary. Congregational singing ensures that music in worship is understood not as performance or entertainment but as a participatory liturgical act, offered to God communally by all who are gathered for worship. Moreover, even the music offered by choirs, groups, or individuals in the context of public worship should be understood to be a shared liturgical act offered in praise of God on behalf of the entire congregation.

Finally, we offer a brief word about the use of instrumental music, music without words. While the fit of sound and sense imparts to hymns much of their affection-forming power, the sound of music alone also has an important affection-forming role. Instrumental music focuses our attention on the power of sound and rhythm apart from human words, and like silence it prompts us to quiet ourselves, to set aside the drive for cognitive mastery and rational control that is often ingredient in our use of words. Instrumental music, like silence, awakens us to receptivity before the sovereign God who gives meaning to all things. It honors God's self-disclosure as mystery, as that which cannot be fully spoken, exhausted, or controlled by our speech and thought. It thus also cultivates in us a renewed sense of our own finitude and creatureliness, and this in turn schools us in humility before God. It reawakens in us a sense of our proper place in the broader rhythms and harmonies of a cosmos oriented not around ourselves but around the glory of the sovereign God.

MUSIC AND THE FULL RANGE OF
THE RELIGIOUS AFFECTIONS

In spite of a general Protestant reticence about the presence of beauty in worship, most of us willingly and reflexively acknowledge and appreciate the power of beauty in the music of worship. We recognize intuitively how this beauty draws us in, fixes our attention, and points us toward God, who is the source of all beauty. If the whole of public worship functions to redirect the desire and sense of dependence that run through and bind together the religious affections, then the beauty of music in worship has an important role to play in achieving this. Music, with its "incredible power" to move the heart, helps us to *feel* our dependence on God and awakens in us a more intense desire for divine beauty. When music draws us toward God as the source of all that is good and beautiful, we begin to give up our idolatrous attachments to other creatures and are purified. When through music we lean into our dependence on God as sustainer of our lives and as the giver of all meaning and purpose, we learn to value other creatures according to their belonging to God and are illuminated. As we find in God the preeminently beautiful One whom we desire and depend upon, we acquire a coherent, stable center of identity that reorders our religious affections and brings harmony to our relationships with other creatures. The beauty of music in worship contributes powerfully to the lifelong process of purification and illumination in which God overcomes our inner and outer fragmentation.

The desire and dependence that course through all of the religious affections, though, is redirected and reoriented only through the cultivation of individual religious affections. This means that music, as with all of the elements of worship, will need to address the full range of the religious affections, reordering each of them theocentrically. A worship service in which the musical selections consist entirely of praise choruses will fail to acknowledge that our gratitude and delight are linked to obligation and mutuality. It will likely also fail to honor the way in which our delight expresses itself as anguish in the face of the continued brokenness of creation. Likewise, a worship service dominated with music designed to elicit a "decision for Christ," especially when it interprets that conversion experience in terms of "going to heaven," will distort our sense of hope and blunt our senses of rightness and well-being. Worship services that select a narrow range of music designed to move us toward social action oriented toward justice also may fail to cultivate the full range of religious

affections, because an almost exclusive focus on developing our senses of obligation and contrition may cause our senses of gratitude and delight to atrophy. If
the music of worship is to cultivate a full range of religious affections and to
contribute to their proper ordering, we need both the songs of praise and
awe and the hymns of contrition, both "O for a Thousand Tongues to Sing"
and "O Sacred Head, Now Wounded." We need "Joyful, Joyful, We Adore
Thee" and "There Is a Balm in Gilead."

We need an expansive scope of hymnody that addresses the full range of
human affections, and we need those hymns to shape these affections with
specifically Christian content that orders them toward the glory of God. Music
that orders our religious affections to the glory of God will necessarily locate
human life and meaning within the broad scope of God's purposes for the
whole creation. It will place limits on the ways in which human goods and
interests may determine the value and purpose of other creatures. Hymns and
psalms that invite us to sing the praise of God on behalf of a speechless creation are especially well-suited to this theocentric reordering of the religious
affections. In Erik Routley's rendition of Psalm 98, for example, we sing,
"Rivers and seas and torrents roaring, / Honor the Lord with wild acclaim; /
Mountains and stones, look up adoring, / And find a voice to praise God's
name."[7] Here we stand as creatures in the midst of the creation, singing with
our fellow creatures and on their behalf. We do not stand as the arbiters of
value or as the highest of God's achievements. We take our place within a vast,
good cosmos that was made to glorify and to enjoy its maker. That experience
of taking our place, of singing our place, within God's beautiful creation evokes
in us a deep sense of awe at God's great works, a humble assessment of our own
value, a grateful acknowledgment of the goodness of all that flows from God's
creative and abundant goodness, delight in the wondrous splendor of the
works of God's hand, and renewed senses of rightness and well-being. The
theocentric reordering of the religious affections that arises from the "mysterious relationship" between them and music works its way deep into the structures of our being so that we are renewed and transformed, so that our hearts
are moved toward the glorification and enjoyment of God.

A FINAL WORD

Throughout this book we have explored how the work of the church as it gathers in worship renews and transforms who we are "at heart." If we are to understand the true nature of Christian worship, we must attend to the ways in which
it expresses, evokes, shapes, sustains, directs, and orders the religious affections, those deeply seated dispositions that orient us in the world as creatures

who were made to glorify and enjoy God. The deepest structures of our personhood are constituted by a nexus of desire and dependence that is formed through social and communicative life and that issue in a patterned set of religious affections that interpenetrate all human knowledge and action. In worship, the beauty of the incarnate Christ attracts, disrupts, and transforms worshipers, whose affections suffer from the fragmentation and distortion of the fall. We have sought to understand the integral relationship between emotions and affections in a way that values both without confusing them.

Our hope is that this new understanding of the nature of the religious affections sheds light on the nature, function, and value of concrete worship practices. When we gather for worship, abide together in the peace of Christ, and are sent out into the world to live doxological lives, we encounter the attractive, disruptive, and transformative power of the incarnation, which purifies and illuminates us. We find ourselves shaped by prayers, sermons, sacraments, and songs into a new way of being. We find ourselves becoming persons who are constitutionally open and dispositionally ready to meet the world as a place that properly calls for awe and gratitude, as an arena that places obligations on us and that provides for our well-being, and as a place that is both delightful and humbling. Through the particular worship practices of the church as we gather around Pulpit, Table, and Font, as we offer prayers of thanksgiving and intercession, as we confess our sins, and as we are charged and blessed to live lives of peace, we learn to lean into our identities as the beloved children of God.

Notes

Foreword

1. Karl Barth, *The Humanity of God* (Richmond: John Knox Press, 1960), 90.

Chapter 1: An Introduction to the Religious Affections

1. "Praise God, from Whom All Blessings Flow," in *The Presbyterian Hymnal: Hymns, Songs, and Spiritual Songs* (Louisville, KY: Westminster/John Knox Press, 1990), hymn #592.
2. As we explore these two impulses in the following paragraphs, we are deeply indebted to H. Richard Niebuhr's essay "Toward a Recovery of Feeling," in *H. Richard Niebuhr: Theology, History, and Culture*, ed. William Stacy Johnson (New Haven, CT: Yale University Press, 1996), 34–49.
3. Niebuhr, "Toward a Recovery of Feeling," 39.
4. Don E. Saliers, *The Soul in Paraphrase: Prayer and the Religious Affections* (Cleveland: OSL Publications, 1991), 6–16.
5. James M.Gustafson describes a disposition as "a readiness to act in a particular way" in his *Can Ethics Be Christian?* (Chicago: University of Chicago Press, 1975), 40–42.
6. In the first volume of his *Ethics from a Theocentric Perspective*, James M. Gustafson enumerates six "senses" or "aspects of religious affections": dependence, gratitude, obligation, remorse and repentance, possibility, and direction. Our own analysis of gratitude, obligation, contrition, hope, and direction is indebted to Gustafson's work: *Ethics from a Theocentric Perspective*, vol. 1, *Theology and Ethics* (Chicago: University of Chicago Press, 1981), 129–36. Gustafson also treats these six senses in *Can Ethics Be Christian?* 94–114.
7. For drawing our attention to the senses of rightness and well-being, we are indebted to Herbert W. Richardson, *Toward an American Theology* (New York: Harper & Row, 1967), 57–59.

Chapter 2: Four Features of the Religious Affections

1. *Book of Common Worship* (Louisville, KY: Westminster /John Knox Press, 1993), 69.
2. "I Greet Thee, Who My Sure Redeemer Art," in *The Presbyterian Hymnal: Hymns, Psalms, and Spiritual Songs* (Louisville KY, Westminster/John Knox Press, 1990), hymn #457.
3. "Joyful, Joyful, We Adore Thee," *Presbyterian Hymnal*, hymn #464.
4. James M. Gustafson, *Can Ethics Be Christian?* (Chicago: University of Chicago Press, 1975), 101.

5. Don E. Saliers, *The Soul in Paraphrase: Prayer and the Religious Affections* (Cleveland: OSL Publications, 1991), 10.

6. This definition of a sacrament is traditionally attributed to Augustine.

7. John Calvin, *Institutes of the Christian Religion*, ed. John T. McNeill, trans. Ford Lewis Battles, 2 vols. (Philadelphia: Westminster Press, 1960), 1.5.10; 1.5.1; 1.5.9; 1.5.2; 3.2.8; 3.2.26.

8. Rosemary Radford Ruether, *To Change the World: Christology and Cultural Criticism* (New York: Crossroad, 1981), 14.

9. The Westminster Shorter Catechism, in *The Book of Confessions* (Louisville, KY: Office of the General Assembly, Presbyterian Church (U.S.A.), 2002), 175. We have altered the text for purposes of inclusive language.

10. See, for example, Immanuel Kant, "What Is Enlightenment?" in *On History*, ed. and trans. Lewis White Beck (New York: Macmillan, 1963), 3–10.

11. Lindbeck uses the term "experiential-expressivist" to characterize a particular understanding of Christian doctrine. We are borrowing the term and expanding it to include a particular understanding of the Christian life and worship. See George A. Lindbeck, *The Nature of Doctrine: Religion and Theology in a Postliberal Age* (Philadelphia: Westminster Press, 1984), 15–45.

12. Friedrich Schleiermacher, *On Religion: Speeches to Its Cultured Despisers*, trans. John Oman (London: Kegan Paul, Trench, Trübner & Co., 1893), 9.

13. For a groundbreaking work that offers a social model of the self as an alternative to the Enlightenment model of autonomous individualism, see George Herbert Mead, *Mind, Self, and Society from the Standpoint of a Social Behaviorist* (Chicago: University of Chicago Press, 1962).

14. Friedrich Schleiermacher, *The Christian Faith*, English trans. of 2nd German edition, ed. and trans. H. R. Mackintosh and J. S. Stewart (Edinburgh: T. & T. Clark, 1989), §100.2.

15. Schleiermacher, *On Religion: Speeches to Its Cultured Despisers*, 227.

16. Gordon W. Lathrop, *Holy Things: A Liturgical Theology* (Minneapolis: Fortress Press, 1993), chaps. 3–4.

17. Augustine, *The Confessions*, trans. J. G. Pilkington, in *Basic Writings of Saint Augustine*, vol. 1, ed. Whitney J. Oates (Grand Rapids: Baker Book House, 1976), 3.

18. *Book of Common Worship*, 146.

19. Ibid., 55.

20. "Come, Thou Fount of Every Blessing," *Presbyterian Hymnal*, hymn #356.

21. "I Greet Thee, Who My Sure Redeemer Art," *Presbyterian Hymnal*, hymn #457.

22. Jonathan Edwards, *The Religious Affections*, ed. John E. Smith, *The Works of Jonathan Edwards*, vol. 2 (New Haven, CT: Yale University Press, 1959), 100–101.

23. Martin Buber, *I and Thou*, trans. Ronald Gregor Smith (New York: Charles Scribner's Sons, 1986).

24. Edwards, *Religious Affections*, 96.

25. Herbert W. Richardson, *Toward an American Theology* (New York: Harper & Row, 1967), 57. While we have drawn the concept of participatory knowing from Richardson, Edward Farley's concept of "participative knowing" is quite similar. See Edward Farley, *Good and Evil: Interpreting a Human Condition* (Philadelphia: Fortress Press, 1990), 165–66.

26. "Joyful, Joyful, We Adore Thee," *Presbyterian Hymnal*, hymn #464.

27. James M. Gustafson, *Ethics from a Theocentric Perspective*, vol. 1, *Theology and Ethics* (Chicago: University of Chicago Press, 1981), 113.

28. We have adapted this metaphor from Gustafson, who says that "piety is, in a sense, the hinge which joins the frame of the moral and natural ordering of life to the door of human duties and obligations" (*Ethics from a Theocentric Perspective*, vol. 1, *Theology and Ethics*, 167).

Chapter 3: Fallen Religious Affections

1. "There Is a Balm in Gilead," in *The Presbyterian Hymnal: Hymns, Psalms, and Spiritual Songs* (Louisville, KY: Westminster/John Knox Press, 1990), hymn #394.

2. "Dona Nobis Pacem," in *The United Methodist Hymnal* (Nashville: United Methodist Publishing House, 1989), hymn #376.

3. *Book of Common Worship* (Louisville, KY: Westminster/John Knox Press, 1993), 53.

4. Augustine, *Concerning the City of God against the Pagans*, trans. Henry Bettenson (New York: Penguin Books, 1972), 571–74; Evagrius Ponticus, *The Praktikos and Chapters on Prayer*, trans. John Eudes Bamberger (Kalamazoo, MI: Cistercian Publications, 1981), 16–20; Jonathan Edwards, *Charity and Its Fruits: Christian Love as Manifested in the Heart and Life*, ed. Tryon Edwards (Carlisle, PA: Banner of Truth Trust, 1986), 158; Tertullian, *De idolatria*, trans. J. H. Waszink and J. C. M. Van Winden (Leiden, Netherlands: E. J. Brill, 1987); Søren Kierkegaard, *The Sickness unto Death*, trans. Howard V. Hong and Edna H. Hong (Princeton, NJ: Princeton University Press, 1983); Reinhold Niebuhr, *The Nature and Destiny of Man*, 2 vol. (New York: Macmillan Publishing Co., 1964).

5. Pseudo-Dionysius, "The Divine Names," in *Pseudo-Dionysius: The Complete Works*, trans. Colm Luibheid (New York: Paulist Press, 1987), 72.

6. Ibid., 122.

7. This formulation of good relationships reflects the description of hierarchy offered by the Pseudo-Dionysius in "The Divine Names," 83.

8. Shel Silverstein, *The Giving Tree* (New York: Harper Collins, 1964).

9. John Calvin, *Institutes of the Christian Religion*, ed. John T. McNeill, trans. Ford Lewis Battles, 2 vol. (Philadelphia: Westminster Press, 1960), 1.11.8.

10. For a detailed exploration of this dynamic of idolatry, see Edward Farley, *Good and Evil: Interpreting a Human Condition* (Philadelphia: Fortress Press, 1990), esp. chaps. 6–14.

11. See, for example, the influential article by Valerie Saiving that was initially published in 1960, "The Human Situation: A Feminine View," in *Womanspirit Rising: A Feminist Reader in Religion*, ed. Carol P. Christ and Judith Plaskow (San Francisco: Harper & Row, 1979), 25–42. For more contemporary treatments of sin from the perspectives of feminist and womanist theology, see Judith Plaskow, *Sex, Sin, and Grace: Women's Experience and the Theologies of Reinhold Niebuhr and Paul Tillich* (Washington, DC: University Press of America, 1980) and Jacquelyn Grant, "The Sin of Servanthood and Deliverance of Discipleship," in *A Trouble in My Soul: Womanist Perspectives on Evil and Suffering*, ed. Emilie Townes (Maryknoll, NY: Orbis Books, 1993).

12. "Love Divine, All Loves Excelling," *Presbyterian Hymnal*, hymn #376. For a treatment of the emergence of the "cult of domesticity" or the "cult of the true womanhood," see Barbara Welter, "The Cult of True Womanhood: 1820–1860," *American Quarterly* 18 (1966): 151–74.

Chapter 4: Redeemed Religious Affections

1. *Book of Common Worship* (Louisville, KY: Westminster/John Knox Press, 1993), 68; Luke 13:29.
2. The character George makes a similar point in Tom Stoppard's *Jumpers* (New York: Grove Press, 1972), 53.
3. Jonathan Edwards, "The Excellency of Jesus Christ," in *The Works of Jonathan Edwards*, ed. Sareno E. Dwight, vol. 2 (Carlisle, PA: Banner of Truth Trust, 1990), 686.
4. Ibid., 680–86.
5. Ibid., 688.
6. Elisabeth Schüssler Fiorenza, "Feminist Spirituality, Christian Identity, and Catholic Vision," in *Womanspirit Rising: A Feminist Reader in Religion*, ed. Carol P. Christ and Judith Plaskow (San Francisco: Harper Collins, 1979), 136–48. For a more fully developed vision of the church grounded in the notion of power as "empowerment," see Letty M. Russell, *Household of Freedom: Authority in Feminist Theology* (Philadelphia: Westminster Press, 1987).
7. Horace Bushnell, *Christian Nurture* (New York: Charles Scribner's Sons, 1912), 10.
8. The Westminster Shorter Catechism, Question 88, in *The Book of Confessions* (Louisville, KY: Office of the General Assembly, Presbyterian Church (U.S.A.), 2002), 183.
9. John Leith, *Introduction to the Reformed Tradition: A Way of Being the Christian Community* (Atlanta: John Knox Press, 1981), 74.
10. Karl Barth, *The Humanity of God*, trans. John Newton Thomas and Thomas Wieser (Atlanta: John Knox Press, 1960), 41. Barth's phrase the "Godness of God" is rendered "God's deity" in the above translation.

Chapter 5: Religious Affections and the Work of the Church

1. Throughout this work, we are deeply indebted to the theocentric and affectional theology of James M. Gustafson. See esp. James M. Gustafson, *Ethics from a Theocentric Perspective*, vol. 1, *Theology and Ethics* (Chicago: University of Chicago Press, 1981) and vol. 2, *Ethics and Theology* (Chicago: University of Chicago Press, 1984).
2. John Calvin, "Defensio contra Pighium," in *Iannis Calvini Opera quae supersunt omnia*, ed. Wilhelm Baum, Eduard Cunitz, and Eduard Reuss, vol. 6 (Brunswick and Berlin: C.A. Schwetschke, 1863–1900), 278. Translated and quoted in Brian A. Gerrish, "Continuity and Change: Friedrich Schleiermacher on the Task of Theology," in *Tradition and the Modern World: Reformed Theology in the Nineteenth Century* (Chicago: University of Chicago Press, 1978), 13.
3. Our discussion of the relationship of memory, Scripture, and identity is indebted to H. Richard Niebuhr, *The Meaning of Revelation* (New York: Macmillan Publishing Co., 1941). For a more contemporary discussion of similar issues, see Allen Verhey, *Remembering Jesus: Christian Community, Scripture, and the Moral Life* (Grand Rapids: Wm. B. Eerdmans Publishing Co., 2002).
4. Vigen Guroian, *Incarnate Love: Essays in Orthodox Ethics* (Notre Dame, IN: University of Notre Dame Press, 1987), chap. 3. For an excellent set of essays connecting worship and ethics, see E. Byron Anderson and Bruce T. Morrill, eds., *Liturgy and the Moral Life: Humanity at Full Stretch Before God* (Collegeville, MN: The Liturgical Press, 1998).

5. For an extended discussion of how Christian faith shapes moral agency, see James M. Gustafson, *Can Ethics Be Christian?* (Chicago: University of Chicago Press, 1975).
6. For an extended discussion of the relationship between worship and the generation of meaning, see Graham Hughes, *Worship as Meaning: A Liturgical Theology for Late Modernity* (New York: Cambridge University Press, 2003).
7. In two works Don E. Saliers addresses the ways in which worship both expresses and shapes our religious affections. See *The Soul in Paraphrase: Prayer and the Religious Affections* (Cleveland: OSL Publications, 1991) and *Worship as Theology: Foretaste of Glory Divine* (Nashville: Abingdon Press, 1994).

Chapter 6: The Structure of Worship

1. For a more extensive explanation of the theological significance of the liturgical calendar, see James F. White, *Introduction to Christian Worship*, 3rd ed. (Nashville: Abingdon Press, 2000).
2. White, *Introduction to Christian Worship*, 170.
3. Gregory of Nyssa, *The Life of Moses*, trans. Abraham J. Malherbe and Everett Ferguson (New York: Paulist Press, 1978); Pseudo-Dionysius, "The Mystical Theology," in *Pseudo-Dionysius: The Complete Works*, trans. Colm Luibheid (New York: Paulist Press, 1987).
4. A. Daniel Frankforter, *Stones for Bread: A Critique of Contemporary Worship* (Louisville, KY: Westminster John Knox Press, 2001), 122.
5. *Book of Common Worship* (Louisville, KY: Westminster/John Knox Press, 1993), 82.
6. See, for example, Immanuel Kant, *Religion within the Limits of Reason Alone*, trans. Theodore M. Greene and Hoyt H. Hudson (New York: Harper, 1960) and Immanuel Kant, *Critique of Practical Reason*, ed. and trans. Mary Gregor (New York: Cambridge University Press, 1997).
7. "Blessed Assurance," in *The Presbyterian Hymnal: Hymns, Psalms, and Spiritual Songs* (Louisville, KY, Westminster/John Knox Press, 1990), hymn #341.

Chapter 7: Prayer

1. Karl Barth, "The Strange New World within the Bible," in *The Word of God and the Word of Man*, trans. Douglas Horton (Gloucester, MA: Peter Smith, 1978), 28–50; Karl Barth, *The Epistle to the Romans*, trans. Edwyn C. Hoskyns (New York: Oxford University Press, 1933), 35.
2. Calvin uses the term "mystical union" primarily with reference to the sacrament of the Lord's Supper. John Calvin, *Institutes of the Christian Religion*, ed. John T. McNeill, trans. Ford Lewis Battles, 2 vol. (Philadelphia: Westminster Press, 1960), 3.11.10; 3.20.5.
3. Don E. Saliers, *The Soul in Paraphrase: Prayer and the Religious Affections* (Cleveland: OSL Publications, 1991), 31.
4. Friedrich Schleiermacher, "On the Power of Prayer in Relation to Outward Circumstances," trans. Mary F. Wilson, in *Selected Sermons of Schleiermacher* (New York: Funk & Wagnalls, 1890), 39.
5. *Book of Common Worship* (Louisville, KY: Westminster/John Knox Press, 1993), 146.
6. Ibid., 53.
7. *The Book of Common Prayer* (New York: Seabury Press, 1979), 836.

8. Calvin, *Institutes*, 1.5.10.
9. Saliers, *The Soul in Paraphrase*, 41.
10. *The Book of Common Prayer*, 388 with concluding collect 394.
11. Schleiermacher, "On the Power of Prayer." Schleiermacher's sermon is based on the Matthew 26:36–46 version of the story.

Chapter 8: The Service of the Word

1. Fred B. Craddock, *Preaching* (Nashville: Abingdon Press, 1985), 51.
2. H. Richard Niebuhr, *The Meaning of Revelation* (New York: Macmillan Publishing Co., 1941), 80. Throughout this chapter, but especially in this section, we are deeply indebted to this work.
3. John Calvin, *Institutes of the Christian Religion*, ed. John T. McNeill, trans. Ford Lewis Battles, 2 vol. (Philadelphia: Westminster Press, 1960), 1.1.1.
4. Niebuhr, *The Meaning of Revelation*, 83.
5. Ibid.
6. Ibid., 111, 112.
7. Garrett Green, *Imagining God: Theology and the Religious Imagination* (San Francisco: Harper & Row, 1989), 62.
8. Ibid., 66.
9. Ibid., 84.
10. Ibid., 6. See esp. chap. 6.
11. Calvin, *Institutes of the Christian Religion*, 1.4.1. We are indebted to Garrett Green's careful appropriation of Calvin's spectacles metaphor in terms of the religious imagination. See Green, *Imagining God*, 106–13.
12. For an early exploration of the interplay between religious language and the religious imagination, see Horace Bushnell, "Our Gospel a Gift to the Imagination," in *Building Eras in Religion* (New York: Charles Scribner's Sons, 1881), 249–85 and "A Preliminary Dissertation on the Nature of Language as Related to Thought and Spirit," in *God in Christ* (Hartford, CT: Brown & Parsons, 1849), 9–117. For a treatment of the nature of religious symbols, see Paul Tillich, "Symbols of Faith," in *Dynamics of Faith* (New York: Harper & Row, 1957), 41–54. For a treatment of metaphor, meaning, and narrative, see Paul Ricoeur, *Interpretation Theory: Discourse and the Surplus of Meaning* (Forth Worth, TX: Texas Christian University Press, 1976); Paul Ricoeur, *Time and Narrative*, 3 vol. (Chicago: University of Chicago Press, 1984–88); Paul Ricoeur, *The Rule of Metaphor: Multi-Disciplinary Studies of the Creation of Meaning in Language* (Toronto: University of Toronto Press, 1977).
13. Ricoeur, *Interpretation Theory: Discourse and the Surplus of Meaning*.
14. Gerard Manley Hopkins, "God's Grandeur," in *Modern Poetry*, 2nd ed., ed. Maynard Mack, Leonard Dean, and William Frost (Englewood Cliffs, NJ: Prentice-Hall, 1961), 31.
15. Craddock, *Preaching*, 79.
16. Friedrich Schleiermacher, "Christ in the Temple," in *Servant of the Word: Selected Sermons of Schleiermacher*, ed. Dawn DeVries, Fortress Texts in Modern Theology (Philadelphia: Fortress Press, 1987), 122; "Blessed Assurance" in *The Presbyterian Hymnal: Hymns, Psalms, and Spiritual Songs* (Louisville, KY, Westminster/John Knox Press, 1990), hymn #341.
17. Gordon W. Lathrop, *Holy Things: A Liturgical Theology* (Minneapolis: Fortress Press, 1993), 24–27.

Chapter 9: Sacraments

1. In this chapter, we assume that there are two sacraments of the church, baptism and the Lord's Supper. We recognize, however, that some traditions include more than these two. For a brief history of the development of the nature and number of the sacraments, see James F. White, *Sacraments as God's Self Giving* (Nashville: Abingdon Press, 2001), 84–89.

2. John Calvin, *Institutes of the Christian Religion*, ed. John T. McNeill, trans. Ford Lewis Battles, 2 vol. (Philadelphia: Westminster Press, 1960), 4.14.7.

3. Ibid., 4.14.9.

4. Pseudo-Dionysius, "The Ecclesiastical Hierarchy," in *Pseudo-Dionysius: The Complete Works*, trans. Colm Luibheid (New York: Paulist Press, 1987), 201.

5. This claim must be qualified in two ways. First, sometimes in the New Testament, baptism seems to have occurred simply in the name of Jesus Christ (see, for example, Rom. 6:3), though even here the Trinity is implied. Second, there have been times in the history of the church when some individuals chose to reserve baptism until nearly the end of life.

6. *Book of Common Worship* (Louisville, KY: Westminster/John Knox Press, 1993), 407.

7. Ibid., 406.

8. Ibid., 411.

9. Geoffrey W. Bromiley, "The Meaning and Scope of Baptism" in *Major Themes in the Reformed Tradition*, ed. Donald K. McKim (Grand Rapids: Wm. B. Eerdmans Publishing Co., 1992), 236–38.

10. The Heidelberg Catechism, Question 1, in *The Book of Confessions* (Louisville, KY: Office of the General Assembly, Presbyterian Church (U.S.A.), 2002), 29.

11. *Book of Common Worship*, 406.

12. Iris Marion Young, in *Justice and the Politics of Difference* (Princeton: Princeton University Press, 1990), points out that we are prone to accept the flawed idea that concepts such as justice and power are goods that can be divided and distributed.

13. "Come, Thou Fount of Every Blessing," in *The Presbyterian Hymnal: Hymns, Psalms, and Spiritual Songs* (Louisville KY, Westminster/John Knox Press, 1990), hymn #356.

14. For an example of a Prayer of Great Thanksgiving that uses this phrase, see *Book of Common Worship*, 138.

15. "Come, Thou Fount of Every Blessing," *Presbyterian Hymnal*, hymn #356.

16. Orestes A. Brownson, "The Mediatorial Life of Jesus: A Letter to William Ellery Channing, D.D." and "The Convert: Or, Leaves from My Experience," in *Orestes A. Brownson: Selected Writings*, ed. Patrick W. Carey (New York: Paulist Press, 1991), 205–31, 242–49.

17. Calvin, *Institutes*, 4.17.1–33. In *Institutes* 4.17.18–19 and 4.17.31, Calvin discusses the nature of Christ's presence in the bread and wine and rejects views that either identify Christ too closely with the elements (i.e., transubstantiation and consubstantiation) or separate Christ from them (i.e., memorialism). While Calvin opts for the notion that Christ is really spiritually present in the Lord's Supper, he encourages his readers to focus not on how Christ's body can come down into the elements, but rather on how through the sacrament the hearts of believers are elevated into Christ's heavenly presence for sanctification. Calvin's tendency is to avoid excessive metaphysical speculation about the nature of Christ's presence in the elements and instead to focus attention on

the practical benefits of the sacrament in effecting sanctifying, mystical union between believers and the resurrected Christ who dwells in heaven.

18. Quotations from the Alexandrine Liturgy of St. Basil are from *Book of Common Worship*, 146, 147.

Epilogue: Some Concluding Reflections on Music

1. Augustine, *The Confessions*, trans. R. S. Pinecoffin (New York: Penguin Books, 1961), book 10, chap. 33, p. 238. Quoted in Paul Westermeyer, *Te Deum: The Church and Music* (Minneapolis: Fortress Press, 1998), 88.

2. John Calvin, *Institutes of the Christian Religion*, ed. John T. McNeill, trans. Ford Lewis Battles, 2 vols. (Philadelphia: Westminster Press, 1960), 3.20.31. Quoted in Westermeyer, *Te Deum*, 156.

3. Charles Garside Jr., "Calvin's Preface to the Psalter: A Re-Appraisal," *The Musical Quarterly* 37:4 (October 1951), 569. Quoted in Westermeyer, *Te Deum*, 156.

4. Throughout this chapter, we are indebted to Westermeyer, *Te Deum*.

5. Westermeyer, *Te Deum*, 302.

6. Ibid., 318.

7. "New Songs of Celebration Render," in *The Presbyterian Hymnal: Hymns, Psalms, and Spiritual Songs* (Louisville, KY, Westminster/John Knox Press, 1990), hymn #218.

Index of Biblical Citations

Unless otherwise noted, all biblical citations and quotations are from the New Revised Standard Version

Index of Subjects and Names